Religious Organizations in Community Services

A Social Work Perspective

Terry Tirrito, PhD, is Associate Professor and Director of the Doctoral Program in the College of Social Work at the University of South Carolina, Columbia, South Carolina. Dr. Tirrito is a graduate of Fordham University in New York with a degree in gerontological social work. Dr. Tirrito was a visiting professor at Australian Catholic University, Canberra, Australia and at Masey University in New Zealand.

Dr. Terry Tirrito has written three books, *ElderPractice: A Multidisciplinary Approach to Working with Older Adults in the Community* (1996), *Gerontological Social Work: Theory into Practice* (1997), and *Aging in New Millennium* (in press, 2003). She presented at over 100 international, national and regional conferences. Dr. Tirrito lectured on aging issues in Korea, Australia, New Zealand, Europe, Argentina, Canada, and the United States.

Toni Cascio, PhD, LCSW-C, is an Associate Professor at the University of Maryland School of Social Work in Baltimore, Maryland. Dr. Cascio teaches clinical practice courses and has published extensively in the areas of spirituality and social work practice and teaching methods in social work education.

Religious Organizations in Community Services

A Social Work Perspective

Terry Tirrito, PhD
Toni Cascio, PhD
Editors

 Springer Publishing Company

Springer Publishing Company, Inc.
536 Broadway
New York, NY 10012-3955

Acquisitions Editor: Sheri Sussman
Production Editor: Jeanne Libby
Cover design by Joanne E. Honigman

03 04 05 06 07 / 5 4 3 2 1

Library of Congress Cataloging-in-Publication Data

Religious organizations in community services : a social work perspective / Terry Tirrito, Toni Cascio, editors.
    p. cm.
  Includes bibliographical references and index.
  ISBN 0-8261-1548-9
  1. Social service—Religious aspects—History. 2. Social service—United States—Religious aspects. 3. Social workers—Religious life—United States. 4. Spiritual life. 5. Church and social problems—United States. I. Tirrito, Terry. II. Cascio, Toni.
  HV530 .R25 2003
  361.7'5—dc21   2002030682
                                                CIP

Printed in the United States of America by Sheridan Books.

This book is dedicated to Phyllis and Nick Maldarelli, June and Lenny Aronica, Vic and Terry Tirrito, and Shannon and John Nicols who became my family. I would like to thank them for their faith in my ability to share my knowledge to help others. Barbara and Peter Creighton, Caroline and Michael Pais, Marilyn Aldoroty, Angela and Bob Alfano, and Lou and Henrietta Adduci were so generous in listening to my ideas. I thank them for their time and friendship.

We must thank our editor, Sheri Sussman, who believed in the importance of this book and encouraged us to continue when it seemed impossible to do any more. I would like to thank the chapter contributors who eagerly agreed to write chapters for this book because they believed as strongly as we did in the value of religious organizations in community service. We were fortunate to work with experts who finished their work in a timely manner and with such skill.

I would like to thank my daughter, Catherine, and my son, Sal, for their unfailing enthusiasm in my work. I deeply appreciate my husband, Sal, for his sense of humor and patience with my many, many activities.

Terry Tirrito

I would like to dedicate this book to my parents, Anthony and Marilyn Cascio, for a lifetime of encouragement, support, and love.

Toni Cascio

CONTENTS

Introduction by Terry Tirrito

Part I The Historical Role of Faith Organizations and Religion

Chapter 1   Religious Foundations of Charity   3
             Toni Cascio

Part II The Contemporary Role of Religious Organizations

Chapter 2   American Congregations and Their Social Programs   23
             Terry A. Wolfer and Michael E. Sherr

Chapter 3   Religiosity and Spirituality in Social Work:
             A Retrospective and Contemporary Analysis   51
             Larry P. A. Ortiz

Chapter 4   Spirituality and the Life Cycle   63
             Ilene Nathanson

Chapter 5   Health, Spirituality, and Healing   79
             Connie Saltz Corely

Chapter 6   Mental Health and Religion   91
             John R. Belcher

Chapter 7   Religion and Spirituality in Social Work Education   113
             Leon Ginsberg

Chapter 8   Sectarian Organizations Serving Civic Purposes   137
             Nieli Langer

Part III New Models for the 21st Century

Chapter 9   The Korean American Church as a Social Service
Provider   155
Gil Choi

Chapter 10 The Faith-Based Community Action Model   171
Terry Tirrito

Conclusion   191

Index   193

CONTRIBUTORS

John R. Belcher, PhD, LCSW-C
Professor
University of Maryland, Baltimore
School of Social Work
Baltimore, Maryland

Gil Choi, DSW
Associate Professor
College of Social Work
University of South Carolina
Columbia, South Carolina

Connie Saltz Corley, PhD, LCSW
Professor
Associate Director of Research,
    The Edward R. Roybal Institute
    for Applied Gerontology
California State University, Los
    Angeles
Los Angeles, California

Leon Ginsberg, PhD
Carolina Distinguished Research
    Professor
College of Social Work
University of South Carolina
Columbia, South Carolina

Nieli Langer, PhD
Adjunct Associate Professor
Graduate Division of Human
    Services, College of New
    Rochelle
New Rochelle, New York

Ilene Nathanson, DSW
Professor
Director of Social Work
College of Management
Long Island University-C.W. Post
    Campus
Brookville, New York

Larry P. A. Ortiz, PhD
Associate Professor
University of Maryland, Baltimore
School of Social Work
Baltimore, Maryland

Michael E. Sherr, LMSW
Doctoral Candidate
College of Social Work
University of South Carolina
Columbia, South Carolina

Terry A. Wolfer, MSW, PhD
Associate Professor
College of Social Work
University of South Carolina
Columbia, South Carolina

INTRODUCTION

Terry Tirrito

The purposes of this book are to review the historical role of religious/ faith organizations in providing social services to those in need, to propose that religious/faith organizations can assume this responsibility again in the 21st century, to explain how the Korean church has successfully provided social services to its congregations, and to provide a model for religious organizations to use to develop community action programs.

Political changes in the United States and around the world demonstrate that most developed and underdeveloped societies are not meeting the social needs of their people. After a long history of informally providing services to those in need, in the 20th century, the church in the United States emerged as an institution that had relinquished this responsibility of helping the poor and underprivileged in local communities, and federal and state governments assumed this role.

In this new millennium economic and political conditions demand a new perspective, and religious/faith organizations are being asked to once again become involved in providing social assistance. Throughout this book "the church" is frequently used to refer to religious/faith organizations. The authors wish to remind readers, however, that religious organizations include temples, synagogues, and mosques as well as churches.

In Part I, the historical role of faith organizations in relation to social welfare is discussed. In the first chapter Cascio describes the major religions of the world and provides a foundation of the historical details that explain the basis for charity. In particular the teachings of Protestantism, Catholicism, Judaism, and Islam regarding charity and their approaches to the poor are highlighted. In looking at historical figures such as Moses and Maimonides in Judaism, Saint Thomas of Aquinas in Catholicism, and Mohammed in Islam, Cascio examines their roles in the shaping of charitable institutions.

Part II presents recent trends in social welfare in the United States and the potential for re-involvement of religious/faith organizations in this arena. We look at the contemporary role of religious organizations regarding social programs, social work education, health and mental health, and the importance of spirituality in the life cycle of the individual. It is essential to explore the role of sectarian organizations serving civic purposes.

Chapter 2 describes how religious/faith organizations may supplement the federal government's broad services to meet the social service needs of the population, and Wolfer and Sherr offer examples of faith organizations providing social services. In chapter 3 Ortiz explores religiosity and spirituality and discusses the religious/faith organization's role in shaping a new concept of spirituality for people. This chapter examines the importance of religion among various ethnic groups such as African Americans, Hispanics, and Asian Americans.

In chapter 4 Nathanson describes the importance of spirituality throughout the life cycle and connects the social work profession's renewed interest in spirituality to the practitioner's need to understand the spiritual life of a client in the helping process. Corely, in chapter 5, illustrates the importance of religiosity and spirituality and its impact on physical health, especially in the healing process.

In chapter 6 the relationship between religion and mental health is explored, by Belcher. Examples include the influence of spirituality on lower incidences of depression, and its beneficial effect on hypertension and recovery from alcoholism. Ginsberg looks at the rift between religion and social work education and offers a discussion for the resolution of these issues in chapter 7. In chapter 8 Langer examines sectarian organizations serving civic purposes such as religiously motivated aid, and the separation of the sacred and the secular. Examples of faith-based programs are provided.

In Part III new models for religiously-based social services are described. In chapter 9, Choi presents the Korean-American church as a model of a religiously-based ethnic church that provides social services to its immigrant congregation. Tirrito, in chapter 10, describes a 12-step model, The Faith-Based Community Action model (FBCA), that religious/faith organizations can adopt to develop social service programs in local communities. These 12 steps are based on community organization principles and are specifically adapted for the use of faith-based organizations.

The editors of this book are grateful to the contributing authors, who competently described how faith-based social services are involved in local communities; how these organizations may fill the gaps in services that currently exist; and how their continued involvement will be necessary to provide adequate social service delivery to the communities.

PART I

THE HISTORICAL ROLE OF FAITH ORGANIZATIONS AND RELIGION

Chapter 1

RELIGIOUS FOUNDATIONS OF CHARITY

Toni Cascio

Religious values, traditions, and beliefs significantly contributed to the establishment of American social welfare (Leiby, 1978; Marty, 1980; Ortiz, 1995). In fact, according to Leiby (1978), "Religious ideas were the most important intellectual influence on American welfare institutions in the nineteenth century" (p. 12). Religious motivations, such as love, altruism, and salvation fostered the development of early sectarian welfare agencies. Similarly, other social work ideals, such as social justice, the worth of the individual, and the responsibility of the individual to the greater society "are synonymous with corresponding religious values" (Siporin, 1986, p. 36). These values have been steeped in centuries of tradition dating back to the Biblical era. In order to understand the mission of social work and to further illustrate the tremendous potential of religious and social service agencies to work in consort, it is necessary to understand the origins of social welfare. Therefore, this chapter will explore early Jewish, Christian, and Islamic foundations for charity that, centuries later, evolved into formal welfare institutions.

JEWISH FOUNDATIONS OF CHARITY

The Jews have long been a unique people. Their beliefs, customs, and rituals have distinguished them from their neighbors in a myriad of ways.

3

Social welfare is but one arena where these differences have played out. At the heart of Jewish social welfare is *tzedakah*—a combination of charity and justice (Cascio, 1996; Hofstein, 1974; Kutzik, 1959). Over the centuries, *tzedakah* has remained an ideal and has been observed to varying degrees, depending on the cultural, political, and economic context of the time. *Tzedakah* is as old as the Jewish people themselves, and its history is intertwined with that of the Israelite nation. Therefore, to understand the notion of *tzedakah*, it is necessary to first examine the cultural milieu in which it was born.

The Jewish religious system was wholly unique at the time that it emerged (around 1200 BCE). For the first time in recorded history, a people had declared the existence of one true God, and monotheism was born. In addition to believing in only one God, the nature of the Israelites' relationship with their God differed markedly as well. First, the Israelites had a direct relationship with God, accessing Him through prayer and ritual sacrifices; there was no need for an intermediary. Furthermore, in polytheistic religions, ritual sacrifices were performed as an attempt to influence a god and/or to provide sustenance to the gods (Zeitlin, 1984). Jews, however, practiced ritual sacrifices as a sign of thanksgiving and devotion to Him. God, in turn, accepted these offerings out of love for His children of Israel. Furthermore, this idea that the Israelites were the children of God and that He was their father, was a unique concept at the time, as well as a very crucial one. For, if God was the father and humans His children, then by extension, there was a familial relationship among men as well; this relationship was the brotherhood of mankind, and it stated that all men, as brothers, had a responsibility to care and provide for one another. Such an idea was strengthened by the belief that this patriarchal God "whose will was the supreme law for human action . . . commanded that people be kind, merciful, and just in their dealings with one another" (Handel, 1982, p. 47). This idea, that "individuals have a positive obligation to perform acts of helping or doing good for other" was, according to Morris (1986), revolutionary (p. 70).

THE *TORAH*

Guidelines for the implementation of these commandments were found in the first five books of the *Bible*, known as the *Torah*. Several passages in these books directly commanded the Hebrews to tend to their neighbors' needs. Deuteronomy 15:7–8 stated, "If there be among you a needy man, one of thy brethren, in thy land, thou shalt not harden thy heart nor shut thy hand unto him." It is noteworthy that this passage did not specify any characteristics of the recipient of aid; need alone was to be sufficient basis for help. Therefore, the interpretation inferred from this passage was that *tzedakah* was to extend to everyone and was not to be based upon race, religion, gender, or physical infirmity. Other passages, however, high-lighted the need to care for certain groups of people deemed especially vulnerable, such as widows, orphans, and strangers. In fact, in Exodus 22:20–23, God threatened retribution should the Israelites fail to follow this admonition and protect and provide for the widow and orphan (Morris, 1986). In addition, Deuteronomy 24:14 stated, "Thou shalt not oppress a hired servant that is poor and needy whether he be a brother or the strangers that are in thy land within thy gates." This passage addressed the issue of the stranger, which was referred to several times throughout the *Torah*. The stranger, to the ancient Israelites, was an individual who was not part of one's immediate family or kinship group, as the clan was the basic unit of social organization. In effect, the term stranger encom-passed not only the traveler, but the widow and orphan, and even daughters who, by marrying outside of the kin group, "became 'strangers' in that they were no longer part of a close group attached to 'its' land" (Morris, 1986, p. 73). Therefore, the term "stranger" was used to refer to any member of society made vulnerable through separation from kin and potentially in need of assistance.

In addition to these blanket statements directing the Israelites to perform *tzedakah*, there were several specific instructions enumerated in the *Torah* as to how to provide charity. For example, the book of Leviticus instructed farmers to leave the gleanings of their fields and vineyards for the poor. This same book also detailed the precepts of the Sabbatical and Jubilee years. According to Leviticus, the Sabbatical year was to take place every 7 years from Rosh Hashanah (Jewish new year) to Rosh Hashanah and was to be a year of "solemn rest" for the land (Ausubel, 1964). By neither tilling the soil nor pruning the branches, the Jews were to allow the soil to become fertile again, and transgression of this ordinance resulted in exile from Judea. Despite the potential for economic disaster, as this was an agricultural society, Jews of the age adhered to this regulation (Ausubel, 1964). In addition, just as the soil was allowed to begin anew, so too, were the people; the Sabbatical year included a provision for the annulment of all financial debt during this time.

Similarly, the book of Leviticus also commanded the institution of the Jubilee year that was to begin on Yom Kippur (the day of atonement) of every 50th year. In addition to encompassing all the provisions of the Sabbatical year, the Jubilee year included the freeing of all those imprisoned or indentured due to debt. Furthermore, "land was returned to the state for reassignment to someone else;" this practice was enacted to prevent the rise of large, powerful estate owners and was based on the idea that all creatures and possessions actually belonged to God alone, as He had created them (Ausubel, 1964). Although the concept of a Jubilee year was rather common in the near Eastern region, Jews were the only ones who, at the time, saw it as a permanent institution and enforced its principles. It was possible to enforce the Jubilee and Sabbatical years due to the pastoral/agricultural nature of the society (Ausubel, 1964). In addition, the communities were so small as to exert peer pressure upon the residents to comply (Morris, 1986).

In fact, in such a small society, a mutual aid system was sufficient for the provision of social welfare. Assistance was very personal and individualized. For example, the wealthy man who fell upon hard times was provided for at the level to which he was accustomed before his financial reversal (Morris, 1986). In part, this was due to the concern for preserving the self-respect of the recipient. Morris (1986) describes a common practice of the time that reflects this idea: "Some Rabbinic leaders used to wrap their alms in a fold trailed over their shoulders so that when they went to visit, the poor could help themselves secretly without him knowing who was helping himself to the 'poor box' " (p. 76). In addition, Jews at this time did not ascribe to the notion of the worthy and unworthy poor. In fact, it was not uncommon for a man to be alternately prosperous and impoverished several times during his lifetime since his livelihood, indeed the whole economy, was agricultural, and therefore subject to the vicissitudes of nature. Furthermore, the Jews at this time believed that if poverty existed, it was society that was principally at fault for permitting such oppression to occur (Ausubel, 1964). The inherent uncertainty of an agrarian society, combined with the idea of social responsibility for the poor, resulted in a belief of the moral right of recipients to aid, and, therefore, this aid bore no stigma (Ausubel, 1964).

Despite the fact that poverty was recognized as being outside of the individual's control, the receipt of charity by the individual was still viewed as a last resort. In fact, "Each person's obligation to work for his own well-being and condition was as important as the obligation to help those in distress" (Morris, 1986, p. 76). Both the book of Genesis and the Psalms established the principle of the work ethic (Morris, 1986). The work ethic, in combination with the fertile land of Canaan, contributed to the growth of this small agrarian society into a profitable nation.

This national prosperity, however, had a tremendous impact on the social structure. During this time—from the 9th to 6th centuries BCE—stark class differences emerged as society became more and more complex (Vriezen, 1963). The population grew exponentially. Industries began to arise, and with them, much greater demands for Jewish social welfare. Religious life was affected by these changes, too, and the interests of the state began to outweigh even fundamental ideals like *tzedakah* (Baron, 1952). After King Solomon's death, however, and the subsequent partitioning of the land into the northern kingdom of Israel and the southern kingdom of Judah, the Hebrews entered into a period of gradual economic and political decline, and injustices that began under earlier rulers intensified. Against this background of social injustice and economic turmoil emerged the voices of the prophets to address these issues. The prophet most concerned with the inattention to the principle of *tzedakah* was Isaiah.

The society that Isaiah lived in was structurally different from that of the preceding period. The tribal or clan system endemic to Israel had dissipated, and the interests of the family were replaced by individual interests, including for the first time, the institution of private property (Lods, 1971). As a result, the observance of the Jubilee year, designed to protect the interests of the smaller farmer, gradually disappeared (Ausubel, 1964). Large landholdings by the elite emerged, while the poor were relegated to small farms and subsistence-wage labor. Isaiah (5:8) addressed this growing practice, declaring "Woe unto them that join house to house, that lay field to field, till there be no room and ye be made to dwell alone in the midst of the land." In addition, a merchant class began to grow at the expense of the poor, while the elders and judges looked the other way (Ausubel, 1964). Finally, peasants, as payment for their debts, often entered into periods of involuntary service, instituting a quasi-slavery among the Jews (Baron, 1952).

Isaiah, enraged at the people's divergence from their religious precepts, reminded the Jews of their obligation to take action against injustice in 1:17 where he urged, "Learn to do well, seek justice, relieve the oppressed, judge the fatherless, and plead for the widow" (Morris, 1986). He later elaborated on the responsibility of the Jews to perform *tzedakah* as commanded by God:

> Is this not the fast that I have chosen? . . . to let the oppressed go free and that ye break every yoke? Is it not to deal thy bread to the hungry and that thou bring the poor that are cast out into thy house? When thou seest the naked that thou cover them? Then shall thy light break forth as the morning and thy healing shall spring forth speedily and thy righteousness go before thee. (Isaiah 58:6–8)

Despite the general inattention to the poor and the oppressed observed by Isaiah, there were a few informal social welfare practices in existence at the time. Jews did continue to leave gleanings in the fields for the poor (Baron, 1952). Also, it became customary for families to display small flags at mealtimes to announce to the poor, the hungry, and the stranger that they were welcome to share in the meal (Ausubel, 1964). Finally, a more formal type of social welfare provision emerged in the form of the *Book of the Covenant*. The *Book of the Covenant* was a small compilation of laws intended to moderate the severity of regulations concerning debt and was believed to be an attempt at restoring ancient fraternal practices (Lods, 1971). Although few in number, these practices tried to address the class polarization of the Israelite society at a time when *tzedakah* was being overshadowed by the quest for private property and wealth.

In the ensuing centuries, Judea was conquered a number of times and ruled by foreign governments, including the Babylonians and Greeks, and they were finally captured by the Romans in the first and second centuries BCE. The Jews responded to this tyranny with a series of unsuccessful riots and rebellions (Applebaum, 1989). In addition to the external military attacks on the Romans, the Jews responded to these events by turning inward; they concluded, as tradition dictated, that their misery was a result of their wayward actions. The rabbinic sages decided that the answer to this dilemma was to return to an ethical way of living, and they attempted to do so by reinforcing the precepts of the *Torah*, one of which is the practice of *tzedakah*.

As the casualties incurred in the Jewish uprisings significantly decreased the number of Jews, a system of mutual aid—the traditional mode of *tzedakah*—was once again possible. Such aid took a number of forms. First, direct financial relief was provided through a community fund called the *kuppah*. The *kuppah* was supervised by two overseers who collected tithings from all persons in the community. These same men then assessed the needs of each individual and dispersed the funds accordingly (Ausubel, 1964). In addition, each Jewish community had a soup kitchen—a *tamhui*— which provided the transient poor with two meals a day (Tanenbaum, 1984). Finally, the rabbinic sages called for the reinstitution of the Sabbatical and Jubilee years.

The sages also participated in the written codification of the precepts of the *Torah*, which became known as the Mishnah. The Mishnah addressed all aspects of Jewish daily living, such as ritual purity, laws concerning damages, and the agricultural support of the poor. The segment of the Mishnah devoted to the latter was known as the Peah, and it contained six tractates dealing with the issue of care for the poor. The general determination was that all food apportioned seemingly by accident had actually been chosen by God for the poor. The produce chosen by God included crops grown in the rear corner of the field, the forgotten sheaf, grapes separated from their bunches, and defective clusters of grapes; also, one tenth of all crops grown during the third and sixth years' harvest in the Sabbatical cycle was allotted for the poor (Neusner, 1990). Particularly germane to this issue of charity were the ideas of Rabbi Moses Maimonides. In the Mishnah, Maimonides emphasized that not only what is given is important but how it is given; thus, he outlined the eight levels of giving, each level of which increases in virtue (Trepp, 1980). These levels are as follows:

> He who gives, but gives grudgingly;
> He who gives less than his share, but does so joyfully;
> He who gives when he is asked;
> He who gives without being asked;
> He who gives without knowing the receiver, yet the receiver knows the giver's identity;
> He who knows the receiver, but the receiver does not know him;
> Neither party knows the identity of the other;
> He who helps the other before the other suffers need, by loans, or by personal guidance in his affairs, or by setting him up in business or profession, allowing him to earn his own living. (Mishnah Torah: Matanot Aniyim 10: 10–14)

Thus, the rabbinic sages specified the exact obligations of the Israelite people with regard to *tzedakah* and other matters. In doing so, they facilitated a return to a life based on the Torah.

CHRISTIANITY AND SOCIAL WELFARE

Christianity shares much with the Jewish traditions. It was, of course, an outgrowth of the Jewish religion. Jesus himself was a Jew, and the Last Supper was, in fact, a celebration of the Passover meal. Therefore, many of the ideas of Christianity had their origins in and bear great resemblance to those found in Judaism (Hamel, 1990; Peterson, 1993). These ideas include "similar views of God, revelation, creation, human duty to God and other humans, sin, salvation, and final judgment" (Peterson, 1993, p. 5). Christian principles of charity and social welfare emerged from these views of human duty and expanded upon them. Similarly, the ways in which charity were collected and dispensed paralleled those of Judaism.

EARLY CHRISTIAN CHARITY

During the first 3 centuries of Christianity, there were notable similarities to Jewish traditions in their approach to caring for the poor. For example, there was a community chest, called an *arca*, and Christian residents were expected to make, at the very least, a monthly contribution to that fund (Dimont, 1910). This money was used to help many of the same groups of people as Jewish community funds, such as widows and orphans, the sick, disabled, and blind, and the imprisoned. There were a few notable differences, however. First of all, this money was also used to help "persons imprisoned, exiled, or working in mines as punishment for their Christian beliefs" (Handel, 1982, p. 48). In addition to the *arca*, there was another form of charity in place called the *oblations*. Oblations were donations of bread and wine collected at the Eucharist service that were then distributed among the poor (Dimont, 1910; Handel, 1982). Other acts of charity included burial of the dead who were unable to afford funeral expenses, the visiting of those imprisoned, providing hospitality to Christian travelers, and helping to provide jobs for those in need of work (Dimont, 1910). Thus, these were the means and functions of the relatively simple Christian charitable system until the fourth century A.D.

In 313 A.D., Constantine, the emperor of Rome, legalized Christianity. This had a significant impact on the nature of Christian charity. First, there was a large influx of Christian converts following this declaration. This momentous decision certainly increased the number of adherents and the amount of donations (Dimont, 1910; Handel, 1982). Since most Christians were from the poorer classes (Morris, 1985), however, it also increased the rolls of the poor. This increase in complexity led to greater formalization in the distribution of alms. While originally, charity was dispensed in individual churches through their clergy, now, "bishops of a diocese had supervisory control over all the churches in his district and control over the revenues" (Handel, 1982, p. 48). Furthermore, the larger number of adherents necessitated a new form of social welfare institution— the hostel. Remember that caring for the stranger was a primary concern, and the increased number of Christian travelers created the need for the first *xenodochium* or hostel, which was established by Julian the Apostate (331–363 A.D.) (Morris, 1986).

Another fundamental change occurred as a result of Constantine's decision that dealt with the underlying motivation of Christian charity. Upon its inception, Christian charity was based upon the principle of love. Early Christians "saw the souls of persons as a reflection of God which gives to persons their intrinsic worth" (Mancoske, 1987, p. 5). This conception reinforced the belief that mankind is a brotherhood, and men had the responsibility to love their brothers. The difference between this and Judaism is that the Jewish ideas of charity were based on the principle of justice, while Christian ideals were bound to love (Morris, 1985). This connection will now be explored.

JESUS AND HIS VIEW OF THE POOR

Jesus' view of the poor was one of the ideas that distinguished early Christianity from its Roman and Jewish neighbors. As previously discussed, the Jews of this time saw taking care of one's neighbor as a duty required by God. This attention to the poor was one of a myriad of duties that God bestowed upon mankind. In fact, Orthodox Jews believe that there are indeed 613 commandments laid out in the Bible as opposed to the 10 commandments with which most people are familiar. Christianity, on the other hand, *highlighted* the care of the poor. Indeed, Morris (1986) states that although the origins of Jesus' message could be found in the Old Testament, "the earlier concepts of mercy and justice were amplified by a new stress upon compassion, pity, and identification with the poor" (p. 101). Maguire (1993) echoes this focus on the impoverished, stating, "Jesus emphasized that what he would be about would be 'good news to the poor' (Luke 4:18)" (p. 135). Therefore, this attention to the plight of the poor was one of the foremost points on his agenda.

In the Gospels of Jesus Christ, there are a variety of references to caring for the impoverished. Three passages in particular depict the Christian approach to the poor. The first is the Golden Rule. Next is the story of the Good Samaritan, and lastly is the Sermon on the Mount. Each of these illustrates a key point as to how Christianity elaborated on the Jewish conceptions of the poor.

Most people in our Judeo-Christian culture are acquainted with the Golden Rule. This passage is found in Matthew 22:38–40: "You shall love the Lord your God with all your heart, and with all your soul, and with all your mind. This is the great and first commandment. And a second is like it, You shall love your neighbor as yourself. On these two commandments depend all the law and the prophets." Here, Jesus states that all that has been taught before and all Jewish laws governing behavior are based on these principles. This sentiment is reiterated in Galatians 5:14: "For all the law is fulfilled in one word, even in this; thou shalt love they neighbor as thyself." What is particularly significant about the phrasing of these statements is the word love. Love was seen as what distinguished Christians from other religious groups of the time (Edwards, 1989). Furthermore, in Christianity, the word love is equated with charity. According to Edwards (1989), the original word used was "*agape*" in the original, which is translated 'charity' . . . So that charity in the New Testament is the very same as Christian love" (p. 129). Paul, in his letter to the Romans (13:8) states that "Love is the fulfilling of the law [of God]," and he expands on this idea in 1 Timothy 1:5, saying "Now the end of the commandment is charity." Therefore, charity and love were inextricably intertwined in Christian doctrine.

In fact, St. Maximus the Confessor asserted that "In charity the whole of Christian life is summarized and contained" (Sherwood, 1955, p. 91). This spirit of charity laid the foundation for all Christian behavior. An important aspect of this charitable spirit is that it was responsible for all pro-social behavior among men. It was believed that if men were infused with Christian charity, they would not cheat, deceive, or besmirch each other (Edwards, 1989; Sherwood, 1955; Swedenborg, 1914). That is, Christian charity predisposes one to behave in a charitable way, and in charitable acts, one sees the essence of Christian love. Edwards (1989) explains this link between Christian love and charitable acts: "We are naturally disposed to pity those whom we love when they are afflicted. This would dispose men to give to the poor, and bear one another's burdens . . . " (p. 136). The need for acting on these charitable impulses is stressed in the Gospel of Luke: "The tree is known by the fruit" (6:44). And, there are two calls for charitable action found in the book of James. First, we read:

> What doth it profit my brethren if a man say that he hath faith but hath not works? If a brother or sister be naked and at a lack of daily food and one of you say unto him go in peace be ye warned and filled and yet ye give him not the things needful to the body what doth it profit? (James 1:27)

In the next chapter, he states, "Show me thy faith by thy deeds" (James 2:18). Thus, it is not enough to feel charitably towards others; one must act on those impulses. Loving your neighbor as yourself, therefore, meant caring for their material and emotional needs in a tangible way.

The question then arises as to how to define one's neighbor. Most cultures at the time, whether Jews, Christians, Romans, or Greeks, each had their own definition of neighbor. The parable of the Good Samaritan directly addressed this question. A lawyer in the crowd directly asks Jesus, "Who is my neighbor?" (Luke 10:29). Jesus responds by telling a story of a man traveling from Jerusalem to Jericho who is accosted by thieves who steal all that he has including his clothing; they leave him wounded and near death by the side of the road. Both a priest and a Levite pass him by and do nothing. The Samaritan, however, one who would be thought of as a foreigner, helps this man despite his nationality. He dresses the man's wounds, puts him on his donkey, and takes him to an inn where he pays the innkeeper to nurse the man back to health. The Samaritan is "moved by compassion and sets out to repair not only the failures of the priest and the Levite but also the evil done by the robbers" (Hamel, 1990, p. 216).

These men who were literally and figuratively the man's neighbor, did not offer any assistance, yet one who could be considered his enemy (in that he was a Samaritan) did help. In this way, the idea of the neighbor is expanded to include potential rivals; indeed, the category of neighbor includes anyone in need. This idea is reinforced in two other places in the New Testament. In both of these instances, the idea of neighbor is expanded through the omission of a specific definition of what constitutes a neighbor. For example, in the Golden Rule mentioned above, there is no discussion of what type of person is a neighbor, implying that there are no limits to this notion. Similarly, in Matthew 25:35–36, Jesus states "For I was hungry and you gave Me food; I was thirsty and you gave Me drink; I was a stranger and you took Me in. I was naked and you clothed Me; I was sick and you visited Me; I was in prison and you came to see Me." He goes on to state that although He himself may not have experienced any of these states "as you did it to one of the least of these my brethren, you did it to me" (Matthew 25:40). According to Hamel (1990), this omission "allowed the new Christians to see people other than their kins (sic) . . . as potentially worth of the kind of charity that did not produce any return" (p. 220). All of mankind is one's neighbor; therefore, all men are worthy of charitable love. This idea is similar to early Jewish notions of the stranger.

It is important to note, however, that another idea springs forth from this discussion. This expanded view of the neighbor implies that all men, including the poor, are a reflection of God and therefore have inherent worth and dignity. This was a revolutionary attitude toward the poor, who were typically vilified in this culture (Hamel, 1990). Indeed, Jesus went one step further and identified with the poor and, along with the apostles, lived a life of austerity:

> Now all who believed were together, and had all things in common, and sold their possessions and goods, and divided them among all, as anyone had need. So continuing daily with one accord in the temple, and breaking bread from

house to house, they ate their food with gladness and simplicity of heart. (Acts 2: 44–46)

Poverty among Christ's followers was seen as a virtue; in fact, "Extreme poverty was the criterion used to recognize the true apostles and prophets" (Hamel, 1990, p. 232). Further, Jesus exalts the poor in the Sermon on the Mount (also known as the Beatitudes). Here, Jesus tells his followers that the poor and meek are blessed, and they shall receive their reward in heaven.

Despite Jesus' embracing of the poor, their acceptance did not last. Following the legalization of Christianity, more and more people came from the upper strata of society, many of them wealthy landowners. While heretofore, the poor had been exalted in Christianity, the idea emerged that "wealth could be ennobling because it allowed the wealthy to do good works that would earn them eternal salvation in the Kingdom of God" (Handel, 1982, p. 49). This idea then laid the foundation for belief that almsgiving could be a means of redeeming oneself from sin and gaining spiritual merit. Another change took place during the fourth century A.D. in that we begin to see references to the worthy and unworthy poor. Both St. Ambrose (340–397 A.D.) and St. Augustine of Hippo (354–430 A.D.) argued for the denial of aid to the able bodied who were capable of work (Morris, 1986). In fact, St. Ambrose believed that there were "special areas of concern" including "age and weakness" and "the needs of the stranger," and he advocated for the investigation of individual cases to determine true need (Morris, 1986, p. 105). Thus, by the end of the fourth century, we see further formalization of charity and a shift in the original Christian attitude toward the poor. Nevertheless, Christianity made important contributions to the social welfare arena. According to Morris (1986):

> The early Christian church enriched and elaborated ideas about care for others by wedding several contradictions, e.g., all men are brothers or family and kin responsibility, open sharing of wealth with prudent caution and formal institutions alongside personal acts of kindness. (p. 107)

ISLAM AND SOCIAL WELFARE

Emerging three centuries later and building upon both Jewish and Christian charitable notions is the religion of Islam. Islam is based on the teachings of Muhammad and means "submission," and "a Muslim is one who has submitted—to Allah, the one and only God" (Hiro, 1989, p. 5). Muhammad was born in 570 A.D. in what is now Saudi Arabia. At age 40, he began having mystical visions, and over the course of the next 23 years, the tenets of Islam were revealed to Muhammad by the angel Gabriel (Haynes, Eweiss, Abdel Mageed, & Chung, 1997). Together, these revelations comprised a complete moral and social order for Muhammad's followers; in this way, Islam differs greatly from both Judaism and Christianity, which sought the separation of the moral/spiritual realm from the state (Haynes et al., 1997; Hiro, 1989). The precepts of Islam were laid out in two texts, the Holy *Qur'an* and the *Sunna*. The *Qur'an* is similar to the *Bible* in that Muslims believe it was divinely inspired; that is, its teachings were revealed to Muhammad by Allah. It is also similar to the *Bible* in that it is the ultimate source of truth and authority for Islam. It contains 114 Suras (chapters), and with the exception of the first Sura, is arranged according to length, with the longest first (Stillman, 1975). The *Sunna*, on the other hand, contains the teachings and collected traditions of Muhammad. It is these two texts which lay the foundation for all of Islamic life.

Since its inception in the seventh century, daily life for the Muslim has been guided by the Five Pillars of Islam. These Five Pillars "offer the Muslim the mechanism for change or social transformation because they provide a structure for positive daily living, with eternal life as the ultimate reward" (Haynes et al., 1997, p. 270). The first of the five pillars is *shahadatain* or faith. There are two components to this tenet. Islam is a monotheistic religion, so *shahadatain* declares that there is one God, Allah, who is the creator and therefore worthy of worship. The second part of this proclamation is that Muhammad is the true messenger of God (Haynes et al., 1997). The second pillar is *salat* or prayer. Muslims are required to pray five times a day while facing Mecca. Fasting is the third pillar of Islam in which adherents are obligated to fast during the holy month of Ramadan. The fourth pillar is *hajj*, which requires Muslims to make a pilgrimage, at least once in their lives, to Mecca. The last pillar is *zakat* whose literal translation is "purification"; *zakat* "is the Muslim's worship of God by means of his wealth through an obligatory form of giving to those in need" (Haneef, 1993, p. 48). Muslims believe that human beings must share their wealth because all things truly belong to Allah and not man; therefore, they are not man's to keep (Haneef, 1993; Haynes et al., 1997). This idea is similar to the Jewish belief that the land and its fruits were created by God and therefore His. According to Haneef (1993) "A Muslim is supposed to be always responsive to human needs and distress, and to regard his wealth as a trust from God which is to be used not only for himself and his family but for other human beings in need as well" (p. 50). Another way in which Islamic charity resembles that of Christianity and Judaism was that its acceptance was viewed as a last resort. The first line of defense in terms of poverty was the family. According to Stillman (1975), "the extended family did all it could to take care of its less fortunate members and thereby avoid humiliating the entire clan by having them seek public charity" (p. 112).

Zakat is actually comprised of two types of charity and is distinguished from *sadaqa*, or voluntary almsgiving. *Zakat* is comprised of "institutionalized, obligatory alms collected by a government treasury official" (Stillman, 1975, p. 106), and a 2.5% tax is levied on property and income. In fact, non-payment of *zakat* was a punishable offense, and a judge could exact a sentence on those refusing to pay zakat (Williams, 1961). The specifics of *zakat* were precisely laid out for Muslims. For example, *zakat* on animals were due on "camels, cattle, sheep and goats," while those on agricultural products pertained to "wheat, barley, millet, sorghum, rice, . . . lentils, chickpeas, vetches, beans and peas" (Williams, 1961, pp. 109–110). *Zakat* was also collected on gold and silver. It was then distributed to eight groups of people. These included the tax collectors themselves, the poor, the needy, slaves (to pay for their freedom), debtors, travelers, "those who fight in 'The Way of God,' " and "those whose hearts it is necessary to conciliate," meaning "those whose conversion is hoped for" (Williams, 1961, p. 112). It is important to note that unlike Christians and Jews, charity was used for purposes other than the care of the needy. While certainly, Muslims cared for the widowed, orphaned, and ill, they also used this money in pursuit of the active propagation of Islam.

It is also important to note that Islam differed from its Jewish and Christian counterparts in the purpose of charity. In Jewish tradition, charity was based on an obligation to take care of one's fellow man out of a sense of justice, while in Christianity, it was based on the idea of love of one's fellow man. In Islam, on the other hand, observing *zakat*

> purifies his remaining possessions and makes his ownership of them legal and permissible. It also purifies his heart from greed and selfishness, and from regarding what God in His bounty has bestowed on him as solely his by right. In turn, zakat purifies the heart of the one who receives it from envy and hatred of others who are better-off. (Haneef, 1993, p. 49)

Therefore, purification, of both possessions and the soul, is the object of charity in Islamic tradition.

Another difference between Islamic and Judeo-Christian tradition is the method of distribution of charity. Both Judaism and Christianity initially distributed charity through their religious congregations at the synagogue and church. Muslims, on the other hand, did not share this concept of a congregation (Stillman, 1975). Therefore, a civic group, the *waaf*, emerged to meet this obligation. According to Stillman (1975), "The institution of *waaf* is traced by Muslim tradition back to the prophet even though it is not specifically mentioned in the Koran" (p. 108). This institution also reflects the lack of separation between church and state in the Muslim tradition.

The *waaf* became a very important social welfare institution. By the middle ages, *waaf* funds were used for a variety of establishments beneficial to the community, including public soup kitchens, schools, hospices, orphanages, and hospitals, among others (Stillman, 1975). Of particular importance in Muslim charitable life was the care of the orphan, as Muhammad himself was an orphan. This care was mainly provided through schools which provided financial aid to orphans. In fact, some of the most well known Muslim philanthropists sought to care for the orphan. For example, Sultan al-Mansur Qalaun funded a charitable complex that still stands today; established in 1284, it included a Sufi hospice, hospital, and a school for orphans (Arjomand, 1999; Stillman, 1975). The Sultan's granddaughter went on to establish "an orphan's school where the children received every day five flat loaves of bread and a number of copper coins" as well as clothing (Stillman, 1975, p. 112). By the middle ages, the distribution of food had also become institutionalized. It was customary to distribute food at the end of Ramadan (the holy month) as well as other holy days throughout the year; furthermore, "every family of means had its clientele of needy persons who appeared on specific dates to receive charitable gifts which were considered their due" (Stillman, 1975, p. 114).

All such Islamic social welfare practices and institutions trace their foundation to references for the need to engage in charity in the *Qur'an*. Indeed, the *Qur'an* instructs Muslims to "practice regular charity" (Ali, 1993). Charity was a required practice for the righteous man. Sura 3:92 explains, "You cannot attain righteousness until you give to charity from the possessions you love. Whatever you give to charity, God is fully aware thereof." And the rewards to and behavior of the righteous are detailed in Sura 51:15–19:

> The righteous have deserved gardens and springs. They receive their Lord's rewards for they used to be pious. Rarely did they sleep the whole night. At dawn they prayed for forgiveness. A portion of their money was sat aside for the beggar and the needy.

Sura 93:10 supports the practice of charity and contains the "religious injunction not to rebuff the beggar" (Stillman, 1975, p. 114).

Much as in the old and new testaments of the *Bible*, the *Qur'an* outlines the recipients of charity. Sura 22, verse 177 deems that "Out of love for Him [Allah]" charity should be provided "For your kin, For orphans, For the needy, For the wayfarer, For those who ask, And for the ransom of slaves." Similarly, Sura 2:215 states: "They ask you about giving: say, 'The charity you give shall go to the parents, the relatives, the orphans, the poor, and the traveling alien. Any good you do, God is fully aware thereof." Even more explicit is Sura 9:60 which states,

> Charities shall go to the poor, the needy, the workers who collect them, the new converts, to free the slaves, to those burdened by sudden expenses, in the cause of God, and to the traveling alien. Such is God's commandment. God is omniscient, most wise.

Thus, the *Qur'an* establishes the need for charity, explains the benefit to the giver, and provides for the care of special classes of people.

Although there are many similarities between Islamic charity and its Judeo-Christian predecessors, these practices differ in some very fundamental ways. Unlike these earlier traditions, *zakat* was mandatory and enforced. Its purpose also differed in that its benefit was primarily for the giver than the receiver. Further, charitable funds were used for the spread of the Islamic faith, which represented a departure from previous systems. However, the most fundamental difference was the interconnection between church and state. Nevertheless, *zakat* served much the same function in Islamic society as it did in both Judaism and Christianity; these charitable practices provided care for the most vulnerable members of society. Charity was seen as an essential part of a civilized society and was imbedded in these religions which insured its practice.

CONCLUSION

From the earliest of civilization, man has recognized the need to care for those unable to provide for themselves. Thus, social welfare is as old as society itself. Social welfare originated under religious auspices that gave reasons for caring for the vulnerable, definitions of need, and guidelines for enacting charitable practices. Further, early religions gave us ideas and practices concerning charity that we still ascribe to today, including the notion of worthy and unworthy poor, soup kitchens, community chests, and widow's pensions. Beliefs about personal responsibility, social justice, and compassion similarly emerged in this early context. Charity was established as an integral part of Jewish, Christian, and Islamic society. Their ideals and charitable practices endured throughout the centuries. They evolved and changed and were eventually brought to the United States to lay the foundation for the American social welfare system.

REFERENCES

Ali, A. Y. (1993). *The meaning of the Holy Qur'an*. Brentwood, MD: Amana.

Applebaum, S. (1989). *Judea in Hellenistic and Roman times*. New York: E. J. Brill.

Arjomand, S. A. (1999). The law, agency, and policy in medieval Islamic society: Development of the institutions of learning from the tenth to the fifteenth century. *Comparative Studies in Society and History, 41,* 263–293.

Ausubel, M. (1964). *The book of Jewish knowledge*. New York: Crown Publishers.

Baron, S. (1952). *A social and religious history of the Jews* (Vol. 1). Philadelphia: The Jewish Publication Society of America.

Cascio, T. (1996). *Continuity and change: The organizational culture of Jewish Family and Children's Service of Philadelphia, 1822–1996*. (Unpublished doctoral dissertation.)

Dimont, C. T. (1910). Charity, almsgiving (Christian). In J. Hastings (Ed.), *Encyclopedia of religion and ethics* (Vol. 3, pp. 382–386). New York: Charles Scribner's Sons.

Edwards, J. (1989). Love: The sum of all virtue. In P. Ramsey (Ed.), *Ethical writings* (pp. 129–148). New Haven, CT: Yale University Press.

Hamel, G. (1990). *Poverty and charity in Roman Palestine, first three centuries, C.E.* Berkeley, CA: University of California Press.

Handel, G. (1982). *Social welfare in western society*. New York: Random House.

Haneef, S. (1993). *What everyone should know about Islam and Muslims*. Chicago: Kazi Publications.

Haynes, A. W., Eweiss, M., Abdel Mageed, L. M., & Chung, D. K. (1997). Islamic social transformation: Considerations for the social worker. *International Social Work, 40,* 265–276.

Hiro, D. (1989). *Holy wars: The rise of Islamic fundamentalism*. New York: Routledge, Chapman, & Hall, Inc.

Hofstein, S. (1981). Introduction: The Jewish poor. In G. Berger (Ed.), *The turbulent decades: Jewish communal services in America 1958–1978* (Vol. 2, pp. 1098–1101). New York: Conference of Jewish Communal Services.

Kutzik, A. (1959). *Social work and Jewish values: Basic areas of consonance and dissonance*. Washington, DC: Public Affairs Press.

Leiby, J. (1978). *A history of social welfare and social work in the United States*. New York: Columbia University Press.

Lods, A. (1971). *The prophets and the rise of Judaism* (S. H. Hooke, Trans.). Westport, CA: Greenwood Press.

Maguire, D. (1993). *The moral core of Judaism and Christianity*. Minneapolis, MN: Fortress Press.

Mancoske, R. (1987). The early development of the social work paradigm: Relationship and effectiveness themes in direct service in Catholic Charities. *Social Thought, 13,* 3–11.

Marty, M. (1980). Social service: Godly and Godless. *Social Service Review, 54,* 463–481.

Morris, R. (1986). *Rethinking social welfare: Why care for the stranger?* New York: Longman.

Neusner, J. (1990). *The economics of the Mishnah*. Chicago: University of Chicago Press.

Ortiz, L. P. (1995). Sectarian agencies. In R. Edwards (Ed.), *Encyclopedia of social work* (19th ed., Vol. 3, pp. 2109–2116). Washington, DC: NASW Press.

Peterson, R. D. (1993). *A concise history of Christianity*. Belmont, CA: Wadsworth Publishing Company.

Sherwood, P. (trans.). (1955). *St. Maximus the Confessor. The ascetic life: The four centuries on charity*. Westminster, MD: Newman Press.

Siporin, M. (1986). Contributions of religious values to social work and the law. *Social Thought, 12,* 35–50.

Stillman, N. A. (1975). Charity and social service in medieval Islam. *Societas—A Review of Social History, 5,* 105–116.

Swedenborg, E. (1914). The second act of charity. In J. Whitehead (Ed.), *Posthumous theological works of Emanuel Swedenborg* (pp. 239–243). New York: Swedenborg Foundation.

Tanenbaum, M. (1984). The concept of the human being in Jewish thought: Some ethical implications. In M. Tanenbaum, M. Wilson, & A. Rudin (Eds.), *Evangelicals and Jews in an age of pluralism* (pp. 47–63). Grand Rapids, MI: Baker Book House.

Trepp, L. (1980). *The complete book of Jewish observance*. New York: Summit Books.

Vriezen, T. (1963). *Religion of ancient Israel*. Philadelphia: The Westminster Press.

Williams, J. A. (Ed.). (1961). *Islam*. New York: George Braziller.

Zeitlin, I. (1984). *Ancient Judaism*. Cambridge: Polity Press.

PART II

THE CONTEMPORARY ROLE OF RELIGIOUS ORGANIZATIONS

Chapter 2

AMERICAN CONGREGATIONS AND THEIR SOCIAL PROGRAMS

Terry A. Wolfer and Michael E. Sherr

One of the most enduring features of the American landscape is the steeple, a landmark signaling the presence of a congregation. Whether small and simple or towering and ornate, whether soaring alongside skyscrapers or rising out of the rolling hills of the countryside or subtly blending into the sameness of a suburban housing development, the spaces set aside by Christian crosses, Jewish Stars of David, Muslim minarets, and other religious markers are the single most pervasive public gathering places in American society. From the moment Europeans landed on these shores, they began constructing meetinghouses—places for worship and for deliberation, for instruction in citizenship for this world and the next. Native Americans, of course, had their own sacred meeting places before the Europeans came. But by the time Alexis de Tocqueville arrived in 1831, voluntary organizations of all sorts—especially congregations—had become the center of American spiritual and democratic vitality. (Ammerman, Farnsley II, Adams, Becker, & Brasher, 1997, p. 1)

Until recently, social work scholars have tended to overlook the role of religious congregations in people's lives. This is ironic, given the social work profession's ecological and social systems perspectives. The oversight parallels, however,

an enormous cartographic failure by both local congregational leaders and experts on religion to locate American congregations precisely. . . . Leaders of local congregations seemed to work with idiosyncratic local maps that extended no further

23

than their property lines or perhaps ones that extended in diminishing detail into a nearby neighborhood or out towards one particular denominational mission field. Scholars of American religion and their colleagues in the social sciences and history employed maps drawn to a much larger scale, but these seldom contained any traces of local congregations. (Wind & Lewis, 1994, p. 10)

SPIRITUALITY, RELIGION, AND CONGREGATIONS IN SOCIAL WORK

In the last several years, however, social work literature has given increasing attention to spirituality and religion (Scales, Wolfer, & Sherwood, 2002). "Spirituality" is typically used in a fairly broad sense as referring to the human sense of and search for transcendence, meaning, and connectedness beyond the self. An example of this is provided by Canda and Furman (1999), who define spirituality as "a universal and fundamental aspect of what it is to be human—to search for a sense of meaning, purpose, and moral frameworks for relating with self, others, and the ultimate reality" (p. 37). "Religion" clearly relates to spirituality, but refers to a more formal organization and embodiment of spirituality into relatively specific belief systems, practices, and organizational structures. According to Canda and Furman (1999), religion is "an institutionalized pattern of beliefs, behaviors, and experiences, oriented toward spiritual concerns, and shared by a community and transmitted over time in traditions" (p. 37). For the most part, scholars have tended to focus alternately on the micro level of individual spiritual experience or the macro level of religion as cultural institution. Granted, a few have mentioned local congregations as possible resources for direct practice, particularly in relation to minority communities (e.g., Ellor, Netting, & Thibault, 1999). Overall, though, little attention has been given to the meso level of religion: local congregations. Even in its local form, "organized religion" is generally considered a pejorative expression.

In this chapter, we provide information about religious congregations in American life. In the first part, we define congregations, outline their major purposes and activities, and briefly argue for their centrality in understanding American religion. In the second part, we review empirical research on the ways congregations contribute to American life and the extent of these contributions. From a systems perspective, we identify and summarize measures of congregations' inputs, outputs, and community linkages.

DEFINING "CONGREGATION"

Recently, sociologist of religion Stephen Warner asserted: "After a period of neglect by scholars and denominational leaders, the *congregation*—a term this chapter uses to speak of local religious assemblies in general—has returned to the spotlight. Despite neglect, the congregation remains the bedrock of the American religious system" (1994, p. 54).

Interestingly, Warner argues that the significance of congregations is *increasing*, that there is a convergence across religious traditions in the United States toward de facto congregationalism.

> This convergence toward de facto congregationalism is happening despite, indeed partly because of, the increasing divergence of religious cultures in the United States; it constitutes both assimilation to a deep-seated interdenominational American religious model and selective adaptation of normative elements contained in the various religious traditions that make up our pluralistic mosaic. (Warner, 1994, p. 54)

The historical and sociological factors for the prominence of congregations in America are beyond the scope of this chapter. Suffice it to say that congregations comprise the primary site for collective religious experience in America, the key to understanding religion in America, and a major factor in the social system of American society (Putnam, 2000; Warner, 1994). For these reasons, we devote this chapter to describing congregations and their various activities.

Congregations can be defined most simply as "local gatherings for religious purposes" (Harris, 1998, p. 602). Drawing on work by Hopewell (1987), Harris (1998) suggests that congregation can be defined

> as a local organization in which people "regularly gather for what they feel to be religious purposes" and as "a group that possesses a special name and recognized members who assemble regularly to celebrate a more universally practiced worship but who communicate with each other sufficiently to develop intrinsic patterns of conduct, outlook and story." (p. 616)

Furthermore, as the introductory quotation suggested, congregations are typically associated with a building, and the congregation and this physical meeting place are often referred to synonymously (Moberg, 1984, p. 16). Defined in this way, congregations include what we commonly refer to as local churches, synagogues, temples, and mosques, all of which comprise groups of people who share religious activities and interpersonal relationships. To go a bit further, sociologist R. Stephen Warner (1994) asserts,

The typical American congregation is a voluntary religious community. To say that the congregation is a *religious* community is to say that it is ordinarily a face-to-face assembly of persons who together engage in many activities, all of them somehow understood as having "religious" meaning, few of them lacking emotional significance. To say that the congregation is a *voluntary* community is to say that mobilization of members must rely on idealism or personal persuasion rather than coercion or material incentives, but *voluntary* also signifies, particularly in the U.S., that the congregation cannot assume the loyal adherence of its members as if they were all part of the same tribe; it must actively recruit them. (p. 63)

Congregations, however, cannot be adequately understood as mere social gatherings. As a *religious* organization, a congregation "is one of the few places in our culture where persons regularly engage in the enduring human attempt to relate to the holy or transcendent, and 'the relationship of these universal human concerns to the particularities of one local place of worship is what makes congregational [life] so interesting' " (Wind & Lewis, 1994, p. 9).

For research purposes, an operational definition brings greater clarity and precision. Borrowing from Wind and Lewis (1994), Boddie, Cnaan, and DiIulio (2001) define as a congregation any religious gathering that meets the following seven criteria (pp. 9–10): It is a group of people that

1. has a shared identity;
2. meets regularly on an ongoing basis;
3. comes together primarily for worship and has accepted teachings, rituals, and practices;
4. meets and worships at a designated place;
5. gathers for worship outside the regular purposes and location of a living or work space;
6. has an identified religious leader; and
7. has an official name and some formal structure that conveys its purpose and identity.

These criteria effectively exclude informal, temporary, and occasional religious gatherings and religiously oriented groups that do not meet primarily for worship.

OTHER RELIGIOUS ORGANIZATIONS

Finally, from a systems perspective, it is also helpful to identify congregations' relationships with other parts of the religious world. Within the religious world, congregations may be distinguished from other types of religious organizations. In this regard, Cnaan, Wineburg, and Boddie (1999) provide a typology of religiously-based social service organizations "based on the geographical locus of service and, by default, the organizational complexity" (p. 27):

1. Local congregations: as defined above.
2. Interfaith agencies and ecumenical coalitions: "organizations, local congregations from different religions, and denominations join together for purposes of community solidarity, social action, and/or providing large-scale services that are beyond the scope of a single congregation" (p. 32).
3. Citywide or regionwide sectarian agencies: "the one most often identified with religious-based social service delivery. . . . Sectarian agencies often employ social workers as service providers and managers and serve as placement sites for social work students" (pp. 33, 34).
4. National projects and organizations under religious auspices: "have multiple affiliates or chapters throughout the nation and even the world [and] have become a major force in provision of services to communities" (p. 36).
5. Paradenominational advocacy and relief organizations: "serve or advocate for people in need and are concerned with improving educational opportunities for people . . . although the organizations are not officially affiliated with any religion or denomination, they are based on religious principles and have strong theological undertones in their mission statements. Their goal is to improve the social condition by applying religious principles to a secular world" (p. 41).
6. Religiously affiliated international organizations: "the emphasis of today's religiously affiliated international organizations is to bring relief and aid to underserved peoples of the world's poorest nations. In many countries . . . they are defined as and operate as nongovernmental organizations (NGOs); in other countries they take the form of missionary agencies" (p. 43).

Of these, local congregations are by far the most numerous and most widely dispersed in American society. Typically, the other types of religious organizations have linkages with numerous congregations. In fact, local congregations usually provide the base of support, in terms of both finances and personnel, for religious organizations serving larger geographic areas or focusing on particular populations or needs. How do congregations do this? The core activities of congregations help to address this question.

CORE ACTIVITIES OF CONGREGATIONS

Across religious traditions, a congregation's basic goal is the spiritual well-being of its members (Ammerman, 2001). Related to this goal, the core activities of congregations include: worship, education, mission, steward-ship, and fellowship (Warner, 1994, p. 64). Though the core activities may take many forms in various religious traditions, they are all geared toward addressing this basic goal. Does this goal suggest an exclusively inward focus for congregations? No, because in most religions, congregational outreach is understood as an integral part of the spiritual life. At least two of the core activities specifically include an outward focus: mission and stewardship. A third, education, may also be related because it socializes people, especially children and newcomers, into the spiritual life.

Two of the core activities most distinguish congregations from other types of voluntary associations, though, and also emerge as most important in congregations. Perhaps surprisingly, both have special relevance for the relationship between congregations and the communities in which they reside. "Across every tradition and in every region, congregations agree— their *highest priority is providing opportunities for vital spiritual worship.* That is where leaders put the most energy, and that is the first thing members look for when seeking a place to join" (emphasis in original; Ammerman, 2001, p. 6). This is the activity that most readily distinguishes congregations from other forms of voluntary association.

Such "otherworldly" concern may seem irrelevant for the larger community. But as Ammerman (2001) points out, worship regularly provides opportunity for reflecting on their personal priorities, recommitting to what's really important, reminding people they are not the center of the universe and ought to care for others, and reinforcing a moral framework to guide their behavior. Less cognitively, worship can help establish a relational context that reassures people they are loved and have reason to hope. This love empowers people to take risks and persist in difficult circumstances. This may be especially true for marginalized and oppressed people (Billingsley, 1999).

That is not all. "The work congregations put second on their list—right behind worship and spiritual life—is 'fellowship.' They see themselves as a family, a community of people who care for each other and do things together" (Ammerman, 2001, p. 7). Leaders work hard to provide a family-like atmosphere, what members indicate they desire when choosing a congregation. Even the new breed of megachurches, congregations with more than 2,000 weekly participants, intentionally develop small groups and other structures to provide ample face-to-face relationships for their members (Thornburgh & Wolfer, 2000).

The inward look of fellowship may also seem irrelevant for the larger community. But it is the basis for development of "social capital," defined as the "connections among individuals—social networks and the norms of reciprocity and trustworthiness that arise from them" (Putnam, 2000, p. 19). For many people, participating in congregational life builds the networks that help to hold society together and also provides opportunities for them to develop civic skills (Ammerman, 2001; Marty, 1994; Putnam, 2000).

From another perspective, the worship and fellowship activities of congregations roughly exemplify the two general contributions that religion makes in society. It has long been understood that "Religious ideals are potentially powerful sources of commitment and motivation" that, for good or ill, lead human beings to "make enormous sacrifices if they believe themselves to be driven by a divine force" (Wald, 1987, pp. 29–30, as cited in Putnam, 2000, p. 67). These religious ideals are often emphasized during worship. But, Putnam argues, "the social ties embodied in religious communities are at least as important as religious beliefs per se in accounting for volunteerism and philanthropy. Connectedness, not merely faith, is responsible for the beneficience of church people" (p. 67). Connectedness grows out of fellowship. For these reasons, congregations play an essential role in people's religious lives, but one that, until recently, has been generally underappreciated. Indeed, as one social scientist concluded recently, "faith communities in which people worship together are arguably the single most important repository of social capital in America" (Putnam, 2000, p. 66).

SCHOLARLY STUDY OF CONGREGATIONS

H. Paul Douglas and Edmund deS. Brunner initiated study of congregations in 1935 (Chaves, Konieczny, Beyerlein, & Barman, 1999). The structures and activities of congregations, however, were largely ignored by social scientists for the next 45 years. During the 1980s, though, marked changes in the human service system brought renewed attention to congregations. Federal cuts in social spending shifted much of the responsibility for providing social programs to states and localities. An assumption contributing to the federal cuts was that social problems might be better handled by religious congregations and other mediating institutions. President Reagan urged religious congregations to help compensate for cutbacks in government spending by increasing their involvement in human service activity (Salamon & Teitelbaum, 1984). These events spurred a renewed interest in determining the variety and extent of services provided by religious congregations. Little was known about the characteristics of congregations, their social service delivery structure, or their willingness and capacity to take on this added responsibility.

Salamon and Teitelbaum (1984) were the first to study religious congregations in the new era of federal cutbacks. They recognized the need to examine the social service programs already being provided by congregations, in order to determine congregational capacity for more responsibility. Their survey of 2,200 congregations from 16 areas of the country achieved a 37% response rate (n = 801). Their study offered an initial look into the involvement of congregations in social service activities, though Salamon and Teitelbaum's conclusions seem too skeptical. For example, despite finding large amounts of service activities by congregations, they assert the absolute value of these services was quite limited. In general, Salamon and Teitelbaum (1984) appeared to approach their research question with a negative bias:

> Despite the fact that religious congregations absorb almost half of all charitable resources in the country, we know precious little in any solid, empirical way about what they do with these resources, and in particular what portion of them find their way into the provision of human services. (p. 62)

Despite significant shortcomings, the study was groundbreaking. It brought awareness of the need to investigate the role of congregations in social service delivery. Indeed, the study sparked increasing study of congregations. It also foreshadowed the difficulty other scholars would have accurately measuring and describing the social service activities of congregations.

DEMOGRAPHICS OF AMERICAN CONGREGATIONS

Although this chapter focuses on congregations, it may be helpful to summarize overall membership and participation rates for the U.S. population.

Since before de Tocqueville, the United States has sustained comparatively high rates of religious involvement (Holifield, 1994). Despite predictions of decline based on secularization theory, religious involvement has remained relatively steady throughout U.S. history: "For most of the past three hundred years, from 35 to 40 percent of the population has probably participated in congregations with some degree of regularity" (Holifield, 1994, p. 24). Recently, Hodgkinson, Weitzman, and Kirsh (1990) suggested that roughly one third of Americans attend services regularly, one third attend occasionally, and one third attend rarely or not at all.

More precisely, the annual *Yearbook of American and Canadian Churches* indicates that American denominations report more than 150 million members (Linder, 2001). Because the *Yearbook* is primarily limited to major Christian denominations, however, it omits many smaller denominations. In addition, an estimated 10% of churchgoers attend nondenominational congregations (Chaves et al., 1999), a group not counted by the *Yearbook*. More significantly, though, the *Yearbook* does not include congregations from most non-Christian religions, a growing sector of American religious life. In addition to these sampling issues, the *Yearbook* suffers from the limitations of denominational statistics: "denominations vary in the strictness of their definition of membership, membership figures are only irregularly updated, self-reports may be inflated, and not all churches keep or report accurate records" (Putnam, 2000, p. 69). In most denominations, membership rates exceed attendance rates, a more important indicator of congregational involvement.

Several major national polls have inquired annually about weekly congregational participation. For example, since 1939, the Gallup poll has posed a standard question: "Did you yourself happen to attend church [or synagogue] in the last seven days?" (cited in Putnam, 2000, p. 453). Other such polls include Roper, National Election Studies, General Social Survey, and DDB Needham. Summarizing data from these five major polls over much of the last half century, Putnam (2000) reports that "in any given week over these five decades, roughly 40–45 percent of Americans claim to have attended religious services" (p. 70). For reasons that become evident below, data regarding church membership and attendance remain uneven and incomplete.

Membership and attendance rates of individuals provide important information about religious involvement in America. However, focusing on individual level data obscures the significant social and communal dimension of religious life represented by congregations. For that reason, we focus instead on the congregation as the unit of analysis.

NUMBER OF CONGREGATIONS

While no one knows the exact number, the estimates of the number of congregations in the United States range from a low of 200,000 to a high of 450,000 (Ammerman, 2001; Boddie et al., 2001; Dudley & Roozen, 2001). The extreme range hints at the difficulty of accurately counting congregations and making generalizable assertions.

As part of an effort to assess the effects of individuals' congregational involvement on philanthropy, Hodgkinson, Weitzman, and Kirsh (1988) sought to use a stratified random sampling method. To obtain a sampling frame, they manually counted the number of congregations listed in telephone directories for the continental United States. This initial effort to draw a nationally representative sample identified 294,271 congregations.

In a 2-year effort to count congregations in the city of Philadelphia, Boddie, Cnaan, and DiIulio (2001) demonstrate the difficulty of developing a complete list. First, a working list of congregations was identified, by combining congregations listed in the telephone directory with a property tax list from the city. Next, a list of known congregations was requested from every denomination and interfaith organization in the region. A manual comparison of the three lists combined to form one list. In interviews, researchers asked key informants from every congregation to provide the telephone numbers and addresses of every congregation with which they collaborate. Any newly identified congregations were added to the list of those already collected. An advisory board made up of religious leaders throughout the city reviewed the list and identified any missing congregations known to them. Finally, like followup workers for the United States Census, graduate assistants went through the city, walking block by block through neighborhoods to identify unlisted storefront churches and other congregations not on the master list. Their final estimate in Philadelphia was 2,010 congregations.

Quite significantly, Boddie and colleagues (2001) found that the combined list from the telephone directory and property tax rolls identified only 61% (1,218 of 2,010) of the congregations in the city. Though based only on a study of Philadelphia, this finding demonstrates the potential error of conventional approaches to study of congregations and the difficulty of accurately estimating the number of congregations or creating sampling frames from which to draw representative samples. As a result, information gleaned from studies utilizing telephone directories or other traditional approaches must be interpreted with caution.

According to Dudley and Roozen (2001), half of all congregations (52%) are found in rural areas and small towns, with estimates ranging from a low of 116,872 to a high of 200,000 (Boddie et al., 2001). Counting congregations in rural areas may pose special difficulties because many of these congregations are quite hard to find. In fact, Heyer-Gray and Neitz (1998) describe as "invisible" congregations that have "no phone number listed in the phone book, no mailing address, an outdated and inaccurate listing in the local newspaper, no identifiable denominational affiliation, and certainly no website" (p. 4). In addition, some congregations in rural areas employ nonresident clergy. Because many studies use clergy as key informants, these congregations are also less accessible to researchers (Heyer-Gray & Neitz, 1998).

SIZE OF CONGREGATIONS

According to the Independent Sector (which is a membership organization of "leading nonprofits, foundations, and corporations strengthening not-for-profit initiative, philanthropy, and citizen action"), most congregations are comprised of 100 to 400 members (Hodgkinson, Weitzman, & Kirsh, 1993). The congregations they classify as small have less than 100 members and comprise 20% of all congregations. Medium congregations have 100–400 members and comprise 52% of congregations, while large congregations have more than 400 members and comprise the remaining 28%. As suggested above, however, the use of telephone directories as a sampling frame probably overrepresents larger congregations and undermines the validity of these figures.

Other studies report a different distribution of congregations by size. In a massive study, Dudley and Roozen (2001) surveyed congregations from 41 collaborating denominations. Although several large denominations are not represented in the study (e.g., Jehovah's Witnesses, Lutheran Church-Missouri Synod, Salvation Army, Church of God), Dudley and Roozen estimate that the data applies to about 80% of U.S. congregations. Because most denominations with large membership participated, however, they estimate that their data applies to 90% of the worshippers in the United States. The survey was completed by religious leaders from a total of 14,301 congregations. The researchers found that half (50%) of all congregations in the United States have fewer than 100 regularly participating members. Moreover, half of these have fewer than 50 such members. On the other hand, one third (33%) of congregations have 100–349 regularly participating members and the remainder (17%) have 400 or more. Not surprisingly, congregations located in rural areas and small towns tend to be quite small while those in suburbs, especially newer suburbs, tend to be the largest (Dudley & Roozen, 2001).

Methodologically, the National Congregational Study (NCS) was an innovative and perhaps the most rigorous effort thus far to collect data about congregations (Chaves, 1999). Starting with a random sample of individuals selected for the 1998 General Social Survey (GSS), a hypernetwork or multiplicity sampling design was used to randomly select the congregations. A hypernetwork sampling design assumes that organizations attached to a random sample of individuals constitute a random sample of organizations. In the end, the NCS sample consisted of 1,480 congregations. Trained interviewers completed data collection with key informants from 84% of all nominated congregations, a high response rate. The NCS helps to control for the overrepresentation of larger congregations that are more likely to be identified by telephone directories or other non-random sampling frames by estimating the degree to which they are overrepresented.

As a result, the NCS appears to provide a more accurate method for estimating of the size of congregations. Chaves and associates (1999) describe the size of congregations in two ways. The first is a distribution of congregations based on the size of the membership. The second is a distribution of where religious participants tend to worship. This difference may appear arbitrary, however, estimates from either method alone provide an incomplete picture. Like Dudley and Roozen (2001), Chaves and colleagues (1999) found that most congregations are small: 50% of congregations have only 75 regular members, while only 10% of congregations have more than 350 regular members. The second approach yields a different picture. Although a majority of congregations are small, these congregations include only 11% of the weekly religious service participants in the country. In contrast, the few congregations that have more than 350 members contain almost half of the country's religious service weekly participants. Interpreting the results together, while most congregations are small, attendance patterns of regular religious participants reveal that a majority worship in the relatively small number of large congregations. Likewise, small congregations contain a minimal number of American religious participants. Given this finding, the results of other studies that do not account for the size distribution of congregations are most likely not representative of all congregations, though they may adequately reflect data on congregations most participants attend. Nevertheless, this adds to the difficulty of accurately describing the variety and extent of social service activities in congregations.

RELIGIOUS TRADITIONS

American congregations represent all of the major world religions. By various counts, there are more than 200 denominations (Cnaan, 1999, p. 28) or nearly 1,600 denominations (Warner, 1994, p. 58). Within this diversity, Christian denominations can be grouped into some 25 denominational families, with several broader divisions. For example, Ammerman (2001) categorizes denominations into four different clusters. These include mainline Protestant (e.g., Presbyterians, Episcopalians, Methodists, Lutherans, conservative Protestant [e.g., Southern Baptists, Pentecostals, Nazarenes, Seventh Day Adventists]), Roman Catholic or Eastern Orthodox, historic African American (e.g., Church of God in Christ, African Methodist Episcopal, National Baptist), other Christian (e.g., Jehovah's Witnesses, Mormons), and other groups that are not Christian (e.g., Jewish, Muslim, Hindu, Buddhist). Of all American congregations, Ammerman classifies more than half (53%) as conservative Protestant and another quarter (26%) as mainline Protestant. Congregations from historic African American denominations comprise 7% of the total, and Catholic and Orthodox another 6%. Jewish and other non-Christian religions comprise 5% of all congregations, a small but growing proportion.

Studies based on denominational samples, as many are, risk overlooking a substantial number of congregations. As Chaves and colleagues (1999) found, some 19% of all congregations are unaffiliated or "nondenominational" congregations. Together, such congregations would constitute the single largest "denominational" grouping of congregations in America. Again, however, the proportion of congregations may be somewhat misleading (Chaves, Konieczny, Beyerlein, & Barman, 1999). While nondenominational congregations comprise nearly one fifth (19%) of all congregations, they include only 10.7% of regular attenders. Likewise, while 16.1% of congregations are Southern Baptist, they include 11.2% of attenders. In contrast, while only 6.1% of congregations are Roman Catholic, they include 28.6% of attenders (and an even higher percentage of members).

ETHNICITY

Congregations reflect the unusual ethnic diversity of the United States. To a large extent, this means that congregations contain the various ethnic and racial groups present in U.S. society. Increasingly, though, denominations and individual congregations also contain multiple groups: nearly as many congregations are "significantly integrated" as have predominantly Latino, Asian, or African American members (Ammerman, 2001, p. 11). A majority of congregations (52%) are "nearly all white," that is, have more than 90% European-American members (Ammerman, 2001). Ammerman classifies 11% of congregations as "multi-ethnic," those with less than 60% of a single ethnic group. The massive Faith Communities Today (FCT) study found that 76% of congregations contained "most to all" adult White members (Dudley & Roozen, 2001, p. 12). The common adage that "Sunday morning is the most segregated time of the week," however, is not supported by the data. "Sunday morning is neither more (nor less) segregated than Saturday night . . . congregations' participants represent a mirror image of the racial composition of the zip codes in which their congregations are located" (Dudley & Roozen, 2001, p. 12). In other words, the ethnic segregation of congregations essentially reflects that of their neighborhoods.

Furthermore, it appears that ethnic segregation increasingly reflects preferences of minority groups rather than exclusion by dominant groups. Since country-of-origin quotas were abolished in 1965, increasing non-European immigration has produced what Warner (1994) identifies as one of two major trends in American congregations, "the flowering of immigrant religious centers" (p. 57). The new congregations include ethnic congregations of Christian denominations (e.g., Korean and Hispanic congregations of various Protestant denominations) as well as non-Christian religions (e.g., Buddhist, Muslims, Hindus) (Warner, 1994, p. 57). Recent data indicates that there are now more people of Islamic than Jewish faith in America, and a growing number of mosques where Muslims congregate.

Over the last 25 years, congregations with mostly ethnic-minority populations are being established in growing numbers. Presently, 20% of all congregations have a majority of Latinos, Asians, or African Americans (Ammerman, 2001). Establishing congregations serves a variety of functions for ethnic minorities. These congregations help to preserve a group's cultural identity, provide a socially acceptable channel of communication to participate with other societal institutions, and provide a sense of ownership and belonging in the community (Ammerman, 2001; Moon, Wolfer, & Robinson, 2001).

TYPES OF CONGREGATIONAL OUTREACH

Ammerman (2001) categorizes congregational outreach into six areas. The most frequent activities are providing direct services to people in immediate need (e.g., emergency food, shelter, clothing). The second most common activities are various educational, cultural, and health-related activities (e.g., nursery schools, tutoring programs, afterschool programs, Boy Scouts, senior centers). Third, though significantly less common, community development activities (e.g., neighborhood associations and civic groups) are organized by congregations. Congregations also provide outreach support for specific groups of people working to help themselves, that is, self-help groups (e.g., Alcoholics Anonymous). Fourth, although not viewed by social workers as a social service activity, some congregations provide evangelistic outreach activities at home and abroad in hopes of improving the world "one soul at a time." Fifth, these efforts often inspire humanitarian efforts to provide food, shelter, and medical care for third world countries. Finally, some congregations participate in public advocacy. From environment and health care to civil rights, congregations sometimes pursue partnerships with other organizations to address broad political issues (Ammerman, 2001, p. 13).

Despite the diverse settings and methodologies used to study congregations, results about the variety of social services have yielded several similar findings. One common finding is the wide array of different services provided by congregations (De Vita, Printz Platnick, & Twombly, 1999; Hodgkinson, Weitzman, & Kirsh, 1988; Salamon & Teitelbaum, 1984; Wineburg, 1994). In the most thorough assessment to date, Boddie and colleagues (2001) identify a total of 2,432 service programs conducted by religious congregations in Philadelphia. Notably, they excluded solely religious activities. Examples of the counted service programs include food pantries, clothing closets, summer day camp, recreational programs for children and adolescents, day care for children and elderly, soup kitchens for the homeless, educational tutoring, health screening, job counseling and placement, blood drives, drug and alcohol prevention, free transportation, in-home assistance, space for a variety of self-help groups, and financial and volunteer support for local agencies.

In the same study, Boddie and associates (2001) noted that congregational leaders typically underreport service programs on conventional surveys. When responding to open-ended survey questions, leaders apparently do not recall all the services their congregations provide. To counter this problem, Boddie, Cnaan, and DiIulio developed a comprehensive 215-item checklist of services activities based on field research. They then used this checklist to elicit data from congregational leaders.

Another common finding is the high prevalence for certain types of services. Across research studies, emergency relief programs (e.g., food, financial assistance, clothing) emerge as the most common services provided by congregations. Salamon and Teitelbaum (1984) report the most common types of direct services provided by congregations are food (46.1%), cash (32.8%), and clothing (31.9%). In a recent census of the social service programs of religious congregations in Philadelphia, 46.6% of the congregations offered food pantries, 33.5% offered clothing closets, and nearly 20% offered emergency shelter (Boddie et al., 2001). Findings from a survey of community services activities of congregations in New Jersey indicate that more than three quarters (77%) offered emergency programs providing food, cash assistance, clothing, and shelter (De Vita et al., 1999). Likewise, Chaves (1999a) found that congregations favored food projects, clothing projects, and programs providing emergency housing. In a random survey of 635 Black congregations from more than a dozen states across the northern and midwestern U.S., Billingsley and Caldwell (1994) found that food and clothing support services were by far the most frequently provided services.

Scholars differ regarding the reasons for these patterns. Chaves (1999a) asserts that these types of services are more prevalent because they do not require sustained involvement by the congregations to meet local goals. Cnaan (1999) offers a different explanation for this pattern. Historically, religious groups were the nation's sole provider of social services. At the turn of the 20th century, social services gradually traded their religious base for one that was secular, temporal, and professional. As a result, religious congregations shifted their focus to filling the gaps of the secular system, providing emergency relief for people who fell through the cracks of the system, and leaving longer-term services to the government. As Wineburg (1994) indicates, however, religious congregations are willing to make long-term commitments if they are called upon and properly trained. As the federal government continues expanding financial support to congregational efforts to deliver social service programs, the array of services may shift from emergency relief to sustained efforts to address social problems. The need for a safety net of emergency relief, however, will still remain. At this point, it is unclear which institutions will provide this emergency relief.

To varying degrees, congregations also appear to be responsive to the needs of society. Issues such as teen pregnancy, substance abuse, HIV/AIDS, and single-parent households, are making the delivery of social service programs even more challenging. Increasing numbers of congregations are creating programs to address these complex issues. For example, in Philadelphia, 11.4% of congregations offered HIV/AIDS programs, 13.7% offered substance abuse treatment, and 8.5% offered sex education (Boddie et al., 2001). Research in other geographical locations report similar findings (e.g., Castelli & McCarthy, 1998; see also Sherman, 2000).

Going further, Billingsley and Caldwell (1994) sorted congregations based on the particular clusters of activities in which they engage. In their survey of Black congregations, they identified three patterns of social service outreach among the congregations. They classified one third of the congregations as "privativistic." These congregations do not engage in any community programs. Another third of the congregations engage in minimal community programs. These programs tend to be food programs and clothing drives. Finally, another third of the congregations engage in substantial social programs that tend to be sustained. This last group of congregations is also more likely to offer programs that promote social and economic justice. As other researchers have confirmed, social and economic justice programs are especially concentrated among African American congregations (Ammerman, 2001; Cnaan & Boddie, 2001).

EXTENT OF SOCIAL SERVICE ACTIVITY

The literature on religious congregations describes the extent of social service activity in a variety of ways. For present purposes, we categorize the research findings into five groups:

1) the number of programs offered by congregations;
2) the amount of volunteerism;
3) the use of facilities;
4) collaboration with outside organizations; and
5) the economic value.

Number of Programs

Although several studies attempt to calculate the number of programs offered by congregations, the findings have yielded inconsistent estimates. The early survey by Salamon and Teiltelbaum (1984) indicated that only 54% of congregations offer social service programs. In contrast, the study of historic religious congregations in six large metropolitan cities, found that 91% reported providing at least one social service (Cnaan et al., 1999). Likewise, 87% of the congregations in an inclusive Philadelphia survey reported offering at least one social program that serves the community (Boddie et al., 2001). From another angle, Castelli and McCarthy's (1998) analysis of the 1992 Independent Sector study indicates that only 7% of congregations did not have any form of social service programs. But Chaves (1999a) estimates that only 57% of congregations, containing 75% of religious participants, participated in some type of social service projects. Chavez recognizes that his estimates are substantially lower than reports in the studies mentioned above. He posits that the other studies failed to control for sampling bias toward larger, urban congregations. This bias may have caused these studies to overestimate the proportion of congregations involved in social service programs. Researchers agree on the need for more precise measurements of congregational programs before designing and implementing new welfare policies (Boddie et al., 2001; Castelli & McCarthy, 1998; Cnaan et al., 1999; Wineburg, 2001).

Not only are most congregations involved in such programming, they have multiple commitments. In addition to prevalence of programming, some researchers have focused on average numbers of programs per congregation. For example, congregations in Philadelphia reported providing 2.33 different programs (Boddie et al., 2001). In contrast, Ammerman (2001) reported that the average congregation provided money, volunteers, space, and in-kind donations to six community outreach programs. More specifically, Ammerman found that the average congregation provided resources for two direct service programs; one community development or political/social advocacy program; and two educational, health, or cultural programs. Among the one quarter of congregations involved in evangelistic and mission work, each supports two such organizations. The remainder have connections with other civic and social programs, including personal growth and self-help groups.

Volunteerism

Volunteerism is another way congregations support their local communities (Ammerman, 2001; Wineburg, 1992). In general, volunteerism refers to a set of activities in which people engage, usually without pay, on behalf of others in need (Wilson & Janoski, 1995). Hodgkinson (1990) identifies volunteerism in congregations as one component of stewardship. Stewardship involves the use of time, talent, and wealth of individuals to serve a community. Hodgkinson points out that stewardship thrives when there is voluntary participation with programs internal to the congregation as well as with external programs. Hodge, Zech, McNamara, and Donahue (1998) describe the scope of volunteer activity in terms of the types of services to which congregational members give their time, their opportunity cost, and the cost for agencies and churches to operate without volunteers. Congregations contribute to volunteer activity in a community by directly recruiting and organizing volunteers for organizations, by encouraging individual members of the congregation to engage in volunteer activities on their own, and by supporting clergy who use a percentage of their time to assist social service programs.

On average, congregations contribute volunteers to three organizations (Ammerman, 2001). Although some congregations send dozens of volunteers to certain organizations, an average of five members are involved with each organization (Ammerman, 2001). Overall, individual congregants contribute 1 to 4 hours of volunteer labor each month to internal congregational activities (Hodge et al., 1998). Religious participants contribute to the internal welfare of congregations by volunteering to help teach religious classes, serving on a committee, leading part of the worship service, and maintaining the grounds. Furthermore, paid staff usually earn below market wages and engage in activities that go beyond their job descriptions (Murnion, 1992).

Hodgkinson (1990) indicates that 45%–54% of members of congregations between 18 and 64 years of age volunteer, and 38% of members 65 years of age and older volunteer. She finds that these volunteers contribute 107 million hours of service per month. Of that total, 51 million hours are devoted to internal operations of the congregations, and 56 million hours are devoted to activities outside the congregation including human services and welfare, education, arts and culture, international causes, and environmental improvement.

In a six-city study, Cnaan (1998) reported that the average total hours of volunteer work per congregation per month was 147.6. For congregations in two cities, Indianapolis and Mobile, the average hours of volunteer work per month was more than 160 hours. This finding indicates that volunteer service in each of the six cities is equivalent to nearly one full-time employee per program. Assessing the value of each volunteer hour to be $11.58 (Hodgkinson et al., 1993), the estimated value of 49,892.18 volunteer hours per month was $577,751.44, or $6,933,017.33 a year. This is a conservative estimate since many congregations surveyed did not provide information on volunteer hours.

Wuthnow (1990) explains why attempts to calculate the quantity of volunteer activity from members of congregations will generate conservative figures. He suggests that many religious congregations believe that it is important not to talk about their volunteer activities or their motivation for participating. Furthermore, he warns of the danger of examining volunteerism too closely. He believes the process of collecting empirical information about volunteerism may obscure efforts to understand the deepest roots of altruism.

Research attempting to explain and predict volunteer activity provide support for Wuthnow's (1990) comments. After Wilson and Janoski (1995) failed to find a single statistically significant causal relationship, they concluded, "The data presented in this paper indicate that the relation between religion and volunteering is much more complex than previously believed" (p. 148). Cnaan, Kasternakis, and Wineburg (1993) found no association between religious motivation and volunteer work. However, Hodgkinson, Weitzman, and Kirsch (1990) observed an association between the frequency of congregational attendance and increased volunteerism. Specifically, their findings suggest members of congregations who attend religious services weekly are the individuals most likely to volunteer. Overall, their findings reveal that members of congregations are more likely to volunteer (51%) than nonmembers (33%). This hints at the central role congregations have in generating and channeling volunteerism.

Facilities

Religious congregations meet in buildings that have rooms used for other purposes, in addition to worship services. As mentioned above, the work of "fellowship" is seen as very important to congregations. This is evident by the amount of space set aside for such work. Oftentimes churches, mosques, and synagogues will have several fellowship halls, kitchens, and classrooms. Larger congregations may even have their own school buildings and gymnasiums. Furthermore, congregations may own other property used for shelters, food storage, and other social service programs. Schaller (1988) estimates that three times more people use the facilities of congregations during the week than on Sundays.

Often, congregations allow outside organizations to use the space of their buildings free of charge (or they may charge a minimal fee). On average, there are nearly two outside organizations that use the space of each congregation (Ammerman, 2001). Though generally skeptical about the potential contribution of congregations, even Salamon and Teitelbaum (1984) recognized that 66% of congregations make their facilities available for use by outside groups. Likewise, other researchers have found that about six out of ten congregations make their facilities available to other organizations in the community (e.g., Ammerman, 2001; Boddie et al.,

2001; Hodgkinson et al., 1988). Typical "outside" uses of congregational facilities include nursery schools, adult day care, aerobic classes, mutual self-help groups, adult literacy education classes, and committee meetings.

From another perspective, many public and private social service agencies and self-help groups depend upon use of congregational facilities. For example, Wineburg (1996) found that 91 of 183 social service agencies and self-help organizations in Greensboro, North Carolina routinely operate aspects of their programs in congregational facilities. If congregations did not provide free or affordable space, it appears that many social service programs offered by community agencies would have to be reduced or made less accessible (Wineburg, 1996).

Allowing other agencies to use their facilities can be costly. Cnaan (1998) estimates the average monthly value of the space provided by congregations is $561.67 per program. The annual contribution for congregations providing space to organizations in his study was $1,455,848.64. This figure is conservative given that it does not include the cost of utilities. Furthermore, Cnaan points out that it is difficult to calculate the fair market value of the space provided by congregations because there is usually no other property in the same area with so many large rooms and a full size kitchen.

Providing space for outside organizations appears to be a substantial contribution made by more than half of all congregations. At a time when the amount of meeting space in general has declined, by offering their space to other organizations, congregations play an important role in creating and maintaining a sense of community (Hodgkninson, 1990).

Estimating the Economic Value of Congregational Contributions

The economic value of social services provided by religious congregations is unclear. As stated earlier, Salamon and Teitelbaum (1984) reported that less than 10% of the congregations in their study devoted as much as $25,000 to the direct provision of services. They concluded, quite appropriately, that the absolute value of congregational services, compared to the need, was minimal. But other studies suggest much higher amounts of support. For example, Hodgkinson, Weitzman, and Kirsch (1990) reported that congregations in 1986 allocated $19.1 billion (46% of $41.6 billion) to the direct provision of social services. In their analysis of the 1992 Independent Sector study of congregations, Castelli and McCarthy (1998) estimated that congregations spend roughly 20% of their budgets on social service programs.

The ambiguity of the above figures is due to the way in which scholars have attempted to define and measure the economic value of programs. Some studies use formulas that focus on the costs of specific aspects of social programs (e.g., Hodge et al., 1998; Wineburg, 1990). Other studies include aspects that are more difficult to calculate in terms of monetary value. Hodgkinson (1990) points out that congregations help build community cohesion, provide informal training for a pool of leadership, and improve the quality of life in a community. These contributions to the community are not measurable in monetary value; however, it is obvious that the absence of these benefits would be costly to replace.

In an effort to reflect the direct and indirect monetary benefits to society, Cnaan and his colleagues (Boddie et al., 2001; Cnaan et al., 1999) conceptualize the value of services in terms of their "replacement value," that is, the cost of replacing the social and community services provided by congregations. The "replacement value" includes calculating the direct financial support from the congregation, the in-kind support, the cost of utilities, the estimated value of space used for the programs, and the value of clergy, staff, and volunteer hours. In the Philadelphia study, they estimated that the annual replacement value of services per congregation was $115,009. The combined estimate for all congregations in the city was $230,018,400 (Boddie et al., 2001).

CONCLUSIONS

From this selective review of congregational research, we draw several conclusions. First, we conclude that understanding the congregation is essential for understanding religious life in the United States. Congregations are far more than the sum of their individual members. Focusing on individuals and their religions, in the absence of their congregational involvement, betrays a pervasive American individualism. Such a perspective does not adequately comprehend religious life for most Americans.

Second, perhaps most strikingly, the American religious world is decentralized in the extreme. In that regard, it resembles the business world in a free market economy. There are national franchises (i.e., denominations), and "Mom and Pop" shops (i.e., storefront congregations). With no good sampling frame, it is difficult if not impossible to measure various aspects of congregational life.

The business analogy has another troubling implication, however. To some extent, any effort (including ours), to measure what congregations contribute or produce reduces their activities to mere commodities. That works better for some contributions than others but consistently falls short. For example, it is relatively easy to establish the market value of a congregation's physical property but harder to determine it's worth as a certain kind of semi-public space. As such, a congregation's physical property provides more than a concrete place to meet. It also provides a protected place for providing care to marginalized people (whether inside or outside the congregation), nurturing vision, ideals, and creativity, and developing moral critique. Likewise, it is hard enough to establish the market value of a congregational program, with particular facilities, resources, volunteers, and funding, but much more difficult to calculate the benefits of such programs for recipients, their families and social networks, volunteers and their networks, congregations themselves, social service agencies and other systems in a community, and so on. Professional social workers in time-limited and relatively well-conceptualized programs have difficulty identifying and measuring the outcomes of their interventions. In contrast, the nature of what happens in congregations is typically so diffuse that attempts to measure outcomes will always be incomplete and inadequate.

Based on his extensive local experience, Wineburg (2001) offers excellent suggestions regarding needed research in this area. For example, we need to know more about the capacity of congregations to handle service responsibilities and ways to build those capacities, how congregations become involved in helping, the (actual and in-kind) costs of services, the effectiveness of services, and so on (pp. 176–179).

When conducting any such research, we think congregations deserve our professional self-awareness and restraint. Despite their considerable contributions, congregations are not social service agencies. Our professional standards do not always apply. Beyond simply quantifying congregational outputs, we need to focus more on congregational inputs and transactive processes and seek to better understand the full context of service provision. For example, we agree with Wuthnow (1990) and Garland (2000) that researchers must pay greater attention to a) how members of congregations benefit from volunteering in social programs; b) how the process of giving nurtures the spark of faith and hope on which the spirit of altruism thrives; and c) how recipients transition from receiving services to providing future services themselves. We think it is also important to learn these things for the benefit of congregations and their members, not merely to maximize their contributions. Finally, when we bring our professional perspectives to bear, we must at least do so with humility and respect for a social structure that predates our profession and may well outlast it.

Because they have so long been "unheralded" (Boddie et al., 2001), the efforts of congregations may surprise us. As this brief review makes clear, there's a lot going on out there, and much more for us to learn.

REFERENCES

Ammerman, N. T. (2001). *Doing good in American communities: Congregations and service organizations working together* (research report). Hartford, CT: Hartford Seminary, Hartford Institute for Religious Research.

Ammerman, N. T., with Farnsley II, A. E., Adams, T., Baker, P. E., Brasher, B., & Clark, T. (1997). *Congregation and community*. New Brunswick, NJ: Rutgers University Press.

Billingsley, A. (1999). *Mighty like a river: The Black church and social reform*. New York: Oxford University Press.

Billingsley, A., & Caldwell, C. H. (1994). The social relevance of the contemporary church. *National Journal of Sociology, 8*(Summer/Winter), 1–23.

Boddie, S. C., Cnaan, R., A., & DiIulio, J. J. (2001). *Philadelphia census of congregations and their involvement in social service delivery: Methodological challenges and findings* (unpublished manuscript). Philadelphia, PA: University of Pennsylvania.

Canda, E. R., & Furman, L. D. (1999). *Spiritual diversity in social work practice: The heart of helping*. New York: Free Press.

Castelli, J., & McCarthy, J. D. (1998). *Religion-sponsored social services: The not-so-independent sector* [On-line]. Available: http://members.aol.com/jimcast/aspfn97.htm

Chaves, M. (1999). *Congregations' social service activities*. Washington, DC: The Urban Institute, Center on Nonprofits and Philanthropy.

Chaves, M., Konieczny, M. E., Beyerlein, K., & Barman, E. (1999). The National Congregations Study: Background, methods, and selected results. *Journal for the Scientific Study of Religion, 38*(4), 458–476.

Cnaan, R. A. (1998). *Social and community involvement of religious congregations housed in historic religious properties: Findings from a six-city study* (research report). Philadelphia, PA: University of Pennsylvania.

Cnaan, R. (1999). Our hidden safety net. *Brookings Review, 17*(2), 50–53.

Cnaan, R. A., & Boddie, S. C. (2001). *Black church outreach: Comparing how Black and other congregations serve their needy neighbors* (research report). Philadelphia, PA: University of Pennsylvania, CRRUCS.

Cnaan, R. A., Kasternakis, A., & Wineburg, R. J. (1993). Religious people, religious congregations, and volunteerism in human services: Is there a link? *Nonprofit and Voluntary Sector Quarterly, 22*(Spring), 33–51.

Cnaan, R. A., Wineburg, R. J., & Boddie, S. C. (1999). *The newer deal: Social work and religion in partnership.* New York: Columbia University Press.

De Vita, C. J., Printz Platnick, T. J., & Twombly, E. C. (1999). *Report to the human services faith-based organizations task force.* Washington, DC: Urban Institute.

Dudley, C. S., & Roozen, D. A. (2001). *Faith communities today: A report on religion in the United States today* (research report). Hartford, CT: Hartford Seminary, Hartford Institute for Religion Research.

Ellor, J. W., Netting, F. E., & Thibault, J. M. (1999). *Understanding religious and spiritual aspects of human service practice.* Columbia, SC: University of South Carolina Press.

Garland, D. R. (2000). *Service and faith: The impact on Christian faith and congregational life of organized community caring.* Unpublished research proposal, Baylor University, Waco, Texas.

Harris, M. (1998). A special case of voluntary associations? Towards a theory of congregational organization. *The British Journal of Sociology, 49*(4), 602–618.

Heyer-Gray, S., & Neitz, M. J. (1998, August). *Finding rural churches: Methodological and practical consequences of invisibility.* Paper presented at he 1998 meetings of the Association for the Sociology of Religion. Retrieved October 30, 2001, from http://hirr.hsartsem.edu/about/about_orw_heyerartcle.html

Hodge, D. R., Zech, C., McNamara, P., & Donahue, M. J. (1998). The value of volunteers as resources for congregations. *Journal for the Scientific Study of Religion, 37*(3), 470–480.

Holifield, E. B. (1994). Toward a history of American congregations. In J. P. Wind & J. W. Lewis (Eds.), *American congregations* (Vol. 2, pp. 23–53). Chicago: The University of Chicago Press.

Hodgkinson, V. A. (1990). The future of individual giving and volunteering: The inseparable link between religious community and individual generosity. In R. Wuthnow & V. Hodgkinson & Associates (Eds.), *Faith and philanthropy in America: Exploring the role of religion in America's voluntary sector.* San Francisco: Jossey-Bass.

Hodgkinson, V. A., Weitzman, M. S., & Kirsch, A. D. (1988). *From belief to commitment: The activities and finances of religious congregations in the United States* (findings from a national survey conducted by the Gallup Organization). Washington, DC: Independent Sector.

Hodgkinson, V. A., Weitzman, M. S., & Kirsch, A. D. (1990). From commitment to action: How religious involvement affects giving and volunteering. In R. Wuthnow & V. A. Hodgkinson & Associates (Eds.), *Faith and philan-*

thropy in America: Exploring the role of religion in America's voluntary sector (pp. 93–114). San Francisco: Jossey-Bass.

Hodgkinson, V. A., Weitzman, M. S., & Kirsch, A. D. (1993). *From belief to commitment: The community service activities and finances of religious congregations in the United States.* Washington, DC: Independent Sector.

Holifield, E. B. (1994). Toward a history of American congregations. In J. P. Wind & J. W. Lewis (Eds.), *American congregations* (Vol. 2, pp. 23–53). Chicago: The University of Chicago Press.

Hopewell, J. A. (1987). *Congregation: Stories and structures.* Philadelphia, PA: Fortress Press.

Linder, E. W. (Ed.). (2001). *Yearbook of American & Canadian churches 2001* (Vol. 69). Nashville, TN: Abingdon Press.

Marty, M. E. (1994). Public and private: Congregation as meeting place. In J. P. Wind & J. W. Lewis (Eds.), *American congregations* (Vol. 2, pp. 133–168). Chicago: University of Chicago Press.

Moberg, D. O. (1984). *The church as a social institution: The sociology of American religion.* Grand Rapids, MI, Baker Book House.

Moon, S. S., Wolfer, T. A., & Robinson, M. A. (2001). Culturally-based Korean American family conflict, and how churches can help: An exploratory survey. *Social Work & Christianity, 28,* 106–123.

Murnion, P. J. (1992). *New parish ministers: Laity and religious on parish staffs.* New York: National Pastoral Life Center.

Putnam, R. D. (2000). *Bowling alone: The collapse and revival of American community.* New York: Simon & Schuster.

Salamon, L. M., & Teitelbaum, F. (1984, September/October). Religious congregations as social service agencies: How extensive are they? *Foundation News, 62*–65.

Schaller, L. E. (1988). The coming boom in church construction. *Clergy Journal, 16,* 36–37.

Sherman, A. (2000). Should we put faith in charitable choice? *The Responsive Community, 10,* 22–30.

Sherwood, D. A., Wolfer, T. A., & Scales, T. L. (2002). Introduction: Spirituality and religion, decision cases, and competent social work practice. In T. L. Scales, T. A. Wolfer, D. A. Sherwood, D. R. Garland, B. Hugen, & S. Pittman (Eds.), *Spirituality and religion in social work practice: Decision cases with teaching notes* (pp. 4–14). Alexandria, VA: Council on Social Work Education.

Thornburgh, G., & Wolfer, T. A. (2000). Megachurch involvement in community social ministry: Extent and effects in three congregations. *Social Work & Christianity, 27,* 130–149.

Warner, R. S. (1994). The place of the congregation in the contemporary American religious configuration. In J. P. Wind & J. W. Lewis (Eds.),

American congregations (Vol. 2, pp. 54–99). Chicago: University of Chicago Press.

Wilson, J., & Janoski, T. (1995). The contribution of religion to volunteer work. *Sociology of Religion, 56*(2), 137–152.

Wind, J. P., & Lewis, J. W. (Eds.). (1994). *American congregations: New perspectives in the study of congregations* (Vol. 2). Chicago: University of Chicago Press.

Wineburg, B. (1990). Volunteers in service to their community: Congregational commitment to helping the needy. *Journal of Volunteer Administration, 9*(1), 35–47.

Wineburg, B. (1992). Local human services provision by religious congregations: A community analysis. *Nonprofit and Voluntary Sector Quarterly, 21*(2), 107–118.

Wineburg, B. (1994). A longitudinal case study of religious congregations in local human services. *Nonprofit and Voluntary Sector Quarterly, 23*(2), 159–169.

Wineburg, B. (2001). *A limited partnership: The politics of religion, welfare, and social service.* New York: Columbia University Press.

Wineburg, R. J. (1996). An investigation of religious support of public and private agencies in one community in an era of retrenchment. *Journal of Community Practice, 3*(2), 35–55.

Wuthnow, R. (1990). *Improving our understanding of religion and giving: Key issues for research.* San Francisco: Jossey-Bass.

Chapter 3

RELIGIOSITY AND SPIRITUALITY IN SOCIAL WORK: A RETROSPECTIVE AND CONTEMPORARY ANALYSIS

Larry P. A. Ortiz

Religion as a plausibility structure, as a codification of spirituality, is at all times shaping and being shaped by culture. Religion provides the cultural mechanism to experience spirituality. As such, it incorporates the values and ideology of a culture reflecting place and time. In diverse societies religion as an artifact of culture is not monolithic; rather it appears differently as it is influenced by such factors as age, sex, ethnicity, socioeconomic class, sexual orientation and no doubt a host of other personal and group characteristics. Consequently, the complexion of how religion and/or spirituality motivate social work service may be vastly different, not only from one historical period to another but during the same time frame by cohorts in the same generation. For example, Garland (1994) identifies two groups of social workers guided by Christian convictions who externalize their faith in very different ways. One group is more inclined to focus on the individual person's psychological needs, interpret their distress in spiritual terms, and believe a closer more intimate relationship with Jesus is the answer to the problems confronting the person. This approach, ideologically and theologically conservative, can be juxtaposed to another Christianity-motivated social worker who works tirelessly on many different fronts to eliminate social structural barriers that are unjust and serve as obstacles to the well-being of communities, families, and individuals. These social workers pattern their action after the teachings of Jesus and the Old Testament prophets that decry the corruptness and evil inherent in social institutions that benefit the rich over the poor.

What accounts for this difference in Christianity-motivated social work? Members of these two groups read the same Bible, worship the same God and follow the same Jesus. One potential explanation: ideology. Shaped by the values of society, one's experiences, and status in society, ideology is a powerful force that influences all areas of social life. It serves as an interpretive lens that filters the sights and sounds of the world, and motivates one to act accordingly.

Religiously motivated social workers do not speak with one voice in this country. In some instances, it appears they may have little in common, as in the case of abortion, for example. Whereas one social worker may cite the "thou shall not kill" commandment as the reason to restrict a woman's right to choose, another cites the God given endowment of humans to make choices, as reason to support a woman's right to choose. Which approach is right, more spiritually or religiously motivated, or truly Christian? It all depends.

Therefore, writing a section on religiously and spiritually motivated social work is itself an ideological exercise that will leave some examples out while including others that could be vociferously contested. As my guide for which examples to include in the section that follows was the reference to services and activities that not only have a religious or spiritual basis but also reflect the values of the social work profession as well. Ergo, in the examples that follow, all have in common a spiritual/religious basis and a reflection of social work values.

SPIRITUALLY AND RELIGIOUSLY BASED SERVICES: SECTARIAN AGENCIES

Sectarian agencies have not vanished from the social services landscape. They still thrive and have found unique and compelling ways of integrating their spiritual and religious motivations with professional social work practices. Although it is seldom possible to simultaneously maximize all values and beliefs, these agencies have approached this dialectic with hermeneutic guidance, spiritual passion, and a respect for the values of the profession that celebrates a diverse culture. Large numbers of sectarian agencies employ professionally educated social workers and adhere to the

National Association of Social Workers (NASW) code of ethics. They may also have a sectarian code of ethics that emphasizes their unique identity.

In the United States, religiously affiliated agencies are organized along the lines of either Christian or Jewish. Christian agencies are often affiliated with particular denominations and may be administered by a central office, commission, or dioceses. Catholic and Jewish agencies tend to be organized nationally. The National Conference of Catholic Charities is a national coordinating body designed to provide support dioceses that oversee the operations of local agencies. Under the auspices of the Council of Jewish Federations, local Jewish social service agencies obtain coordination and consultation. The Federation provides no authoritative role or fiscal support to local agencies (Ortiz, 1995).

Other protestant services exist as local entities or on a smaller national scale as compared with Catholic and Jewish auspices. For example, Lutheran Social Services offers a wide range of services in areas of the country where Lutheran immigrants tended to migrate. Mormon services operate out of the Church of the Latter Day Saints. Baptist hospitals and children's homes still exist in regions of the country where there is a large Baptist interest. As well, the Salvation Army, which is actually a church, operates a wide range of services to alcoholics, drug addicts, and the indigent in most municipalities. All of these endeavors tend to be more localized in their administration, fund-raising, and program offerings to the community. Generally, these groups will have some connection to their original denominational sponsor in terms of purpose and mission, board of director representation, and financial support. For the most part, however, they operate autonomously with regard to staffing, programming, and fiscal operations.

Adaptation to changing times, demographics, and population needs, has been the hallmark of many sectarian agencies. Caring for the needy with a sense of spiritual purpose has changed for many agencies as immigrant populations have changed, demographics in cities and rural areas altered, and cultural movements and social changes taken place. The type of service delivered in the early, mid, and late 20th century has changed considerably. For example, as immigrant patterns have changed in urban areas and as different ethnic groups have replaced other ethnic groups in areas of the city, the sectarian agencies in the neighborhoods have had to face the question of either following their historic clientele, going out of business, or adapting their programming to the needs of the new population. Most agencies have adapted. For example, as families and clientele have gotten older, so have their needs changed; sectarian agencies initially developed to support young families, have had to retool to serve an aging population. With the diminishing population growth in this country, the availability and use of contraceptive devices, the need for children's homes and adoption agencies has changed. Some sectarian homes for children, that historically served to care for orphans, now provide residential treatment services for troubled adolescents. These examples of adjustments in service delivery are not always simple, but remain true to the original purpose of the agency, to do the good work of the faith. Creative alliances and coalitions have also been employed to continue the work. For example, sectarian agencies have formed coalitions with other religious groups to increase their resources to deliver service, found ways to obtain governmental funding in a manner that does not compromise their mission, and deliver fee-based services to help offset the costs of operation. Sectarian agencies, the hallmark of religiously motivated social work in this country are thriving, dynamic, and at all times an integral part of the profession. These agencies play a major role in filling the gap of services created by a society that does not view human services as a right.

SPIRITUALLY AND RELIGIOUSLY BASED SERVICES: SOCIAL MOVEMENTS

Although not social work in the professionally defined manner, social movement endeavors are designed to promote enhanced well-being for groups or classes of people that have historically been among the clientele of the profession. Often these endeavors are designed to empower people who are disenfranchised because of characteristic or social status. These activities often have religious or spiritual foundations because the clients, or perceived beneficiaries of these efforts, are well integrated in faith systems. Social workers, along with religious or spiritual leaders have functioned in these movements as leaders, facilitators, consultants, or promoters. The examples used in this section illustrate both the history of these social movements, and the promise of future potentialities.

AFRICAN AMERICAN EXPERIENCE

From its very beginning, the African American church stood for liberation and social justice. As the exodus themes of the slave years gave way to liberation, the church took on the position of social justice. Thus the church developed as a separate institution from the White church. This was " . . . necessary to ensure a sense of community, control over decision making, accumulation of wealth and property, black [sic] leadership, and an institutional basis to influence and challenge the dominant social and economic and political order" (Maton & Wells, 1995, p. 185). The civil rights movement in the late 1960s began in African American churches (Cnaan, 1999). In addition, the call for justice rooted in the truths of scripture, " . . . [was] spoken from the pulpits, sung from the choir lofts and written on the walls of African American churches," and seeped through the walls of the church and into all communities of color and diversity who were oppressed, disenfranchised, and the victims of injustice (Ortiz & Smith, 1999, p. 315). "The result was a political movement that brought on constitutional changes, anti-discrimination laws and an ethos of inclusiveness" (p. 315) and celebration of diversity that has changed the very definition of modern America.

The message of liberation has not been the only message proclaimed by the Black church. Historically, and still today, it serves as the basis for mutual a support network. As a mechanism of social support it functions to provide prayer and counsel to those going through difficult times. In the form of mutual aid, it provides basic services to its members and those in the community, who are hungry, need clothing, or lack other basic human necessities. As a source of information, the Black church has provided information to its members on how to connect to needed services, as well as important health and educational information. It has also served as an important place to develop community leadership using models more consistent with African American culture than that of the dominant society. Tapia (1996) has noted that the Black church has lost some of the momentum it enjoyed in the 1960s and 1970s. Evidence for this is the decrease in church attendance from a generation ago, down from 80% to 40% (Tapia, 1996, p. 27). However, the church has also shown signs of maturity, however, by focusing on initiating economic and social structural changes that are empowerment oriented as seen through, " . . . setting up schools, insurance companies, building housing, automobile refurbishing and retailing, credit unions, and economic development corporations" (Ortiz & Smith, 1999, p. 315).

LATINO EXPERIENCE

Latinos are not a monolithic group; therefore, one cannot speak of a Latino experience in this country; rather, we must speak of experiences. As a whole, Latinos are composed of several different ethnic groups, each with their own histories, culture, dialect, customs, and political orientations. The three dominant Latino groups in the United States, Mexicans, Puerto Ricans, and Cubans, are distinctively different in the aspects mentioned above. They do share religion and language in common; yet, that is generally where similarities end. Religiously, most Latinos are Roman Catholic, although there has emerged in the last decade a growing number of Pentecostal type churches that are experiencing tremendous growth among Latinos, Mexican and Central Americans in particular. With the exception of Cuban Americans, Latinos tend to fall toward the lower end of the socioeconomic scale. They are more likely to live in poor or substandard housing in either rural or urban areas, have fewer years of formal education, work longer hours for lower wages, and experience more obstacles in attaining quality health care (Cornellis & Ortiz, in press). Yet, despite the increasing number of Latinos in this country (at present the largest minority group of color), there has not emerged, since the Chicano movement days of the 1970s, a widespread concerted organized movement to address their social plight. Nevertheless, there are many pockets of endeavors designed to improve the conditions of Latinos in not only the temporal sense, but also to empower through educational, economic, and political enfranchisement. Following are two examples of these as emerging from the efforts of social workers from a religious/spiritual orientation.

In the early 1990s a group of Mennonites and Presbyterians organized recently displaced clothing manufacturing workers living in a barrio in San Antonio, Texas around their common experiences, those of being Christian and unemployed. Organizing the community around Bible studies and support groups the church volunteers implemented a " . . . praxis of collaboration as a model of community governance, [that] . . . focused on raising the level of consciousness of its members regarding their plight, contextualizing their collective experiences, visualizing opportunities for themselves and taking action" (Ortiz & Smith, 1999, p. 316). In the last decade since this endeavor was implemented, members from the community have moved toward economic independence, become involved politically, continued to organize their community, and pursued trade and college education. They have realized their visions of what can be, gaining strength from their spirituality and the collective support from their compadre/as.

Cnaan (1999) reports on Nueva Ezperanza in Philadelphia, Pennsylvania, a religiously-based nonprofit organization serving the Latino community. Developed by a minister and seminary professor, this group originally organized by bringing together various church groups serving the Latino community. Putting aside doctrinal differences this group organized as a truly ecumenical coalition to address the needs of this underserved community. The result of this endeavor has been to raise the political visibility of the Latino community, obtaining millions of dollars of allocations through empowerment zone funding, and developing the community into a commercial center. As an organized community, Latinos have gained a voice in the political and economic development of Philadelphia, " . . . due to the efforts of organized religion . . . the social, political, and economic rights of the Hispanic people are currently being protected and advanced" (Cnaan, 1999, p. 331).

No discussion on the Latino experience and empowerment would be complete without a reference to Liberation Theology. Although not a North American experience, it is certainly western hemispheric and prevalent in most Latin American countries. The essence of this theology " . . . is practiced through the instruments of a socialanalytical reflection of the [context], a Biblical reflection concerning the poor and a practical . . . discovering [of] the steps to implement a plan of action to overcome oppression" (Ortiz & Smith, 1999, p. 314). Consisting of three systematic steps, Liberation Theology begins with a social and political analysis of the condition of the poor and their context; the theology assumes a position consistent with Old Testament prophets and Jesus who sided with the poor, viewing their plight as the result of oppression and injustice. Second, a Biblical hermeneutic is developed to read the experience of the poor through scripture as a means of developing direction, a course of action to liberate the poor from the hands of the unjust. Third is the step of praxis, that requires the community to determine the course of theologically-based action to pursue. Liberation Theology suggests that spirituality is rooted in the everyday experience—where we live, play, and work. Consequently, spirituality is the lived experience, not an existentially sequestered state. As such it has to have meaning, relevance, and saliency to the real condition of those living the experience. It is a seamless experience that does not view the Old Testament prophet Micah's words as being separate commands, but an integrated proclamation wherein which loving God and others tenderly, and pursuing justice is the integrated essence of spirituality.

Uniquely Latin American, this theology-based approach to liberation and justice for the poor and oppressed, has tremendous potential for organizing the poor and other victims of oppression who have a spiritual and religious commitment. This theology, that has grown out of the Roman Catholic Church, is not without its critics, including the pontiff; in some countries it has become the enemy of the state. The criticisms usually emerge from those who have something to protect, however, such as wealth and power. It is shamelessly ideological, assuming a Biblical mandate to take the position of the oppressed against the mighty. As the U.S. Latino population grows, this approach has great relevance to our society. Separation of church and state, the secular from the sacred, is a false dichotomy for Latin cultures. The concept of personal and political, secular and spiritual are not stretches of the imagination, culturally speaking. Therefore, it seems perfectly logical and appropriate for social workers engaged with a Latino population to use an approach modeled after Liberation Theology as a means of community organization and empowerment.

WOMEN'S EXPERIENCE

Historically, women have lived a second class role in society. Even with changes that resulted from the civil rights and feminist movements of the late 20th century, women remain at risk in several areas. They are more likely to be victims of crime, suffer from various forms of discrimination, and earn less pay than their male counterparts. In the late 19th century woman had very few career choices, but social work was an area that provided women with career opportunities. Traditional ministry was closed to women, however, outside of the role of clergy there were several opportunities open to them. For example, they could work in church sponsored children's homes or hospitals, or travel abroad as missionaries serving in roles in foreign lands that they were excluded from in the United States, such as physicians and teachers (Cnaan, 1999). Such capacities abroad served as fruitful training ground for women who were later able to apply their learning in this country. Social work was one of those arenas in which woman could use their education and skill, and fulfill a career calling to serve others. As the profession grew in the late 19th century, it was increasingly attractive to woman as a career, and remains so at present.

Besides career opportunities, the church has historically provided services to women, and social work as a profession has played a role in responding to needs. For example, the Salvation Army has historically offered services to women who were "wayward," pregnant outside of marriage, drug or alcohol dependent, or abused. The Catholic Church with its St. Jude society has played a similar role, as well as other countless religious orders that have provided services specifically to women in need. Contemporarily, churches across the nation have been involved in serving women with needs concerning health care, child care, shelter, emergency welfare, drug and alcohol addictions, escaping from poverty, and assistance in immigration.

Outside of the church there are many other examples of spiritually guided work with women. For example, " . . . [F]eminist spiritual support groups combine therapy, group work, spirituality and ritual to empower women individually and as a group" (Ortiz & Smith, 1999, p. 315). Neu (1995) describes the characteristics of these groups as focusing on " . . . placing women at the center, reverencing the Earth and all creation, valuing women's body and bodily functions, seeking an interconnectedness with all living things and placing an emphasis on ritual" (Neu, 1995, p. 189). These celebrations of womanhood are outside of traditional religious entities. They are designed, however, to use collective feminist spirituality as a means of connecting with others, the Earth, and the cosmos, and thus become empowered in capacities not previously encountered.

Specific examples of religiously- and spiritually-based services for women, by women, could fill volumes of text. The intersect between social work and religion and spirituality is quite evident in this area. It is noteworthy in these endeavors, though, that the motivation to help is spiritual, and the methods for implementing caring, are social work.

GAY AND LESBIAN EXPERIENCE

One of the more ongoing areas of controversy in the church is the rightful role of gays and lesbians in the church, and also their treatment in society. The reaction in the church ranges from outright contempt and damnation to the embracing of the lifestyle as a legitimate orientation reflective of God's holy creation. In between these two positions are a range of positions and actions taken on this issue by churches, temples and synagogues. Some more conservative, but not fundamentalist groups, reject the gay and lesbian lifestyle as sin, yet are compassionate to gay and lesbian people. While believing that the behavior is wrong, they also believe in loving, supporting, and responding to the needs of the person. However, they are not likely to allow known practicing gay or lesbians opportunities to serve in formal church capacities. Yet another position taken by the more moderate religious is one of acceptance and welcoming of gay and lesbians into the congregation, but requiring celibacy of those who serve in formal church roles such as ministers, rabbis, or teachers. A more liberal position is complete nondiscrimination of gays and lesbians, welcoming them into the congregations with the full rights and privileges to serve and participate in fellowship. Finally, probably the most liberal approach is the position taken of the United Fellowship of the Metropolitan Community Church and its founder Troy Perry, who in essence has developed a gay and lesbian theology that celebrates one's ordained sexuality and spirituality in the context of the Christian church.

As noted earlier, other than the abortion, this issue is probably one that has served to be the most divisive between organized religion and the social work profession. This is an area that continues to require dialogue and visualization of how to work together on this issue, so that the church does not neglect the needs of gay and lesbian persons in the name of religion.

CONCLUSION

There is a rich history of a relationship between formal religion and the social work profession. The history dates back much further than that of the profession of social work, to origins of the modern theistic religions of Judaism, Christianity, and Islam. I think it not an overstatement to say that social work is inherently a spiritual enterprise. As such it is a calling to which one responds to care for others, serve communities, and work diligently for the well-being of both, with a sense of purpose not rooted in self-interest but one that transcends mortal experience.

REFERENCES

Cnaan, R. (1999). Empowerment through organized religion. In W. Shera & L. Wells (Eds.), *Empowerment practice in social work* (pp. 320–346). Toronto, CA: Canadian Scholar's Press.

Cornellis, L., & Ortiz, L. (in press). Is being the "largest" Latino ethnic group enough to ensure Mexican American equity of access to health care? In K. E. Davis & T. B. Bent-Goodley (Eds.), *The color of social policy*. Alexandria, VA: Council on Social Work Education.

Garland, D. R. (1994). *Church agencies: Caring for children and families in crisis*. Washington, DC: Child Welfare League of America.

Maton, K. I., & Wells, J. (1995). Religion as a community resource for well-being: Prevention, healing, and empowerment pathways. *Journal of Social Change, 51*(2), 177–192.

Neu, D. (1995). Women's empowerment through feminist rituals. *Women and Therapy, 16*(2/3), 185–200.

Ortiz, L. (1995). Sectarian agencies. In R. Edwards et al. (Eds.), *Encyclopedia of social work* (19th ed., 3, pp. 2109–2116). Washington, DC: NASW Press.

Ortiz, L., & Smith, G. (1999). The role of spirituality in empowerment practice. In W. Shera & L. Wells (Eds.), *Empowerment practice in social work* (pp. 307–319). Toronto, CA: Canadian Scholar's Press.

Tapia, A. (1996). Soul searching: How is the black church responding to the urban crisis? *Christianity Today, 40*(3), 26–33.

Chapter 4

SPIRITUALITY AND THE LIFE CYCLE

Ilene Nathanson

The purpose of this chapter is to identify the relationship of spirituality to human development, the impact of age on spiritual consciousness, and the variations in spiritual outlook associated with gender and other demographic factors. Age cohort distinctions based on transforming cultural and technological contexts are also addressed.

The importance to social workers of understanding these connections relates to the area of spiritual assessment. Hodge (2001) describes spiritual assessment as an underdeveloped area in social work. He notes that the growing acceptance of the strengths perspective in social work practice, which draws on the centrality of the client's strengths in the helping process, supports the need to clarify spiritual strengths as well as other strengths in engaging the capabilities of the client. In this chapter the author seeks to identify the changing nature of spirituality over the life span and how the spiritual perspective is mediated by other factors in the hope of shedding light on this overlooked aspect of human development. Hodge (2001) identifies certain areas in which spirituality is an important force in recovery, such as substance abuse or sexual assault. Spirituality appears to also play an important role in moral and cognitive development. An appreciation of the association of an individual's spiritual perspective to other aspects of personality is vital to comprehensive needs assessment and the development of a strategic plan for intervention, as this author will attempt to demonstrate. The individual perspective is inexorably linked to the social perspective and can only be understood in relation to social vicissitudes. The author starts from the premises that aging today is not the same as aging yesterday; and, the role of spirituality in the life of the human being is in flux.

As evidence of our changing perspectives, "being spiritual" has come to replace "being religious" as the context for demonstrating faith in a transcendent source of meaning. People used to be religious, now they are spiritual. In fact, the author changed the title of this chapter from the original, "Religion and the Life Cycle," to reflect this trend. What is the basis for this trend? Also, how can we explain the surge in spiritual awareness among the baby boom generation? Are the aging boomers merely playing out some sort of phylogenic ancestral recapitulation or is this spiritual awakening reflecting some new socially constructed twist on an old theme?

There are different views on the nature of spiritual development, but before getting to that it is important to explain some of the concepts and assumptions that frame the discussion. To begin with, it is impossible to consider the role of spirituality in human experience without reference to the social construction of ideas. The human perspective is shaped by cultural factors. This point it reiterated by scholars, such as Mannheim, Scheler, and Marx. Peter Berger and Thomas Luckmann (1967) make the case for the social construction of reality in a book by the same title. Their clearly developed argument leads to the conclusion that our social context shapes our thoughts and views. This author would like to propose that physical factors of human development equally shape our perspectives. We are molded by biological as well as cultural factors. Changing spiritual outlooks can trace their roots to changes in the human physiological condition as impacted by advances in biotechnology. We can look forward to long lives today because of improvements in our health and functioning. Certainly, these improvements rely on advances in medicine and technology, perhaps most importantly on improved standards of public health and use of a wide spectrum of vaccines, drugs, and medical devices. We are healthier than previous generations. The media constantly reminds us that we can attain octogenarian status if we follow the proper regimen of diet, exercise, and preventive care. Death seems a long way off throughout the early and middle phases of life. We have an exaggerated sense of time, an attenuated attention to the finite reality of our personal time. Spirituality may not beckon us in the same way as it did our ancestors who faced death on a daily basis. Spiritual awakening often follows from adversity. In contemporary America, the mainspring of adversity may be mental anguish, rather than physical suffering. However, a quick review of American history puts our aches and pains into a decidedly favorable perspective if we only compare the existence of an average industrial worker today with that of a factory worker 100 years ago. Adversity is not the same as it used to be. It was a daily fact of life, and religion, that what we called faith related activities back then, played a central role in most people's consciousness.

The assumption that different biological and cultural conditions are at the root of changing spiritual perspectives underlies this discussion. Our consuming reliance on science and technology defers the opportunity or need for spiritual reflection. Many people require a wake-up call to alert them to life's spiritual dimension. Aging with its associated challenges can provide such a reminder. On the other hand there are people whose faith seems to transcend ordinary experience. Their faith does not ebb and flow with fluctuations in experience but is a continuous current in their lives.

Another concept that figures into this discussion is the very definition of spirituality. There are many. A popular view of spirituality, based on the Jungian perspective, construes the spiritual quest as a "resacralization" of the self and the world with the goal of each individual to embark on a personal journey with the aim of discovering the transcendent meaning in everyday life and all human relations. The emphasis shifts away from integrating different aspects of the self into one unified perspective, to involving a multiplicity of selves in a meaningful relationship with the surrounding environment. In other words, according to Paul Wink (1999), the aim of spirituality is to develop the ability to find the sacred at every point in time and in everything one does. This does not necessarily imply an experience of God as divine, but rather assumes placing the immediate experience into a larger framework of meaning that transcends objective reality or the simple experience of the senses. Fowler describes faith as involving that which tests or shapes the defining directions of people's lives or relationships with others in accordance with coordinates of value and power recognized as ultimate (Fowler: In Koenig, 1994). Harold Koenig (1994) challenges Fowler's conception of faith on the basis that the coordinate of value or power could be something as banal as money, and more importantly does not include the notion of a Supreme Being. Koenig believes that only belief in a Supreme Being provides the ultimate meaning upon which faith development is based. Although this author agrees with Koenig that true faith development should involve belief in a framework of meaning that transcends objective reality, the source of transcendent meaning does not have to be God. Frankl, Fromm, and Maslow are examples of humanistic theorists who extol beliefs outside the traditional religious ideologies. Maslow observed that "the human being needs a framework of values, a philosophy of life, a religion or religion-surrogate to live by and understand by, in about the same sense he needs sunlight, calcium or love." Maslow believes all people need to understand and have a validated, usable system of human values (Maslow: In Sermabeikian, 1994, p. 181).

Further complications abound when addressing the concept of spiritual or faith development. This author draws on Koenig, Fowler, Erikson, and Jung as well as her own observations in presenting a framework in which to highlight the relationship of spiritual development to other areas of human development. The belief that faith is subjective serves as a primary assumption of the discussion that follows. Whether a person follows an independent path or strict religious doctrine reflects on beliefs that do not lend themselves to scientific analysis. All we can conclude from studying beliefs is whether or not they seem to facilitate or restrict the attainment of human satisfaction or peace of mind. There is no right or wrong answer. Faith needs no proof or justification. One either believes or does not. The questions pursued in these pages are simply: Does faith development follow a pattern? Do men and women seem to vary in their faith development? What other factors seem to impact faith development; and, what seems to account for cohort differences?

PATHWAYS TO FAITH

Two authors who have distinguished themselves in their treatment of the subject of faith development are James Fowler and Harold Koenig. Both authors agree that the processes involved in the growth of faith complement growth phases in cognitive, psychosocial, and moral development. In other words, as children grow in mental capacity, social experience, as well as in conscience development, they experience corresponding developments in faith or spiritual awareness. Fowler describes several stages of faith development (Fowler: In Koenig, 1994):

> *Intuitive-Projective (ages 2–7):* In this phase the child begins to form pictures of God. The child is oriented toward punishment.
>
> *Mythic-Literal (ages 7–12):* The child begins to use logic. The child is literal. The world operates on the undefiable rule of reciprocity. God gives good things to good people, bad things to bad people.

Synthetic-Conventional (adolescence onward): The adolescent locates authority outside the self (primarily with the peer group) and demonstrates adherence to group norms. Fowler argues that most of church life in America works best when members are at this faith stage.

Individuative-Reflective (early to mid-20s or beyond): The individual must now re-construct a personal ideology or belief system independent of the confines of class, tribe, or religion.

Conjunctive Faith (midlife and beyond): The individual who achieves this level of faith development develops a more open attitude toward other religious traditions. The self is caught between the need to preserve its own being and fulfill its own needs, and a more universal concern that is willing to lay down one's life for others.

Universalizing Faith (late life): The individual who achieves this level develops a readiness for fellowship with persons regardless of religious tradition. This individual further experiences total commitment to a vision; a willingness to give up oneself and one's life for justice and a transformed world, in order to make the kingdom of God actual on this earth.

Koenig (1994) criticizes Fowler's reliance on structure rather than content. Fowler does not emphasize belief in God or in any source of transcendent meaning as the basis of faith development. Faith development in Fowler's paradigm is predicated on faith in anything that serves to provide meaning to one's life. Faith is relative. The question that follows for Koenig is this: How then does God achieve "the full weight of ultimacy" as implied in Fowler's phase of Universalizing Faith? In other words, how does Fowler account for the shift from faith in any coordinate of value to faith in God? Koenig takes the seemingly opposing view that faith development is not devoid of content and relies on belief in God as the only valid object of faith development. Belief in God provides ultimate meaning to the directions of our lives, according to Koenig. There is no faith development outside of the context of organized religion. It is the content of the Judeo-Christian religion that determines attitudes and behaviors, which in turn influence the emotional state. Belief in God is outside and apart from man and the universe in contrast to the pantheistic view that does not distinguish God from the universe. Koenig (1994) presents his own stages of faith development:

Early Childhood (0–2): The parents reflect God and it follows from this, if the mother or significant other is perceived as loving, God will be seen as loving.

Middle Childhood (2–6): Images of God depend on parental instruction and example.

Late Childhood (6–12): The child's views are still heavily influenced by parents, teachers, and increasingly, by peers. The child begins to develop a capacity to reflect on religious themes. Rites of passages such as Confirmation and Bar/Bat Mitzvah reinforce faith.

Adolescence and Young Adulthood (12–21): From here onward, religious faith can take several different paths:

1. The individual can establish conventional faith;
2. The individual can reject all previous teachings and abandon further development;
3. The individual can proceed to a post-transition faith (actively struggling to establish a relationship with God that has meaning and value in a personal and individual way, although not necessarily in a way that is different from parents or peers).

These first four stages closely follow Fowler's stages of faith. It is in the final stages that we see a divergence from Fowler:

Adulthood and Later Life: The individual makes the decision to believe in God and enter into a personally meaningful relationship. Mature faith involves a deep, intimate, stable and exclusive relationship with God—placing God at the center of one's ultimate concern and trusting in God with no doubt. If God is at the Center of one's concern then a person's life should reflect this in his or her actions.

According to Koenig, many of the fruits of faith are psychological in nature. The emphasis on relationship is central to these effects—relationship with God and relationship with man. Despite the differences, both authors offer a view of faith development that emphasizes the distinction between the conventional path and the individual path. For both, higher-level faith development involves the attainment of a selfless regard for other people. This view corresponds with Erikson's belief that the realization of personal integrity involves a love of the human ego (not of the self) that conveys "some world order and spiritual sense" (Erikson: In Koenig, 1994). In combination, these beliefs lead to the inference that faith development and character development are parallel growth processes.

Both theories raise the questions: Do you need to place God at the center of ultimate concern to a) have faith or b) achieve mature faith? What differences exist between men and women in their spiritual or religious development? How does social class impact faith development? How does education impact faith development? How are age cohort distinctions related to faith development?

Fowler and Koenig concur that the first four stages of faith development coincide and interrelate with psychosocial, cognitive, and moral development. Neither author accounts for variations in life span development based on such factors as gender and social class. Germaine Greer (1992), for one, would argue that existing life span developmental theories do not describe the general experience of women, because women's limited social opportunities do not promote development of autonomy and elaboration of mental powers. Greer implies that cultural stereotypes and biological imperatives restrict women from enjoying the same developmental opportunities as men. Would this not further suggest that more women than men remain in the adolescent phase of faith development?

Koenig (1994) describes a process in which the individual moves from a concrete representation of God to a conventional view of religion at adolescence. The individual then chooses to deepen belief and relationship with God and with other people based on religious precepts, or not. Deepening one's belief is related to growth in the capacity not only to think, but to think independently. If society has restricted women and other vulnerable groups from evolving these capacities then it would logically follow that faith development would never achieve the mature level described by both Koenig and Fowler. In fact, certain areas of religious inquiry and growth traditionally have been cut off to women, such as the priesthood and Talmudic study. Exclusion from positions of religious power severely limits women's authority in organized religion. Their historic absence from religious hierarchy can be construed as a highly effective political maneuver that keeps them and the children they raise within the narrow confines of doctrine and away from all questioning debate that may lead to a more highly evolved appreciation of religious/spiritual experience. On the other hand, even if pathways to further enlightenment have been cut off to women, is conventional religion less meaningful than advanced individual-reflective practice? Not necessarily; however, many women of today would take the position and do take the position that the options should be the same for both men and women. Religious service attendance does seem to vary with age and gender—with women being a highly representative group in some churches, perhaps indicating their adolescent phase commitment. Religious coping and service attendance are also associated with race and social status with participation high among the lower classes, the poor, and Blacks as well as among women and the elderly (Koenig, 1994). This may reflect social class restrictions on opportunity for independent development, or may just as easily reflect the greater need for consolation and support among people at risk and the impact of adversity upon spiritual consciousness. The church is an important social organization among people of color, serving a variety of community needs. High religious service attendance among the elderly may reflect age cohort differences as well as the increasing need for support and understanding as one encounters the challenges of aging.

Research is being called upon to show the relationship of spirituality or religious practice to health and successful aging, presumably to demonstrate the efficacy of having a religious or spiritual focus. Qualitative research can be useful in elucidating the various ways in which spirituality seems to effect a successful aging outcome. Research that attempts to measure happiness or depression as a function of spirituality may lead to misguided outcomes, however, by assuming that quantitative analysis can be appropriately applied in this area. Research aimed at demonstrating a specific positive consequence may promote the assumption that suffering is bad and that if faith is associated with suffering we should avoid developing a particular brand of faith. As aptly explained by Patrick Glynn (1997) in God the Evidence, "It is worth remembering that religion, or true spirituality, does not promote exemption from suffering; on the contrary it teaches the inevitability of suffering as a means of strengthening the soul and turning it from the world toward God" (p. 93). Belief has to be tested to achieve its full magnitude. Faith development is a struggle. We have to grapple with our own faith in order to deepen our spiritual connections. Yet, according to Koenig, we cannot even enter this arena without a specific religious orientation. His reasoning poses ontological questions that go beyond the scope of this discussion. However, it is patently clear that in order to grapple, you need something to grapple with. Therefore, it is fundamental that spiritual growth involves some spiritual or religious introduction or awakening.

This brings us to the issue of age cohort differences in religious socialization or observance. Although previous generations of Americans were more religiously observant than the current generation, it is less clear whether we have become less spiritual. The oldest age cohorts today are more religiously identified than their children are; however, they introduced these "baby boomers" (born between 1946 and 1964) to religion in their formative years. The rudiments of religious experience exist for this cohort, and thus the foundation for faith development. The children of the baby boomers are growing up in a world of interfaith marriages and diverse religious and cultural influences. Many are experiencing a very different religious orientation than their parents experienced. At the same time, technology is evolving and the life span, expanding. It stands to reason that faith development and the place of spirituality in the life cycle will continue to reflect these changes. Religious or spiritual awareness may rely on parental modeling as proposed by Fowler and Koenig. If a child is not exposed to a set of formal religious or even spiritual principles, he or she can still develop morally as well as cognitively, but there will be a void in spiritual or religious development. Spiritual precepts reinforce conscience development by providing a rationale for right and wrong behavior. Spiritual guidelines may satisfy the child's needs for answers. Certainly, a spiritual base will provide a framework for adolescent questioning and may even reinforce abstract reasoning abilities. The developmental path of a spiritually devoid childhood will be different from one enriched by spiritual exposure and opportunity. How we judge that difference is a function of our values. There is even the possibility that the individual who has experienced a lapse in spiritual exposure may more ardently seek answers to questions regarding the nature of existence to compensate for the gap.

Richard Rohr and Joseph Martos believe that balance and wholeness of self and soul can only result from the "labyrinthine journey of faith." They believe that many men in American society are trapped by an illusion of superiority. They are not aware of what constitutes deep masculinity (the ability to embrace the female soul). Little boys and young men suffer from the lack of grandfathers or contemplative elders to serve as role models for the journey to the center within themselves and the understanding that the Center is not themselves (Rohr & Martos, 1996). Rohr and Martos believe women in America are doing a better job than men in breaking away from stereotypes and moving along a path of enlightenment.

Some scientists, such as Benson, believe that the spiritual drive is absolutely fundamental to human physiology. He believes that human beings are "wired for God" and have to create a belief in God as a survival mechanism (Benson: In Glynn, 1997). Other scientists argue that widespread belief in God is evidence of the existence of God. Either way, Alfons Marcoen (1994) argues that a spiritual outlook on life may help elderly people to cope with the vicissitudes of life. Marcoen puts forth a multidimensional concept of personal well-being that includes the following components: psychological; physical; social; material; cultural; and, existential. As defined by Marcoen, existential well-being results from one's successful reconciliation to the reality of being born and having to die in a still incomprehensible universe. According to Marcoen both young and older people look for answers at hand in their social environment even before questions arise in an articulated way. For Marcoen, life's meaning is expressed in what people do and take care of, in their concerns, goals, and projects. Marcoen concludes that the experiences of well-being with regard to different reality domains are interrelated. He considers existential well-being as "the cornerstone of a person's global well-being," and suggests a person's spirituality is grounded in the experience of a transcendent relationship to something greater than oneself. He draws on the reflections of Elkins and colleagues (1998) and Genia (1990) in proposing a multidimensional construct of spirituality that includes belief in a transcendent source of meaning, commitment to a mission or purpose, as well as the experience of doubt and uncertainty. He goes on to explain how people who have a spirituality that helps them to live hopefully, inherited their spiritual outlook on life from religious or other spiritual systems that were transmitted through their parents and teachers, or developed a private spiritual system based on their own personal experiences. He argues that a spiritual perspective cannot thrive without social support.

Glynn (1997) confirms the resurgence of interest in religious thought in recent years. Whereas psychoanalysis banished religion as a vestige of obsolete thinking, new developments in psychology reflect the reintroduction of religious concepts into therapy. Glynn describes the current trend in spiritually-based psychological literature that deals with such themes as forgiveness, healing, and spiritual growth. What is the source of this resurgence? In his quest to demonstrate the existence of God, he discusses the relationship between faith and reason. Reason seems to have taken precedence over religion for much of the 20th century with secular, rationalistic thinking replacing the religious perspective. Glynn's dialectic is founded on his quest to prove the existence of God. Rather, his discussion can equally be construed as evidence for the Hegelian dialectic of a constantly changing reality with a material base. In other words, as social structures change, values as well as ideas change, resulting in further material changes. Whether the renewal of interest in spirituality is proof of the existence of God or a function of a constantly changing reality is academic. However, this renewal may provide evidence of a transcendent human need to achieve existential well-being. Although the source of meaning may change, the need for meaning may be constant. Reason alone cannot satisfy the need for existential well-being.

Carl Jung, who differed with his mentor, Sigmund Freud, in matters regarding the relationship of spirituality to mental health, was a proponent of this position. Jung observed, "Among all my patients in the second half of my life, there has not been one whose problem in the last resort was not that of finding a religious outlook on life" (Jung: In Glynn, 1997). The popular view of the spiritual quest to discover the transcendent meaning in everyday life and all human relations has its roots in Jungian theory. Paul Wink (1999) illustrates this view, in very imaginative fashion, with the quest of Luke Skywalker of the Star Wars trilogy. This allegory serves well as a model of spiritual growth and development and demonstrates the importance of spirituality in human experience. Wink explains that Luke starts out as a bored young man looking for excitement. He is invited to embark on a journey by two robots, one of which projects an image of Princess Leia. Luke is smitten by the vision of the young woman who exemplifies traits he is lacking. On his journey, Luke meets other characters and is introduced by Obi-Wan Kenobi to the concept of "the force." In order to engage the powers of the force, Luke must be able to suspend rational thought and place trust in the realm of intuition. Luke's journey of individuation includes an encounter with Darth Vader, the personification of evil. Toward the end of his journey, Luke realizes that Princess Leia is his biological sister and Darth Vader, his long lost father. Paul Wink explains the people Luke encounters are projections of his mind, in Jungian terms. Each is an archetype of different aspects of his mind. Princess Leia represents his feminine side, Darth Vader, his capacity for evil, and Obi-Wan Kenobi and the force, his potential for transcendent spiritual experience.

There is one further point that may shed some light on the increasing centrality of spirituality in contemporary culture. The baby boomers are beginning to confront the challenges of middle age and enter a life stage that this author has named transience. Transience is the transition between middle and early old age (beginning at age 50) and seems to bear some association to adolescence. As in the case of the adolescent, the transient individual experiences an awakening from the quiescence or complacency of the immediately preceding years. Quiescence is associated with the successful integration of different aspects of the self into one unified perspective. Successful integration, if achieved, seems to occur at a later age today than in previous generations and may present a greater mental, if not physical, challenge. This greater challenge appears to be associated with the need for the individual to balance many competing role expectations in the process of unifying multiple aspects of the self. For such an individual who reaches this developmental milestone, transience involves the passage to a spiritual state of consciousness in which the emphasis shifts away from integrating different aspects of the self to finding the sacred in everyday life and all human relations. Chronological aging marks this passage and seems to foster the transformation in spiritual perspective. The transient individual awakens to the realities of impending old age with natural trepidation. Although many individuals in this age group are very healthy and physically active, most have begun to experience some limitations in activity level, as well as have endured losses of loved ones. Since the baby boomers in the Western world grew up under the influence of the secular rationalistic worldview, as described by Glynn, many have experienced a lapse in religious or spiritual attentiveness. Longer life and better health expectancies, reduced risk of premature death and biotechnological advances may have served to reinforce an illusion of inviolability, if not immortality. The need for existential well-being has caught this generation unawares. The resulting search for meaning would be a logical consequence of this spiritual shake-up. Differences in the expression of this awakening consciousness may reflect variations in faith development as outlined by Fowler, Koenig, and others. Those individuals who have been consistent in their spiritual practices may experience an expanding, rather than awakening consciousness. Despite the variations, transience seems to be a critical time for spiritual awareness.

The above discussion yields more questions than answers regarding the relationship of spirituality to the life cycle. Besides the ontological questions regarding the existence of God and whether faith development necessitates a belief in God, questions remain regarding the origin of spiritual awareness in the developing human being, and whether certain spiritual experiences transcend cultural or cohort differences. Also remaining are the key questions of whether spirituality is worth promoting as a target of social concern, and whether general spiritual awareness and a loosely arranged system of values and beliefs are as useful as a tightly constructed set of religious precepts in fostering existential well-being?

Some of these questions are unanswerable. They do not lend themselves to rational analysis. Marcoen's (1994) belief, however, that a spiritual perspective cannot thrive without social support implies the possibility, if not the necessity, of human mediation in spiritual processes. It seems clear that children need to be introduced to spiritual concepts in order to include them in their cognitive repertoire. The absence of a framework may not negate a spiritual process of development, but will alter the shape of that development. We do not deprive children of our academic wisdom. For what reason could it be desirable to withhold spiritual wisdom from our children? Glynn (1997) argues that postmodern philosophy in its attempt to demonstrate a value-free morality at best has offered a diluted version of New Testament morality. He believes that an orientation to a religious perspective provides the most comprehensive and truthful orientation and makes the argument there is little variance in basic moral law among Christians, Jews, Muslims, Hindus, Buddhists, and everyone else. A pan-spiritual perspective would seem to lack the consistency a child may require for understanding and serve poorly as an orientation. A well-coordinated humanistic system of values, however, may serve as effectively as formal religion to inspire a sense of existential well-being. In either case, society could contribute to the spiritual development of children by providing opportunities for the expression of spiritual beliefs. Koenig believes that faith needs to be expressed through relationship. Community service, particularly where adolescents are concerned, can provide the opportunity for meaningful activity and serve as an antidote for alienation.

Society can play a role in promoting existential well-being by providing outlets for spiritual and ethical expression across the life span. Erikson's appreciation of social factors in explaining human development set him apart from Freud. Erikson (1980) believed that healthy adult development is as much influenced by opportunities afforded by the social environment as by a positive individual perspective. Erikson helps to explain why individuals in late life may give in to a despair that never manifested itself in their earlier years. Positive people can become negative by virtue of too much loss in later life. Society provides the opportunities or gaps in opportunity for self-expression, the basis of self-esteem. This self-expression may include the need to find the sacred in everyday life through relationship, and thus, may also serve as the basis of existential well-being.

The large population of aging baby boomers can seriously influence their own aging experience by promoting positive social change. Jung (1968) believed "germs of future psychic occurrences" shape the human psyche, as much as past memory. Intimations of the future can serve as guideposts for actions in the present.

Mannheimer (1999) explains how our society is embroiled in a difficult process of casting off stereotypes, including aging. He argues that if social reality is constructed, the hope is that we can deconstruct it. "In the case of aging, we can applaud creative, committed, caring older people who demonstrate in various ways that aging doesn't necessarily mean disengaging" (p. 19). Mannheimer also cautions "life is a process of passage from being to nothingness" and "we cannot insist upon sameness no matter how much we cherish a permanent position in the universe" (p. 17). In his view meaning is the product of temporality, and experiences are only meaningful when reflected upon "within a framework of interpretation that is [my] biography" (p. 17). He wonders whether the perspective achieved in old age can only be achieved in old age. Mannheimer suggests existential well-being in old age comes from a realistic acceptance of the limits of mortality and the need to remain socially engaged.

Ultimately, each individual must ask and find his or her answers to questions regarding the nature of existence and seek his or her own spiritual path. The route to existential well-being is not fixed in stone. It is difficult, if not impossible, to escape the question of the existence of God. The question has become more and more central to what drives this author's personal quest. Is this quest a function of being "wired" to search for meaning or an artifact of aging? A deeper connection with religious practice may have resulted in a different spiritual course. Faith in God, as the source of ultimate meaning, makes the reconciliation of reason with temporality seem possible. Milton Steinberg (1951) offers the following explanation for why this may be so:

> And only with God can we ease the intolerable tension of our existence. For only when He is given, can we hold life at once infinitely precious and yet as a thing lightly to be surrendered. Only because of Him is it made possible for us to clasp the world, but with relaxed hands; to embrace it, but with open arms. (p. 20)

Whether one's faith is founded on a belief in God or some other source of ultimate meaning, clearly, spiritual development is as critical as any other aspect of human development to the individual throughout the life span. Social workers can help individual clients connect with their spirituality to find strength. Social workers can also help communities of people by supporting the development of social structures that promote existential well-being. For social workers, these are not simply tasks. These are also the ways that social workers find meaning for themselves.

REFERENCES

Berger, P. L., & Luckmann, T. (1967). *The social construction of reality.* New York: Anchor Books.

Erikson, E. (1980). *Identity and the life cycle.* New York: Norton.

Glynn, P. (1997). *God the evidence: The reconciliation of faith and reason in a postsecular world.* Rucklin, CA: Prima Publishing.

Greer, G. (1992). *The change: Women, aging and the menopause.* New York: Alfred A. Knopf.

Hodge, D. R. (2001). Spiritual assessment: A review of major qualitative methods and a new framework for spirituality. *Social Work, 46*(3), 203–214.

Jung, C. G. (Ed.). (1968). *Man and his symbols.* New York: Dell Publishing.

Koenig, H. G. (1994). *Aging and God: Spiritual pathways to mental health in midlife and later years.* New York: Haworth Press.

Mannehimer, R. J. (Winter 1999–2000). A philosophical time of life. *Generations.*

Marcoen, A. (1994). Spirituality and personal well being in old age. *Ageing and Society, 14,* 521–546.

Rohr, R., & Martos, J. (1996). *The wild man's journey.* Cincinnati, OH: St. Anthony Messenger Press.

Sermabeikian, P. (1994). Our clients, ourselves: The spiritual perspective and social work practice. *Social Work, 39*(2), 178–183.

Steinberg, M. (1951). *A believing Jew.* New York: Harcourt Brace.

Wink, P. (1999). Addressing end of life issues: Spirituality and inner life. *Generations, 23*(2), 75–80.

Chapter 5

HEALTH, SPIRITUALITY, AND HEALING

Connie Saltz Corley

Health. It is a way we feel that affects how we relate to each other. It is translated into a cost to society, both in government expenditures and out-of-pocket costs. It is a factor that holds great import in perceived life satisfaction, notably among older adults (Palmore, 1995), and is defined as "the condition of being sound in body, mind, or spirit" (p. 558, Webster's Ninth New Collegiate Dictionary).

Spirituality. It is " . . . the personal quest for understanding answers to ultimate questions about life, about meaning, and about relationship to the sacred or transcendent . . . " (Koenig, McCullough, & Larson, 2001, p. 18). For some it is expressed in beliefs and behaviors associated with organized religion.

Healing. It is a word whose root is "wholeness." It is a response to the challenges of life. "To heal often means to make sense of a patient's life and death" (Kinsley, 1996, p. 195).

How do these three words interrelate? Depicted as petals of a lotus flower, spirituality can be seen as nestled between health and healing, with beliefs and behaviors at the heart of the flower (see Figure 5.1). The lotus is a flower depicted in ancient art and has mythical association with contentment.

In this chapter health will be addressed in terms of how spirituality, viewed here as encompassing religion but being a broader concept, is an

FIGURE 5.1   Health, spirituality, and healing.

essential aspect of health and healing, of wholeness. A brief cultural and historical overview of the comingling and clashing of spirituality and health/ mental health practices is first provided. Evidence for the importance of spiritual beliefs and practices in relation to health and mental health is presented. A contemporary perspective is then provided, followed by a discussion of the need for creating new paradigms for practice and training.

HEALING AND HEALERS ACROSS TIME AND CULTURES

Across time and cultures, specialized healers have been consulted by those who are unsettled emotionally, physically, and/or spiritually. Healing practices have included prayers said collectively and privately, the use of herbs (prescription medications are a contemporary example) and other interventions that are intended to alter the connection between the source of illness and the person experiencing it. Attributions of causality have varied greatly ranging from forces of nature to forces within the individual. The intent of healing is to restore the balance of these forces.

Throughout most of history, health and spirituality were seen as strongly connected. For example, asylums were founded starting in the Middle Ages for persons we now define as experiencing "mental illness" as a form of "moral treatment." One of the meanings of the word "asylum" is "sanctuary" which includes in its definition "the most sacred part of a religious building" (p. 1040, Webster's Ninth New Collegiate Dictionary).

Historically, health and mental health have also been seen as coexisting rather than separate, the "split" being the more common approach in contemporary health care delivery and financing in the United States. This split does not exist in the more traditional forms of healing such as qigong (Eisenberg & Wright, 1987) and shamanism (Canda & Furman, 1999; Villoldo, 2000). In fact, ancient healing traditions such as Chinese medicine emphasize the interconnectedness between mind and matter, and sickness and health (Beinfield & Korngold, 1991). Similarly, in major religious traditions there is a role for healing, which "involves restoring harmony, correcting behavior, rebuilding fractured relationships (with gods, ancestors, or the living) . . . " (Kinsley, 1996, p. 2).

In this chapter "health" is addressed as a unified concept including emotional, physical, as well as spiritual aspects. A new paradigm reflecting healing in contemporary society shows that spirituality remains an essential component of health and well-being that can enhance conventional treatment. The specialization of health and mental health services reflected in the medical model has isolated the experience of the person (wholeness) from the diagnosis and treatment of symptoms. An enlightened team approach that works within the current practice context but brings together traditional and advanced wisdom is part of a paradigm that can help "heal the split" that has resulted from the passing off of spiritual matters of healing to specialized practitioners.

IMPACT OF SPIRITUAL/RELIGIOUS BELIEFS AND PRACTICES ON HEALTH

A surge of interest in the influence of spirituality and religion on health has been manifested in both the popular press (e.g., cover page articles in 2001 editions of *Reader's Digest* and *Time* magazines) and in the academic literature. The *Handbook of Religion and Health* written by Koenig, McCollough, and Larson (2001), which examines over 1,200 studies and 400 research reviews, is a demonstration that a sufficient body of evidence exists that religion has an impact on health (including mental health). Yet the authors state, " . . . the relationship between religion and health is certainly a new and sometimes puzzling frontier for medical researchers, health professionals, and religious professionals today" (Koenig, McCollough, & Larsen, 2001, p. vix).

Both positive effects of religion and negative effects (e.g., refraining from life-saving procedures such as transplants among some religious groups) have been explored by researchers. In the realm of mental health, Koenig and associates (2001) have cited a full array of positive effects of religion on both subjective well-being, such as life satisfaction and hope/optimism, as well as rates of different behaviors. For example, reduced rates of suicide, lowered anxiety, lower rates of alcohol and drug use and abuse, and fewer psychotic episodes have been found among those who engage in religious expression. Similarly, reduced rates of various chronic diseases (e.g., coronary artery disease, hypertension, stroke, immune system dysfunction, and cancer) and fewer negative health behaviors are evidenced in the vast majority of studies on religion and health (Koenig et al., 2001).

In the field of aging, there has been a rapid expansion of interest in the multidimensional impacts of spirituality and religion, for example, in reducing stressors that affect overall health; in offering a framework to bring greater meeting to life, buffer stresses, and enhance coping; in providing greater external as well as internal resources (Levin, 1995). "Positive spirituality" as a vital component of successful aging is being discussed (Crowther, Parker, Koenig, Larimore, & Achenbaum, in press). A cross-faith and interdisciplinary effort is called for (Ai, 2000) to better understand spiritual well-being, spiritual growth, and meeting the challenges of adversity across the life span. Understanding these processes will enhance the knowledge base and enrich the opportunities for promoting overall health and well-being of all generations.

Sorting out the relative influences of religious practices and spiritual beliefs remains a challenge for researchers, given the fact that most studies utilize an empirical approach (largely epidemiological in nature). In addition, studies that focus on religion/spirituality among particular racial or ethnic groups rarely explore variations both among and within such groups (Levin, 1995). Further, most research has been conducted among established Western religious traditions (Koenig et al., 2001), leaving much of the world's major spiritual beliefs and behaviors unexplored in the scientific literature. This creates the opportunity to expand the growing knowledge of the vital connections among spirituality, health, and healing. Mystical and paranormal experiences that may occur outside of the realm of formal religious practice and are harder to document by traditional scientific approaches are a further landscape to be explored (Levin, 1995).

Funding by government sources and foundations such as the Fetzer Institute, the Robert Wood Johnson Foundation, and the Templeton Foundation will go far in providing the research support to undergird greater attention to spirituality and religion as vital components of health and well-being and essential in the provision of professional care. The creation of a White House Commission on Complementary and Alternative Medicine under former President Clinton and discussions of faith-based initiatives by President Bush provide national attention to a broader influence of religion/spirituality and the opportunity to explore a greater array of healing modalities than reflected to date in published research. A small but growing part of the federal research budget under the National Institutes of Health (e.g., via the National Center for Complementary and Alternative Medicine under the National Institutes of Health) opens the door for demonstrating the potential of healing approaches based in spiritual traditions (e.g., see Ai, Peterson, Gillespie, Bolling, Jessup, Behling, et al., 2001) to meet the needs of a population that increasingly seeks alternatives to conventional health and mental health care (Eisenberg, Davis, Ettner, et al., 1998).

HEALTH, SPIRITUALITY, AND HEALING IN THE NEW MILLENNIUM

In the conventional health care community in the United States, the role of religion and spirituality in health and well-being is drawing increased attention. At the same time, there is a movement away from conventional health care among many who are alienated by the impersonalization that often accompanies highly technical and specialized treatment approaches. Additionally, the role of self in healing, which underlies Eastern practices such as qigong (Jahnke, 1999), is being brought to greater awareness in the West, where the focus of healing has tended to be on externally prescribed interventions.

Acknowledgement of healing traditions among the increasingly diverse population in the United States is also growing. In the field of end-of-life care, for example, the universal dimension of spirituality in death, dying, and grieving among diverse ethnic groups is recognized (e.g., Irish, Lundquist, & Nelson, 1993). Carl Jung notes that the great majority of the world's religions might be seen as "complicated systems of preparation for death" (1934; 1969, p. 172), as death is seen as the defining condition of being human for many (Thomas & Eisenhandler, 1999).

A case example is useful in highlighting how rituals associated with death in the Jewish tradition are adapted in contemporary life:

> Fredela, an 86-year-old widow suffering from arthritis and a degenerative eye disease, lived independently in her studio apartment in Venice, California, from which she slowly walked each weekday to the senior center. Although her father was a rabbi in the "old country," she no longer kept kosher at home, yet she looked forward to a kosher meal and the camaraderie of her fellow Jewish friends at the center. On Monday she did not appear and the center director called her next of kin in Chicago, to learn that she had died over the weekend and funeral services were being held that day. It is a Jewish custom to bury the dead as soon as possible after the death, in a simple casket not open for public viewing. To honor the dead, members of the family and community pray daily, traditionally for a week (called "shiva"). At the senior center, the custom is adapted by saying the "Kaddish" at lunchtime for the rest of the week. This prayer honors the living as well as the dead. Another marker of mourning is the "Yahrzeit," one year later, when family members again meet to unveil the tombstone at the gravesite. At the senior center, members discuss making plans for that time, noting how many other participants had died the same month and honoring them collectively.

The case study above illustrates how several healing rituals in Judaism are adapted to meet the needs of the family on one hand, and the social community on the other hand, in response to death. Even those who do not have an affiliation with a synagogue find meaning in the group process of mourning. Some of the older participants in the senior center have no surviving family members nearby, and find comfort in knowing that they will be honored and remembered at the center as they contemplate their own death. In contemporary times, returning to rituals that have survived for centuries can still bring meaning to the healing process for those who do not have a formal affiliation with a religious institution, but feel a connection to the spiritual practices of that religion, especially in bringing meaning to death.

Another adaptation of incorporating practices associated with various spiritual traditions into contemporary life is exemplified in the growing area of stress reduction and health promotion. One example is the pioneering work of Jon Kabat-Zinn (1990) and colleagues from the Mindfulness-Based Stress Reduction Program at the University of Massachusetts Medical Center, a program that incorporates meditation and yoga. Also, the "mind-body" approaches promulgated at major institutions such as Harvard (e.g., Benson, 1975) and programs featured by the Center for Mind-Body Medicine in Washington, D.C. (among others) have been adopted by numerous health care organizations across the United States. Acupuncture—a form of Chinese medicine that alters patterns of energy flow in the body, known as meridians—is now routinely covered by medical insurance, giving further evidence that ancient healing traditions once considered unconventional are entering "mainstream American consciousness" (Beinfeld & Korngold, 1991, p. xiii).

As "East meets West" there is a growing effort to understand consciousness and how various spiritually-based approaches, such as yoga, that alter consciousness can promote health and healing (e.g., Mann, 1998; Ruiz, 2001). Understanding spirituality as "divinely focused altered states of consciousness" (Bullis, 1996) allows us to see how changes in brain waves from beta or waking consciousness to deeper states such as alpha (associated with being calm) and theta (where pain control is possible without anesthesia) can have profound implications for expanding the possibilities of controlling and even curing illnesses that may be less responsive to conventional medical treatments. Herein lies greater understanding of mysteries such as "spontaneous remission." Further, there is groundbreaking research on the role of prayer both as a private experience (e.g., Ai, Dunkle, Peterson, & Bolling, 1998) and as it is engaged in by others intentionally for someone (e.g., Sicher, Targ, Moore, & Smith, 1998) in reducing short-term and long-term outcomes of illness and surgical interventions.

The effect of the consciousness of a therapist or other healer on patients is only now beginning to be addressed. For example, Mann (1998) describes a Sacred Healing model where the heightened subtle energy of the therapist can be transmitted to others. Even to be aware of life force energy (known as "shakti" or "prana" in the yogic system) in the self and others can have a powerful effect on the healing relationship. "The process of sacred psychotherapy moves beyond the mind and emotions, as subtle energetic reality becomes a legitimate field of investigation and change" (Mann, 1998, p. 147). Self-awareness of one's spiritual nature as a practitioner then becomes essential in bringing greater energy into the healing relationship.

Extensive discussion of energy healing is beyond the scope of this chapter, but readers are referred to the work of Carolyn Myss (1997a, 1997b) for an in-depth discussion of energy systems. In her book, *Anatomy of the Spirit*, she demonstrates how the life force flowing through the body has been symbolized in major spiritual traditions such as Hinduism (the chakras), Judaism (the Tree of Life) and Christianity (the sacraments). It is considered "an internal roadmap, a spiritual maturation process that can lead us from the unconscious to the conscious mind, then on to the superconscious" (Myss, 1997b, p. 193). Exciting interdisciplinary research on energy healing (qigong), funded by the federal government, and a discussion of the challenges of designing clinical trials involving this ancient art are reported by Ai, Peterson, Gillespie, Bolling, Jessup, Behling, and Pierce (2001). They note, "[T]he blossoming of research on energy healing may eventually enrich methodologies used in clinical research on other types of healthcare" (Ai et al., 2001, p. 99).

Given the exciting developments just described, has professional training kept pace? The answer is no, according to Koenig and colleagues (2001): "There exists almost no research and very little discussion on how physicians, nurses, social workers and other health care providers might address religious issues in a non-offensive, sensitive manner" (p. 477). People may be afraid to discuss their spiritual experiences with professionals (Targ, 2001), which inhibits an opportunity to foster a team approach in healing. The time has come for an open dialogue in the professional community about the role of spirituality/religion in health and healing, including self-awareness. This creates an exciting challenge for the practice of healing and health promotion in a spiritual context and for enhancing professional education.

CREATING NEW PARADIGMS FOR PRACTICE AND TRAINING

At a time when attention to spiritual beliefs and behaviors is highlighted in world events and when the call for healing is ever present, it is essential to "heal the split" between mind and body characterizing research and practice, by embracing the role of spirituality in promoting health and wholeness. Therefore, "spiritual" must become a necessary component of the traditional "bio-psycho-social" approach that is common in health professions training. The inclusiveness of spirituality builds on values of empowerment (e.g., in the Social Work Code of Ethics) and the growing incorporation of the strengths perspective (Hodge, 2001) in professional training (e.g., Miley, O'Melia, & DuBois, 2001).

A model proposed as a paradigm for understanding the dynamics of spirituality has been designed by Thibault, Ellor, and Netting (1991; in Ellor, Netting, & Thibault, 1999). As shown in Figure 5.2, the three-part domain of spirituality (cognitive, affective, and behavioral) is conceptual-

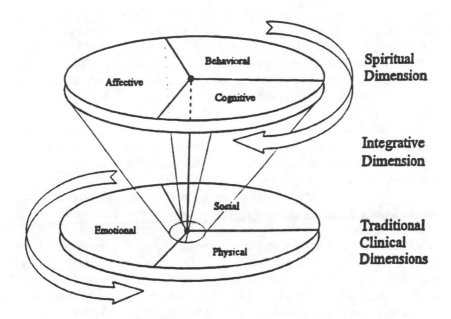

FIGURE 5.2 The whole person: A model.

In Ellor, J., Netting, F. E., & Thibault, J. (1999). *Religious and spiritual aspects of human service practice.* Columbia, SC: University of South Carolina Press.

ized as "a potentially integrative structure that can be visualized as an overlay to the (holistic) physical, emotional, and social domains of the individual" (Ellor, Netting, & Thibault, 1999, p. 117). It is suggested here that culture be added to further expand this "whole person model" to foster assessment and interventions that encompass the "bio-psycho-socio/cultural-spiritual" domains. This allows for greater appreciation of diversity in spiritual/religious expression. Ellor and associates (1999) further highlight the importance of a spiritual self-examination as part of undertaking a career in human services.

Teamwork is essential in healing the mind-body split characterizing conventional care and in incorporating spiritual and sociocultural domains. A proposed advance in interdisciplinary education and practice is "enlightened teamwork" (Corley, 2001), in which some essential spiritual values underlying diverse traditions guide team members (which include the client/patient and the family) as part of an "eightfold path": caring, sharing, listening, leading, lending, reflecting, revising, and resolving. Teams in conventional health care settings have the opportunity to expand their membership to include leaders of religious/spiritual communities (Tirrito, Nathanson, & Langer, 1996), as well as healers who have been considered outside the mainstream but are increasingly part of the health care landscape (e.g., massage therapists). Further, " . . . there is need to create the safety for patients to talk in detail about the role spirituality plays in their lives" (Targ, 2001, p. 8).

The promotion of health and healing is hence a journey that is not one confined to the therapist's office or health care setting. Spiritual and religious beliefs and practices are part of daily life, and awareness and conscious use of self in a professional capacity as part of a larger community (including humanity as a whole) must be cultivated. Daily life in contemporary times involves the processing of an immense amount of information via various external media (television, internet, cellular communication), which heightens our awareness of the "outer world." By promoting greater attention to the immense "inner world" the health care community is well poised to create healing teams that grow beyond the reaches of a physical location such as a health care setting. The responsiveness of healers from all walks of life to tragic events, such as the September 11, 2001 terrorist acts in the United States, which impact global health and well-being, demonstrates that finding meaning in healing is a responsibility we all share.

CONCLUSION

Spirituality and religion are central to the lives of most Americans, perhaps more so than to the professionals they encounter in conventional health care settings. A growing body of evidence points to the powerful impact of spiritual/religious beliefs and practices on promoting health and well-being and influencing the course of illness. Given the high costs of an increasingly specialized health care system, and the growing use of "alternative and complementary" approaches across the diverse spectrum of the population, a broader vision of health and healing that incorporates spirituality and religion is finding its voice.

REFERENCES

Ai, A. (2000). Spiritual well-being, spiritual growth, and spiritual care for the aged: A cross-faith and interdisciplinary effort. *Journal of Religious Studies, 11,* 3–28.

Ai, A., Dunkle, R., Peterson, C., & Bolling, S. (1998). The role of private prayer in psychological recovery among midlife and aged patients following private surgery. *The Gerontologist, 38,* 591–601.

Ai, A., Peterson, C., Gillespie, B., Bolling, S., Jessup, M., Behling, B., & Pierce, F. (2001). Designing clinical trials on energy healing: Ancient art encounters medical science. *Alternative Therapies, 7,* 93–99.

Beinfield, H., & Korngold, E. (1991). *Between heaven and earth: A guide to Chinese medicine.* New York: Ballantine.

Benson, H. (1975). *The relaxation response.* New York: Avon.

Bullis, R. (1996). *Spirituality in social work.* Washington, DC: Taylor & Francis.

Canda, E., & Furman, L. (1999). *Spiritual diversity in social work.* New York: Free Press.

Corley, C. (2001). *The spirit of teamwork and the evolution of interdisciplinary education and practice.* Presented at the Gerontological Society of America annual meeting, Chicago, IL.

Crowther, M., Parker, M., Koenig, H., Larimore, W., & Achenbaum, W. (in press). Rowe and Kahn's model of successful aging revisited: Positive spirituality, the forgotten factor. *Annals of Behavioral Medicine.*

Eisenberg, D., Davis, R., Ettner, S., Appel, S., Wilkey, S., Van, M., & Kessler, R. (1998). Trends in alternative medicine in the United States, 1990–1997: Results of a follow-up national survey. *Journal of the American Medical Association, 280,* 1569–1575.

Eisenberg, D., & Wright, T. (1987). *Encounters with qi.* Bergenfield, NJ: Viking Press/Penguin.

Ellor, J., Netting, F., & Thibault, J. (1999). *Religious and spiritual aspects of human service practice.* Columbia, SC: University of Columbia Press.

Hodge, D. (2001). Spiritual assessment: A review of major qualitative methods and a new framework for assessing spirituality. *Social Work, 46,* 203–214.

Irish, D., Lundquist, K., & Nelson, V. (1993). *Ethnic variations in dying, death and grief: Diversity in universality.* Washington, DC: Taylor & Francis.

Jahnke, R. (1999). *The healer within: The four essential self-care techniques for optimal health.* San Francisco: Harper.

Jung, C. (1969). The soul and death. In *The collected works of C. G. Jung* (2nd ed., Vol. 8). Princeton, NJ: Princeton University Press. (Original work published in 1934)

Kabat-Zinn, J. (1990). *Full catastrophe living: Using the wisdom of your body and mind to face stress, pain and illness.* New York: Doubleday & Co.

Kinsley, D. (1996). *Health, healing and religion: A cross-cultural perspective.* Upper Saddle River, NJ: Prentice Hall.

Koenig, H., McCullough, M., & Larson, D. (2001). *Handbook of religion and health.* New York: Oxford.

Levin, J. (1995). Religion. *The encyclopedia of aging* (2nd ed., pp. 799—802). New York: Springer Publishing.

Mann, R. (1998). *Sacred healing: Integrating spirituality with psychotherapy.* Nevada City, CA: Blue Dolphin.

Miley, K., O'Melia, M., & DuBois, B. (2001). *Generalist social work practice: An empowering approach* (3rd ed.). Needham Heights, MA: Allyn & Bacon.

Myss, C. (1997a). *Anatomy of the spirit: The seven stages of power and healing.* New York: Random House.

Myss, C. (1997b). *Why people don't heal and how they can.* New York: Three Rivers Press.

Palmore, E. (1995). Successful aging. In G. Maddox (Ed.), *The encyclopedia of aging* (2nd ed., pp. 914–915). New York: Springer Publishing.

Ruiz, F. (2001). What is consciousness? *Yoga Journal,* Sept/Oct., 104–107; 173–177.

Sicher, F., Targ, E., Moore, D., & Smith, H. (1998). A randomized double-blind study of the effect of distant healing in a population with advanced AIDS. *Western Journal of Medicine, 169,* 356–363.

Targ, E. (2001). Who's to say who's nuts. *Spirituality & Health,* Fall, 8.

Thibault, J., Ellor, J., & Netting, F. (1991). A conceptual framework for assessing the spiritual functioning and fulfillment of older adults in long-term care settings. *Journal of Religious Gerontology, 7,* 29–46.

Thomas, L. E., & Eisenhandler, S. A. (Eds.). (1999). *Religion, belief and spirituality in late life.* New York: Springer Publishing.

Tirrito, T., Nathanson, I., & Langer, N. (1996). *Elder practice: A multidisciplinary approach to working with older adults in the community.* Columbia, SC: University of South Carolina Press.

Villoldo, A. (2000). *Shaman, healer, sage.* Anzel, NJ: Harmony/Crown Publishers.

Chapter 6

MENTAL HEALTH AND RELIGION

John R. Belcher

Over the last decade there has been increasing discussion about the relationship between mental health and religion (Crossley, 1995). Research into this relationship has explored specific pathologies, such as depression (Kendler, Gardner, & Prescott, 1997), anxiety (Koenig, Ford, George, Blazer, & Meador, 1993), and other DSM codes. On balance, while some studies have shown evidence of higher rates of psychological pathology among some members of faith groups (Gritzmacher, Bolton, & Dana, 1988), other studies have shown less pathology (Hayes, Vining, & Belcher, Unpublished Manuscript). Most studies that have examined relationships between mental health variables and faith have failed to account for theological differences among subjects (Belcher & Vining, 2000). Faith groups have been lumped together, which often provides for negatively skewed differences. Moreover, clients who present with mental health problems and who are also religious have often been assumed to have mental health problems because of their faith. In addition, the missions of faith groups have not been examined to determine whether the mission might attract people with certain kinds of mental health problems.

Suspiciousness of faith groups by mental health professionals was begun by Sigmund Freud (1963) and furthered by such people as Albert Ellis. As a result, mental health professionals are often quick to label clients who are religious as pathological. Mental health professionals who are also Christians have formed associations, such as the American Association of

Christian Counselors, and begun their own journals, such as the *Journal of Psychology and Christianity*, which has often created a gulf between secular mental health professionals and Christian therapists.

This exploration of the relationship between religion and mental health comes at a point in history when the experts (those professionals who allegedly understand human behavior) cannot agree. Jerome Bruner (1990) notes:

> I have written . . . at a time when psychology, the science of mind as William James once called it, has become fragmented as never before in history. It has lost its center and risks losing the cohesion need to assure the internal exchange that might justify a division of labor between its parts. (pp. ix–x)

Religion does not pretend to be a science because it is inexact and based on the unseen. Psychology and psychiatry are also inexact and based on the unseen, yet pretend to be scientific. Consequently, science that attempts to fit its framework over religion is frustrated when it does not fit.

The profession of social work has not been immune from the debate as to the relationship between religion and mental health. In many respects, social work continues to struggle with definition. Should the profession accept as normative beliefs, behaviors, and practices, that the profession has decided to be deviant. Unlike psychology and psychiatry, social work practices within a value-based framework that, in many cases, finds religious belief, behaviors, and practice not normative. There is a growing division between religious mental health professionals, primarily pastoral counselors, and secular mental health professionals. Historically, there has been a rich connection between religion and social work (Derezotes & Evans, 1995). Unfortunately, that connection is beginning to fray with the movement of Christians away from traditional liberal denominational groups. The Jewish community is going through a similar experience, with many Jewish congregations moving toward more conservative or orthodox modes of thinking. The religious landscape is now becoming more complex. In the Christian community, more and more people are not describing themselves in terms of denominational affiliation. Instead, many Christians use broader categories, such as Charismatic, Evangelical, Pentecostal, or nondenominational. Mental health professionals are often less familiar with these distinctions and can become easily overwhelmed by certain forms of Christian practice (Belcher & Vining, 2000). Also confusing is the fact that many people identify themselves as spiritual, but not religious. In many respects, these individuals put together their own form of spirituality, which can borrow from many different religious backgrounds. This chapter will disentangle these relationships and provide a review of research that explores the relationship between mental health and religion.

WELL-BEING

Well-being is not delineated as a mental health condition as defined by the DSM-IV-TR. Most of the DSM-IV-TR diagnoses, however, involve some examination of well-being. Psychological well-being is hard to define. James (1890, p. 19) noted, how to gain, how to keep, how to recover happiness is in fact for most men and at all times the secret motive of all they do. Is the client happy, or are they satisfied with life? These questions are often difficult for clients to answer. They require the client to look at their life holistically and ask himself or herself, when everything is taken into consideration, are they happy?

Religion has been found to produce characteristics, such as social support, being healthy and active, high levels of internal locus of control, a strong sense of purpose and meaning, hopefulness, and optimism (Koenig, McCullough, & Larson, 2001). Most of the studies that have examined psychological well-being and religion have used cross-sectional designs. As a result, the long-term effect of religion psychological well-being is not known.

Religious involvement moves people in directions that promote positive well-being (Ellison & Smith, 1991). Being involved with a religion requires commitment to values, ideas, and behaviors that most often translate into positive changes. Adler (1992) notes that people have the basic need to belong. Part of belonging is a sense of support and well-being.

Studies have found a consistent relationship between marital status and religious involvement. Marital status has been found to predict well-being (Andrews & Withey, 1976; Denier, 1984; Glenn & Weaver, 1979). Religion can also keep unhealthy marriages together, which can promote psychological problems such as depression (Belcher, Unpublished manuscript). In general though, the relationship between religious involvement and marital status is positive.

Research finds negative outcomes for people who abuse alcohol and/or drugs, yet people who are religiously involved do not tend to abuse alcohol and drugs (Cassel, Hoey, & Riley, 1990; Levav, Kohn, Golding, & Weissman, 1997). Less exposure to alcohol and drugs generally lowers the risk of hypertension, heart disease, stroke, cancer, and disability, and generally increase life expectancy. Obviously, good health status promotes greater psychological well-being. Some studies have found significant substance abuse among some religious people, but these findings are confounded by the fact that some religious groups specifically reach out to people who have significant problems, such as depression and addictions (Belcher & Vining, 2000).

Religions tend to promote activities, such as attendance at worship, Bible studies, prayer meetings, volunteer activities, and daily devotionals. As a result, people involved in religious activities are generally active and involved (Cutler, 1976). One of the advantages of activity is that people do not have time to be lonely or depressed. The studies that have found a high rate of depression and anxiety (Koenig, George, Meador, Blazer, & Ford, 1992, 1994) do not account for the fact that certain religious groups specifically reach out to people with problems. Much like a mental health center, these groups will show higher rates of mental health problems among its members. Religion tends to promote the idea that a person should do something for someone else. Helping others also tends to focus someone away from their own problems and can also help the helper by letting them know that their problems pale in comparison to the helped.

Optimism is generally promoted by religion (Koenig et al., 2001). Pentecostals and Charismatics, for example, promote positive expectation among their adherents (Belcher & Hall, In Press; Carson, 1987; Land, 1994). Personality types appear to be drawn to particular faith movements, which in part explains why some faith movements are able to promote optimism and their followers are able to readily accept it. Studies of religious affiliation show other predictors as to why people join religious movements, economic class (Glock, 1964; Hak, 1988); psychological reasons, such as stress (Pargament, 1997); and personality style (Bunker, 1991).

People expect their faith movement to meet a personal need. Jung [1971] articulated four-personality functions, intuiting people, feeling people, sensation people, and thinkers. These personality functions tend to predict their faith needs. People tend to expect that God and their faith movement will create certain kind of environments (Belcher & Gurganious, Unpublished manuscript).

Along with a sense of optimism, religion promotes hope (Belcher & Vining, 2000; Carson, Soeken, Shanty, & Terry, 1990; Herth, 1989). Hope translates into the sense that situations will work out for the best. Such a belief tends to lessen the incidence of both anxiety and depressive disorders. People who look at the "glass as half full" tend to minimize their problems and the problems of the world and believe that situations will work out for the best. While some mental health professionals may criticize such an approach as being naive, it can have both a short- and long-term positive effects.

Religion has been found to enhance coping ability (Courtenay, Poon, Martin, Clayton, & Johnson, 1992). Religious coping techniques are often effective in relation to problem solving and stress reduction (McCrae & Costa, 1986). In fact, religious support often enhances the coping of those people committed to religion (Pargament, 1996; Pargament et al., 1990). Luhmann (1977) notes that religion is way of coping with the unknown. Over time, coping with crises can create a stable system (Vossen, 1993).

Ganzevoort (1998) argues that religious coping is a highly complex process that is interactive and creates support. In fact, religious coping is multidimensional involving the use of experience, interpretation, and behavior (Brown, 1987; Stark & Glock, 1968; Switzer, 1986). Van Uden (1985) notes that some Christians experience, from religion, a maternal role of comfort and consolation. Interestingly, the sense of comfort of consolation comes about most often when support is not the object of faith (Cieslak, 1991; Newman & Pargament, 1990). The person may simply be attending church, but because they are part of a community, they often experience positive relationships.

Commitment to religion most often fosters spiritual growth that in turn fosters psychological growth (DeHoff, 1998). Religion often asks people to closely examine themselves and determine where they need improvement. Such reflection can lead to a person seeking to improve relationships, approach life in a more constructive manner, and realize the continued need for change. Much of the New Testament, particularly the books written by Paul, argues for change and renewal. For many Christians, wanting to draw closer to God coincides with their wanting to engage in self-improvement.

Given the many positive influences of religion on mental health, why are mental health professionals so concerned with the negative relationship between religion and mental health? In fact, the church is full of people in need. Many scholars, pastoral counselors, and theologians argue that the mission of the church is to reach out to the troubled (ref). Therefore, it is not surprising that studies of people who are connected to church often show pathology. It is important to review some of the many studies that have explored the relationship between religion and psychopathology.

RELIGION AND PSYCHOPATHOLOGY

Religion can contribute to psychopathology (Bergin, 1983; Genia, 1997; Ingersoll, 1994; Kendler, Gardner, & Prescott, 1997; Koenig et al., 1993; Koenig et al., 1994; Williams & Faulconer, 1994). Clinebell (1984) for example, noted that some Christians have pathogenic beliefs that contribute to pathology. Studies have shown that people who are members of certain faith groups, such as Pentecostals, appear to exhibit anxiety disorders (Koenig et al., 1993), alcohol abuse, and dependence (Koenig et al., 1994), major depression (Meador et al., 1992) and narcissistic beliefs (Castelein, 1984; Poloma, 1989). These faith groups particularly reach out to people with problems as compared with other faith groups, which is evident in their membership. Some scholars have argued that some faith groups encourage narrow thinking, which can lead to some adherents exhibiting psychological distress (Koenig, McCullough, & Larson, 2001).

Modernistic views of faith that stress openness and criticize those people who engage in conservative Christian thought, have tended to emphasize the pathological contribution of faith (Faupel, 1996). It should be noted that narrow is usually in the eyes of the beholder. In point of fact one person's definition of narrowness is not another person's. If a person believes that it is wrong to engage in premarital sex and another person labels that as negative thinking, the person doing the labeling is acting on bias.

Does religion contribute to psychopathology? The answer depends upon what kinds of theories, instruments, and research methodologies are used to assess psychopathology (Belcher & Cascio, Unpublished manuscript). Modern science often assumes that constructs, such as faith and spirituality are inferior as compared with mental illness, which has been broken down and coded (Williams & Faulconer, 1994). There is also a "split" or tension between extrinsically religious and intrinsically religious people in the way faith and spirituality are understood (Batson & Ventis, 1982). Extrinsically religious people often attempt to separate out spirituality from religiosity and argue that spirituality is valid whereas religiosity is stigmatizing and not valid (Dayton, 1987; Turner, Lukoff, Barnhouse, & Lu, 1995; Zinnbauer et al., 1997). What has emerged, then, is the notion that spirituality has a positive connotation (Spilika & McIntosh, 1996), and religiousness is viewed as negative (Pargament, 1996).

Lowenberg and Dolgoff (1982) note that religion often becomes the means by which pathology is expressed. Meichenbaum (1988) asks the relevant question; How many times do we misinterpret? How often do we infuse our client's behavior with surplus meaning? (p. 85). People for example who are drawn to a particular faith movement because of personality style (Bunker, 1991) may exhibit certain personality styles. Did the individual bring those personality issues to the movement or did the movement cause the personality issues? The question, while difficult to resolve, would seem to be answered by research that indicates that particular personality styles are drawn to particular faith movements.

Williams and Faulconer (1994) describe the use of hermeneutical psychology to better understand the relationship between psychopathology and religion. Hermeneutical psychology does not rely on reductionism or the use of prior assumptions. Religious phenomena are often pathologized; Glossolalia (speaking in tongues) is a case in point (Cutten, 1927; Williams, 1981). However, when people who use Glossolalia (most likely Pentecostals) are studied in context, it has been noted that it is a benefit for some adherents (Copestake & Malony, 1993; Gritzmacher et al., 1988).

Mental health language may not be the best way to understand the language of religion (Polkinghorne, 1983, 1988, 1990; Schrag, 1980, 1990). Mental health professionals pride themselves on being able to select out when a behavior is abnormal, yet in the majority of cases the mental health professionals base their opinions upon the norms by which they live. Is it normal to express joy and excitement during a football game? Most mental health professionals would point out that that behavior is normal for the environment. Yet, when people during worship express similar sentiments, the behavior becomes pathological.

The relationship between psychopathology and faith is particularly interesting in regards to healing. Rudolph Bultmann (1963, p. 5) notes:

> It is impossible to use electric light and the wireless and to avail ourselves of modern medical and surgical discoveries, and at the same time to believe in the New Testament world of demons and spirits.

Bultmans comments underscore the beliefs of some theologians and many mental health professionals. In this age of modernity, how can people believe in what is seemingly not rational as defined by modern science? For many theologians, the answer is a question; how can people, in the vast confusion brought on by modern science, not believe in God? Interestingly, those people who do believe in what is allegedly not rational are by most nonreligious definitions not rational and most likely disturbed.

For many people struggling with faith issues, postmodernists are preoccupied with power struggles that surround language use and social practice (Moreland, 2001). People often come for pastoral counseling to avoid the uncertainty of secular mental health professionals.

Scholarly attempts to separate out the historical Jesus from the divine Jesus have posed particular challenges (Buttmann, 1963; Crossan, 1973; Herzog, 1999). Scholars from the Jesus Seminar and the Q Project argued that the alleged "miracles" of Jesus were symbolic in nature and designed to achieve theological purposes other than actual healing. Despite these criticisms, over forty healing stories have been identified in the Bible (Percy, 1997). Some Christian movements, such as Charismatics and Pentecostals, have incorporated divine healing into their theology (Dayton, 1996), other groups, such as Catholics and Episcopalians, have made the belief in healing a common although not a normative practice.

While the theological debate continues over the proper place for healing (Belcher & Hall, In Press), the fact that it is both widely practiced or believed in, challenges mental health professionals. Many Christians practice praying for healing in which people pray for the divine intervention of God in their lives. The notion of praying for healing fits well with the way Jesus practiced healing. Carrol (1995) notes that healing was practiced broadly in the New Testament. Mental health professionals do not usually seem to have concern over the notion of praying for healing, although Ellis and other theorists deny the presence of divine intervention. What seems to give many mental health practitioners pause, is the use of altar healing (Belcher & Hall, In press). Moreover, the practice of altar healing mixes in the use of exorcism. For many people who believe in altar healing, the Christian walk is a constant struggle against the flesh (Thomas, 1998). Many individuals believe that they can be healed and protected from this struggle. Healing particularly altar healing is a way for members of these faith groups to turn their problems over to God and move on with their lives. This symbolism is much the same thing that takes place when a person talks with a mental health professional.

Altar healing for those not familiar with the practice, takes place when a person wanting healing is invited to the altar, where the pastor and others pray, by laying on of hands, for healing. Oftentimes the person wanting healing feels immediately healed and may throw away crutches or other aides. To many people, the practice of altar healing appears contrived by the healer or at best an act of desperation by the healed. To the healed, however, the practice has delivered them from illness. What confuses many people is that the healing is not designed to be measured in time. Instead, the healing may only last seconds, minutes or years.

Many mental health professionals are also baffled by the fact that many Christians believe in the divine presence of the Holy Spirit (Belcher & Cascio, 2001; Parker, 1996). The problem for many mental health professionals is that the Holy Spirit cannot be seen or measured. Many Christians expect the transformative power of the Holy Spirit in their lives (Carson, 1987). The emotion-experience-centered theology of many Charismatics overwhelms many secular counselors. Prayer becomes a means of communicating with the Holy Spirit. Unlike some secular counselors, many Christians of all theological positions view prayer as normative. Moreover, they accept its usage in psychotherapy (Finney & Malony, 1985; Lange, 1983; Magaletta & Brawer, 1998; Mageletta & Duckro, 1996).

Secular counselors are often confused and frustrated by the fact that people are not consistent in their theology. A person may believe in the Holy Spirit, but not practice altar healing. A Charismatic may be very emotional in worship, but not practice speaking in tongues. Unlike mainline denominations that clearly define their theology, much Christian practice is heterogeneous (Cox, 1995). Christians are increasingly drawn to nondenominational churches that most often practice a diverse charismatic theology. Many of these churches function like mini-mental health centers (Meador et al., 1992). People with emotional needs are often drawn to these movements (Castelein, 1984; Poloma, 1989).

Let's return to the question first asked in this section; does religion contribute to psychopathology? There is no resounding yes or no. Instead, the answer depends upon factors, such as the view of the researcher, the research method used to explore the relationship, and the language used to define the phenomena. An understanding of religious interpretation is important in exploring further the relationship between religion and mental health.

RELIGIOUS INTERPRETATION

Ganzevoort (1998, p. 267) notes, Religious experience is clearly connected to the interpretation of events. How does the client view God? Pargament and colleagues (1988) observed that God could be viewed as passive or active. The choice is largely determined by how the person feels about religion; what is its role in relation to their daily living. Certainly, religious interpretation influences the appraisal process in crisis and coping (Ganzevoort, 1994). Most importantly, religion often provides a set of meanings as to how a person should interpret events and situations (Ganzevoort, 1998; Pargament & Maton, 1991).

Christian theology, the telling of belief, is both written and un-written. The latter theology tends to be characterized by emotion—experience-centered theology (Gause, 1976; Vining, 1995). Interestingly, it is faith groups that practice unwritten theology that often provide the most guidelines about how to interpret events. Many Christians read Romans 14:1–12 and infer that Christians are to behave a certain way in churches. Other Christians do not read Paul in the same way. Why? In most cases, one's theological background and what a particular faith group considers normative will determine the interpretation.

Cieslak (1991) notes that religious interpretation can reduce the threat of a crisis by interpreting events in a non-threatening way. Similarly, some faith groups encourage crisis because it is believed that spiritual growth and development are facilitated during crisis (Land, 1994). A crisis has often been interpreted as a time of religious significance (Croog & Levine, 1972).

Mental health professionals most often view a crisis negatively. The notion that a crisis could promote such things as spiritual growth (Burning & Stokes, 1982) often places religious leaders and mental health professionals at odds with one another. Many religious leaders argue that faith enables someone to better approach a crisis. In addition, the crisis may promote spiritual growth. People often turn to religion in search of meaning and purpose during a crisis (Shandor, Miles, & Brown-Crandall, 1986).

Many people are religiously converted during crises (Gillespie, 1979; Johnson, 1978; Ulman, 1989). There is a literature on conversion, yet many mental health professionals too often assume that conversion is pathological. When a person converts they accept an interpretation of events that normalizes their conversion. Therefore, if their faith community practices water immersion as part of the conversion process, then they accept water baptism.

What determines a crisis and its aftereffect is how someone chooses to interpret events. The religious background of the individual will most likely determine what kind of religious interpretation they use to frame the event (Loewenthal & Cornwall, 1993). A person may decide that God will ultimately lead them successfully through a crisis. Such a position will act to limit the crisis.

Coming though a crisis relatively unscathed, so to speak, becomes possible through religion. Mental health professionals often mistake language or behavior used during the crisis as indicative of pathology. A client may point out, The Lord led me to pray and I immediately received a feeling of peace. The client's statement, often given in the form of a testimony (Belcher & Vining, 2000), is both the client's interpretation of what they can and should expect from God. Moreover, their interpretation of the crisis shows their belief that God is in control of events. Pargament (1996) notes that the client will experience something positive when religion is viewed as central to the person. There can be an interpretation of events that can lead to a negative psychological impact. If the interpretation of events is one of punishment by God, the person will most likely feel depressed and experience despair (Hathaway & Pargament, 1991).

Unfortunately, theology can create an environment in which the person feels punished by God. Charles Finney advocated the notion that if people prayed enough, they would be healed (Finney, 1835). Obviously, there was the not subtle supposition that if a person did not receive healing, they did not believe. It became a tautological argument. Such practices continue today among some pastors and evangelists. Unfortunately, churches that practice healing have not developed a singular view of healing on which all the different factions of the different faith movements could agree (Belcher & Hall, In Press).

RELIGIOUS BEHAVIOR

One of the methods that mental health professionals use to assess or evaluate people is through their behavior. Although such a method is reductive and attempts to fit square pegs in round holes, the practice continues. When examining religious behavior, psychologists frequently count behaviors, such as religious attendance or the number of times a person prayed during the week (Ganzevoort, 1998). Such methods may not have any relevance to a person's actual stance on religion (Wulff, 1991).

People can engage in religious behaviors that can contribute to poor mental health. However, these same behaviors for other people can contribute to positive mental health. Sanders (1989) found that church attendance can lead to suppression of grief. Graham and associates (1978) found that lifestyle prescription can degenerate into strict requirements that can be unhealthy (Ganzevoort, 1998). Other researchers have found that church attendance contributes to positive mental health (Ellison, 1991; Gartner, Larson & Allen, 1991; Williams et al., 1991). The obvious question did people have problems before they started attending church regularly is not often asked by researchers. Gartner, Larson, and Allen's (1991) sample did include psychiatric patients and the results of church attendance were still found to be positive.

Prayer as a religious behavior has been extensively studied (Finney & Malony, 1985; Lange, 1983; Magaletta & Brawer, 1998; Magaletta & Duckro, 1996; Scarlett & Perriello, 1991) and found to generally contribute positively to mental health. The behavior of prayer creates a sense of purpose and belonging that increases the psychological well-being of individuals. Moreover, prayer acts to transcend problems beyond the human condition.

The difficulty in selecting out any religious behavior, such as prayer or religious attendance, is that these behaviors are embedded in the total lifestyle of religious behavior. In the majority of cases it is the totality of religious behaviors that produce effects and not a single behavior. Ganzevoort (1998, p. 268) notes that "religious behavior is not a stable phenomenon" and that religious behavior may change as the culture changes.

For example, the United Methodist church, as time has passed, has become more liberal and many members long for the days when the church spoke out forcefully against alcohol, homosexuals, and pre marital sex. Are those people who have adapted to modern culture and incorporated liberal views toward homosexuals healthier? Some mental health professionals would point out that this change in behavior is a healthy sign of openness. Other mental health professionals would point to the cognitive dissonance experienced by those individuals who believe it is wrong to endorse such lifestyles. Religious views and behaviors change, but it often remains uncertain as to whether the changes or healthy are unhealthy.

It is also important to note that religious behavior varies from faith group to faith group. The religious behavior of United Methodists is far different from the behavior of Pentecostals. For example, the Pentecostal movement has always valued emotional experience over reason (Belcher & Hall, In Press; Gause, 1976). It is also noteworthy that not all members of a faith movement exhibit behaviors that are always indicative of their faith movement. For instance, a mental health professional observes a Catholic praying to St. James and assumes that all Catholics pray to St. James.

For many people, engaging in religious behaviors is a sign that the person has been transformed. They have gone through convictional experiences (Loder, 1981). For many Christians the convictional experience is baptism, which for the vast majority of Christians is growth producing. Once the person has become part of the Christian community, they most likely engage in ritualistic practices that help to maintain their faith. These behaviors may make no sense to mental health professionals who may find the behaviors difficult to understand. Without the rituals, however, the Christian might have difficulty maintaining their faith.

Other religious communities, such as the Orthodox Jewish community, also have religious practices and behaviors that help to define them and show to the outward community that they are members of the community. People consider many of these practices, such as the shaving of a married woman's head, odd in the non-orthodox Jewish community, but they do not understand the symbolic importance that the shaving of the wife's head has for the couple and for the larger Jewish community.

Religious testimonies offer a glimpse into how ritual behaviors maintain faith. For many Charismatics, testimonies describe their unique relationship to God (Belcher & Vining, 2000). Through these testimonies they are able to remind themselves of the fact that God is active in their life. Testimonies are a "crossover" behavior, which usually suggests that someone has become a member of a particular faith community. A testimony usually consists of someone's oral reporting of what God has done for them in their lives. For example, a person might describe how God has delivered them from the sin of addictions.

Understanding religious behavior is a complex process that is made difficult by the people who frequently evaluate it when they themselves are not religious. Instead, they are observers of behaviors that they may find objectionable or simply beyond reason. Freud (1913) argued that religious behavior is developed in the Oedipus complex. In 1927, Freud authored, *Future of Illusion,* in which he argued that, Religion would thus be the universal obsessional neurosis of humanity" (p. 43). The notion that religious belief and behavior are pathological has remained a preoccupation of the health and mental health professions. Despite the obvious bias of such individuals, such as Freud, there are certain religious behaviors that most people would agree is negative.

Religion becomes pathological when it is used to stop life saving medical care. Some overly aggressive faith healers encourage people to stop medical treatments as a "way to demonstrate the faith necessary for divine healing" (Coakley & McKenna, 1986; Koenig et al., 2001, p. 64). In addition, some religious groups may not seek timely medical care (Lannin et al., 1998). There have also been studies that have reported that some faith groups refuse blood transfusions (Swan, 1997), refuse childhood immunizations (Rodgers, Gindler, Atkinson, & Markowitz, 1993), refuse prenatal care and physician assisted delivery (Kaunintz, Spence, Danielson, Rochat, & Grimes, 1984), and abuse children (Bottoms, Shaver, Goodman, & Qin, 1995). All these studies, with the exception of refusing blood transfusions, practiced widely by Jehovahs witnesses, have found the instance of these practices to be isolated as opposed to denominationally or faith movement supported practices.

SUMMARY AND CONCLUSIONS

This chapter has highlighted the fact that faith and/or religion is a strong predictor of positive health and mental health. The fields of religion and mental health use different languages and frameworks to understand life. As a result, the two fields are frequently in conflict with one another.

Social workers and other mental health professionals, frequently work with people when they are in a state of crisis, often make the mistake of misinterpreting individual pathology to be representative and even produced by a particular faith movement. Interestingly, religion and mental health have a great deal in common. Both groups attempt to understand what cannot be seen and is often difficult to rationally explain. Psychopathology, for example, while it can be described, cannot be measured, nor its etiology specifically determined, nor its complexity always understood.

Using caution is the best way to approach the relationship between religion and mental health. There will always be a mystery to both disciplines that will tantalize individuals and scientists. Both disciplines will continue to have their share of highly narcissistic and controversial individuals who will cast both doubt on the validity of the discipline and bring shame upon themselves and their professions. If anything, it is important for people attempting to understand the many complexities of religion and mental health to realize that both disciplines have created great, lasting, and monumental changes, which should earn both disciplines a degree of respect. It is with respect for both disciplines that this chapter closes. Understanding the human mind and its relationship to God has a rich historical tradition, yet despite advanced methods of inquiry, significant challenges in understanding remain. This chapter advances a new paradigm of understanding, a hermeneutical approach that both disciplines can use.

A new paradigm requires that both disciplines learn new respect for one another and realize that it is often better to remark, I am not sure, in response to questions about the relationship between mental health and religion. Rather than begging the question, the statement recognizes that when two different worlds with different languages attempt to relate to each other, there are words, phrases, and behaviors that cannot be translated.

REFERENCES

Adler, A. (1992). *Understanding human nature*. Chatham, NY: Oneworld Publications, Ltd.

Andrews, F. M., & Withey, S. B. (1976). *Social indicators of well-being: America's perception of life quality*. New York: Plenum.

Batson, D. C., & Ventis, L. W. (1982). *The religious experience: A social-psychological perspective*. New York: Oxford University Press.

Belcher, J. R. (Unpublished manuscript). Living as deprived and in the shadow of the Second Coming: Counseling classical Pentecostal couples.

Belcher, J. R., & Cascio, T. (Unpublished manuscript). Exploring religiosity, spirituality and psychopathology: Implications for social work practice.

Belcher, J. R., & Cascio. T. (2001). Social work and deliverance practice: The Pentecostal experience. *Families and Society, 82,* 61–68.

Belcher, J. R., & Gurganious, J. (Unpublished manuscript). Personality factors and spirituality: The Pentecostal experience.

Belcher, J. R., & Hall, S. M. (In Press). Healing and psychotherapy. *Pastoral Psychology.*

Belcher, J. R., & Vining, J. K. (2000). Counseling Pentecostals: The process of change. *Marriage and Family: A Christian Journal, 3,* 383–392.

Bergin, A. E. (1983). Values and religious issues in psychotherapy and mental health. *American Psychologist, 46,* 394–403.

Bottoms, B. L., Shaver, P. R., Goodman, F. S., & Qin, J. (1995). In the name of God: A profile of religion-related child abuse. *Journal of Social Issues, 51,* 85–112.

Brown, L. B. (1987). *The psychology of religious belief.* London: Academic Press.

Bruner, J. (1990). *Acts of meaning.* Cambridge, MA: Harvard University Press.

Bultmann, R. (1963). *History of the synoptic tradition.* John Marsh, Trans. Oxford: Basil Blackwell Publisher. (Original work published 1921.)

Bunker, D. (1991). Spirituality and the four Jungian personality functions. *Journal of Psychology and Theology, 19,* 26–34.

Burning, G., & Stokes, K. (1982). The hypotheses paper. In K. Stokes (Ed.), *Faith development in the adult life cycle* (pp. 17–61). New York: Sadlier.

Carrol, J. T. (1995). Sickness and healing in the New Testament Gospels. *Interpretation, 49,* 130–132.

Carson, D. A. (1987). *Showing the Spirit: Theological exposition of 1 Corinthians 12–14.* Grand Rapids, MI: Baker Book House.

Carson, V., Soeken, K. L., Shanty, J., & Terry, L. (1990). Hope and spiritual well-being: Essentials for living with AIDS. *Perspectives in Psychiatric Care, 26,* 28–34.

Cassel, R. N., Hoey, D., & Riley, A. D. (1990). Chemical dependency rehabilitation where fostering fitness is an integral part of the process. *Journal of Instructional Psychology, 17,* 202–217.

Castelein, J. D. (1984). Glossolalia and the psychology of the self and narcissism. *Journal of Religion and Health, 23,* 47–62.

Cieslak, K. (1991). Religiosity and marital relations. Paper presented at the Fifth European Symposium for the Psychology of religion. Leuven, Belgium.

Clinebell, H. (1984). *Basic types of pastoral care and counseling.* Nashville: Abingdon Press.

Coakley, D. V., & McKenna, G. W. (1986). Safety of faith healing. *Lancet,* February, 444.

Copestake, D. R., & Malony, H. N. (1993). Adverse effects of Charismatic experiences: A reconsideration. *Journal of Psychology and Christianity, 12,* 236–244.

Courteany, B. C., Poon, L. W., Martin, P., Clayton, G. M., & Johnson, M. A. (1992). Religiosity and adaptation in the oldest-old. *International Journal of Aging and Human Development, 34,* 47–56.

Cox, H. (1995). *Fire from heaven: The rise of Pentecostal spirituality and the reshaping of religion in the 21st century.* New York: Addison-Wesley Publishing Company.

Croog, S. H., & Levine, S. (1972). Religious identity and response to serious illness. *Social Science and Medicine, 6,* 17–32.

Crossan, J. D. (1973). *The challenge of the historical Jesus.* New York: Harper and Row.

Crossley, D. (1995). Religious experience within mental illness: Opening the door on research. *British Journal of Psychiatry, 166,* 284–286.

Cutler, S. J. (1976). Membership in different types of voluntary associations and psychological well-being. *Gerontologist, 16,* 335–339.

Cutten, G. B. (1927). *Speaking with tongues: Historically and psychologically considered.* New Haven, CT: Yale University Press.

Dayton, D. W. (1987). *Theological roots of Pentecostalism.* Metuchen, NJ: Hendrickson Publishers.

DeHoff, S. L. (1998). In search of a paradigm for psychological and spiritual growth: Implications for psychotherapy and spiritual direction. *Pastoral Psychology, 46,* 33–46.

Denier, E. (1984). Subjective well-being. *Psychological Bulletin, 95,* 542–575.

Derezotes, D. S., & Evans, K. E. (1995). Spirituality and religiosity in practice: In-depth interviews of social work practitioners. *Social Thought, 18,* 39–56.

Ellison, C. W. (1991). Religious involvement and subjective well-being. *Journal of Health and Social Behavior, 32,* 80–99.

Ellison, C. W., & Smith, J. (1991). Toward an integrative measure of health and well-being. *Journal of Psychology and Theology, 9,* 35–48.

Faupel, D. W. (1996). *The everlasting gospel: The significance of eschatology in the development of Pentecostal thought.* Sheffield, England: Sheffield Academic Press.

Finney, C. G. (1835). *Lectures on revivals of religion.* New York: Leavitt & Lord.

Finney, J., & Malony, H. N. (1985). Contemplative prayer and its use in psychotherapy: A theoretical model. *Journal of Psychology and Theology, 13,* 172–181.

Freud, S. (1913). Totem and Taboo: Some points of agreement between the mental health lives of savages and neurotics. In J. Starchey (Ed. and trans.), *Standard edition of the complete psychological works of Sigmund Freud.* London: Hogarth Press.

Freud, S. (1927). Future of an illusion. In J. Starchey (Ed. and trans.), *Standard edition of the complete psychological works of Sigmund Freud.* London: Hogarth Press.

Freud, S. (1928). A religious experience. In J. Starchey (Ed. and trans.), *Standard Edition of the complete works of Sigmund Freud.* London: Hogarth Press.

Freud, S. (1963). Further recommendations in the technique of psychoanalysis (1913). In P. Rieff (Ed.), *Theory and technique* (pp. 135–156). New York: Macmillan.

Ganzevoort, R. R. (1994). Crisis experiences and the development of belief and unbelief. In D. Hutsebaut & J. Corveleyn (Eds.), *Belief and unbelief: Psychological perspectives* (pp. 21–36). Amsterdam: Rodopi.

Ganzevoort, R. R. (1998). Religious coping reconsidered, Part one: An integrated approach. *Journal of Psychology and Theology, 26,* 260–275.

Gartner, J., Larson, D. B., & Allen, G. D. (1991). Religious commitment and mental health: A review of empirical literature. *Journal of Psychology and Theology, 19,* 6–25.

Gause, R. H. (1976). Issues in Pentecostalism. In R. Spittler (Ed.), *Perspectives on New Pentecostalism.* Grand Rapids, MI: Baker Book House.

Genia, V. (1997). The spiritual experience index: Revision and reformulation. *Review of Religious Research, 38,* 344–361.

Gillespie, V. B. (1979). *Religious conversion and personal identity.* Birmingham, AL: Religious Education Press.

Glenn, N. D., & Weaver, C. N. (1979). A note on family situation and global happiness. *Social Forces, 57,* 960–967.

Glock, C. Y. (1964). The role of deprivation in the origin and evolution of religious groups. In R. Lee & M. F. Marty (Eds.), *Religion and social conflict.* New York: Oxford University Press.

Graham, T. W., Kaplan, B. H., Cornoni-Huntley, J. C., James, S. A., Becker, C., Hames, C. G., & Heyden, S. (1978). Frequency of church attendance and blood pressure elevation. *Journal of Behavioral Medicine, 1,* 37–43.

Gritzmacher, S. A., Bolton, B., & Dana, R. H. (1988). Psychological characteristics of Pentecostals: A literature review and psycho-dynamic synthesis. *Journal of Psychology and Theology, 16,* 233–245.

Hak, D. H. (1988). Deprivation theory. In W. H. Swatos, Jr. (Ed.), *Encyclopedia of religion and society* (pp. 136–137). London: Altamira Press.

Hathaway, W. L., & Pargament, K. I. (1991). The religious dimensions of coping: Implications for prevention and promotion. In K. I. Pargament & K. I. Maton (Eds.), *Religion and prevention in mental health* (pp. 65–92). New York: Haworth Press.

Hayes, M. A., Vining, J. K., & Belcher, J. R. (Unpublished manuscript). Pentecostal's personalities from FFM perspective.

Herth, K. (1989). The relationship between level of hope and level of coping response and other variables in patients with cancer. *Oncology Nursing Forum, 16,* 67–72.

Herzog, III., W. R. (1999). *Jesus, justice, and the reign of God: A ministry of liberation.* Louisville, KY: Westminister John Knox Press.

Ingersoll, R. E. (1994). Spirituality, religion, and counseling: Dimensions and relationships. *Counseling and Values, 38,* 98–111.

James, W. (1890). *The principles of psychology.* New York: Holt.

Johnson, P. E. (1978). Conversion. In W. E. Conn (Ed.), *Conversion: Perspectives on personal and social transformation* (pp. 163–178). New York: Alba House.

Jung, C. G. (1971). A psychological theory of types. In H. Read, M. Fordham, G. Adler, & W. McGuire (Eds.), *The collected works of C. G. Jung, Volume 6, Psychological types* (R. F. C. Hull, Trans, pp. 542–541). Princeton, NJ: Princeton University Press. (Original work published, 1931.)

Kaunitz, A. M., Spence, C., Danielson, T. S., Rochat, R. W., & Grimes, D. A. (1984). Perinatal and maternal mortality in a religious group avoiding obstetric care. *American Journal of Obstetrics and Gynecology, 150,* 826–831.

Kendler, K. S., Gardner, C. O., & Prescott, C. A. (1997). Religion, psychopathology, and substance use and abuse: A multimeasure, genetic, epidemiologic study. *American Journal of Psychiatry, 154,* 322–329.

Koenig, H. G., Ford, S. M., George, L. K., Blazer, D. G., & Meador, K. G. (1992). The relationship between religion and anxiety in a sample of community-dwelling older adults. *Journal of Geriatric Psychiatry, 26,* 65–93.

Koenig, H. G., George, L. K., Meador, K. G., Blazer, D. G., & Ford, S. M. (1994). Religious practice and alcoholism in a southern adult population. *Hospital and Community Psychiatry, 45,* 225–231.

Koenig, H. G., McCullough, M. E., & Larson, D. B. (2001). *Handbook of religion and health.* New York: Oxford University Press.

Land, S. J. (1994). *Pentecostal spirituality: A passion for the kingdom.* Sheffield, England: Sheffield Academic Press.

Lange, M. A. (1983). Prayer and psychotherapy: Beliefs and practice. *Journal of Psychology and Christianity, 2,* 36–49.

Lannin, D. R., Mathews, H. F., Mitchell, J., Swanson, M. S., Swanson, F. H., & Edwards, M. S. (1998). Influences of socioeconomic and factors on racial differences in late-stage breast cancer. *Journal of the American Medical Association, 279,* 1801–1807.

Levav, I., Kohn, R., Golding, J. M., & Weissman, M. M. (1997). Vulnerability of Jews to affective disorders. *American Journal of Psychiatry, 154,* 941–947.

Loder, J. E. (1981). *The transforming moment: Understanding convictional experiences.* San Francisco: Harper and Row.

Lowenberg, F., & Dolgoff, R. (1982). *Ethical decisions for social work practice.* Itasca, IL: F. E. Peacock.

Loewenthal, K. M., & Cornwall, N. (1993). Religiosity and perceived control of life events. *International Journal for the Psychology of Religion, 3,* 39–45.

Luhmann, N. (1977). *Die Funktioin der Religion.* (The function of religion.) Frankfurt, Germany: Suhrkamp.

Magalettta, P. R., & Brawer, P. A. (1998). Prayer in psychotherapy: A model for its use, ethical considerations, and guidelines for practice. *Journal of Psychology and Theology, 26,* 322–330.

Magalettta, P. R., & Duckro, P. N. (1996). Prayer in the medical encounter. *Journal of Family Practice, 44,* 526.

McRae, R. R., & Costa, P. T., Jr. (1986). Toward a new generation of personality theories: Theoretical contexts for the five-factor model. In J. S. Wiggins (Ed.), *The five-factor model of personality: Theoretical perspectives* (pp. 51–87). New York: Guilford.

Meador, K. G., Koenig, H. G., Hughes, D. C., Blazer, D. G., Turnbull, J., & George, L. K. (1992). Religious affiliation and major depression. *Hospital and Community Psychiatry, 43,* 1204–1208.

Meichenbaum, D. (1988). The ubiquity of interpretation: Commentary on Donald P. Spence. In S. B. Messer, L. A. Sass, & R. L. Woolfolk (Eds.), *Hermenuetics and psychological theory: Interpretative perspectives on personality, psychotherapy, and psychopathology* (pp. 215–289). New Jersey: Rutgers University Press.

Moreland, J. P. (2001). A philosophical review of postmodernism for Christian counselors. *Christian Counseling Today, 9,* 3–15.

Newman, J. S., & Pargament, K. I. (1990). The rise of religion in the problem solving process. *Review of Religious Research, 31,* 390–404.

Pargament, K. (1996). Religious methods of coping: Resources for the conservation and transformation of significance. In E. P. Shafranske (Ed.), *Religion and the clinical practice of psychology* (pp. 215–239). Washington, DC: American Psychological Association.

Paragament, K. I. (1997). *The psychology of religion and coping: Theory, research, and practice.* New York: The Guilford Press.

Pargament, K. I., Ensing, D. S., Falgout, K., Olsen, H., Reilly, B., Van Haitsma, K., & Warren, R. (1990). God help me: Coping efforts as predictors of the outcomes to significant life events. *American Journal of Community Psychology, 18,* 793–824.

Pargament, K. I., Kennell, J., Hathaway, W., Grevengoed, N., Newman, J., & Jones, W. (1988). Religion and the problem solving process: Three styles of coping. *Journal for the Scientific Study of Religion, 27,* 90–104.

Pargament, K. I., & Maton, K. I. (1991). Introduction. In K. I. Pargament & K. I. Maton (Eds.), *Religion and prevention in mental health* (pp. 1–9). New York: Haworth Press.

Parker, S. E. (1996). *Led by the Spirit: Toward a practical theology of Pentecostal discernment and decision making*. Sheffield, England: Sheffield Academic Press.

Percy, M. (1997). The gospel miracles and modern healing movements. *Theology, 100,* 8–17.

Polkinghorne, D. E. (1983). *Methodology for the human services: Systems of inquiry*. Albany: SUNY.

Polkinghorne, D. E. (1988). *Narrative knowing and the human sciences*. Albany: Sunny Press.

Polkinghorne, D. E. (1990). Psychology after philosophy. In J. E. Faulconer & R. N. Williams (Eds.). *Reconsidering psychology: Perspectives from continental philosophy* (pp. 92–115). Pittsburgh: Duquesne University Press.

Poloma, M. M. (1989). *The Assemblies of God at the crossroads: Charisma and institutional dilemmas*. Knoxville, TN: University of Tennessee Press.

Rodgers, D. V., Gindler, J. S., Atkinson, W. L., & Markowitz, L. E. (1993). High attack rates and case fatality during a measles outbreak in groups with religious exemption to vaccination. *Pediatric Infectious Disease Journal, 12,* 288–292.

Sanders, C. M. (1989). *Grief: The morning after. Dealing with bereavement*. New York: Wiley.

Scarlett, W. G., & Perriello, L. (1991). The development of prayer in adolescence: In F. K. Oser & W. G. Scarlett (Eds.), *Religious development in childhood and adolescence* (pp. 63–76). San Francisco: Josey Bass.

Schrag, C. O. (1980). *Radical reflection on the origin of the human services*. West Lafayette, IN: Purdue University Press.

Schrag, C. O. (1990). Explanation and understanding in the science of human behavior. In J. E. Faulconer & R. N. Williams (Eds.), *Reconsidering psychology: Perspectives from continental philosophy* (pp. 61–74). Pittsburgh: Duquesene University Press.

Shandor, M. M., & B. Crandall, E. K. (1986). The search for meaning and its potential for affecting growth in bereaved parents. In R. H. Moos (Ed.), *Coping with life crises: An integrated approach* (pp. 235–244). New York: Plenum.

Stark, R., & Glock, C. Y. (1968). *American piety: The nature of religious commitment*. Berkeley, CA: University of California Press.

Spililka, B., & McIntosh, D. N. (1996). Religion and spirituality: The known and the unknown. Paper presented at the American Psychological Association Annual Conference, Toronto, Ontario, Canada.

Swan, R. (1997). Children, medicine, religion, and the law. In L. A. Barness (Ed.), *Advances in pediatrics* (chap. 15). St. Louis: Mosby.

Switzer, D. K. (1986). *The minister as crisis counselor*. Nashville, TN: Abingdon.

Thomas, J. C. (1998). *The devil, disease, and deliverance: Origins of illness in New Testament thought*. Sheffield, England: Sheffield Academic Press.

Turner, R. P., Lukoff, D., Barnhouse, R. T., & Lu, F. G. (1995). Religious or spiritual problem: A culturally sensitive diagnostic category in the DSM-IV. *Journal of Nervous and Mental Disease, 183*, 435–544.

Ullman, C. (1989). *The transformed self: The psychology of religious conversion*. New York: Plenum.

Van Uden, M. H. F. (1985). *Religie in de crisis van de rouw*. (Religion in the crisis of mourning.) Nijmegen, Netherlands: Dekker & van der Vegt.

Vining, J. K. (1995). *Spirit-centered counseling: A pneuascriptive approach*. East Rockaway, NY: Cummings and Hathaway Press.

Vossen, H. J. M. (1993). Images of God and coping with suffering: The psychological and theological dynamics of the coping process. *Journal of Empirical Theology, 6*, 19–38.

Williams, C. G. (1981). *Tongues of fire: A study of Pentecostal glossolalia and related phenomena*. Cardiff, Wales: University of Wales Press.

Williams, R. N., & Faulconer, J. E. (1994). Religion and mental health: A hermeneutic reconsideration. *Review of Religious Research, 35*, 335–349.

Williams, D. R., Larson, D. B., Buckler, R. E., Heckman, R. C., & Pyle, C. M. (1991). Religion and distress in a community sample. *Social Sciences & Medicine, 32*, 1257–1262.

Wulff, D. M. (1991). *Psychology of religion: Classic and contemporary views*. New York: Wiley.

Zinnbauer, B. J., Pargament, K. I., Cole, B., Rye, M. S., Butter, E. M., et al. (1997). Religion and spirituality: Unfuzzing the fuzzy. *Journal for the Scientific Study of Religion, 36*, 549–564.

Chapter 7

RELIGION AND SPIRITUALITY IN SOCIAL WORK EDUCATION

Leon Ginsberg

Spirituality is one of the more difficult areas of discussion and concern for social work education and, for that matter, for many U.S. citizens. The nation has something of a complex relationship with religion and spirituality. Many of our public policy issues are directly associated with spirituality and religion. No matter what they may be, they often devolve into issues of religious identification and spirituality. That was true even before there was discussion of President George W. Bush's Faith-Based Initiative. It is particularly difficult in social work education to deal with spirituality and religion, partly because many social workers, particularly social work educators, often have ambivalent relationships with their religious and spiritual sides.

Historically, the United States was founded on spiritual bases. That is, many of the people who settled the United States came to the New World because it was possible for them to deal with spiritual and religious issues and their own beliefs and doctrines in ways that were not possible in England or their other nations of origin. The Pilgrims were certainly a religious group. The Quakers were and are a religious community. The early American Catholics were, of course, religious.

Furthermore, many of the people who came to the United States to escape oppression in their former nations came because of religious discrimination and persecution. That was true of Jews in the late 19th and

113

early 20th centuries but it was also true of members of many other religious groups. The colony of Rhode Island was noted, for example, for its religious neutrality, for allowing spiritual differences, and for tolerating all religious positions.

By the time the U.S. Constitution was written, the nation was a complex association of many different peoples and religious persuasions. Not the least of the spiritual groups in the United States are the Native Americans, each group of whom has a religion and each of which has spiritual connections of various kinds. The American solution to all of this religious complexity was to simply keep government out of religion, completely.

It is surprising that the U.S. is one of the few nations that takes such a position. Most countries in the Western world make it clear that freedom of religion is the basic posture of each country—however, many of the same countries also have official churches. Some of the British Commonwealth nations, including our neighbor, Canada, as well as England, Australia, and New Zealand, name the Church of England as their official church. No one is persecuted for being of any other faith, of course; however, there is an official national church. Other nations have predominant religions— France is largely Roman Catholic, Greece is Greek Orthodox, Colombia has a special agreement with the Roman Catholic Church, and the Arab nations plus Iran have essentially established Islam as their religion.

Although not well known to Americans or other Westerners, many Eastern nations also support a particular religion. Much of the Asian world is Buddhist. And Buddhist mandates and practices are sometimes built into public law. I recall visiting an official agency in one Asian nation that had, as one of its goals, increased meditation, a Buddhist approach to religion.

Even some countries that have no official religion have special notions about religion that are part of the state. Israel is a religiously Jewish nation but it also protects Christian and Muslim groups. France has a long Catholic tradition but also has active groups from many religions. Germany is largely Roman Catholic. The Russian Orthodox and Romanian Orthodox churches are important factors in their national governments. So the strong emphasis on religious freedom in the United States makes this nation a bit different than many others. Many of the countries that follow our pattern have had organized and established religions, even though they may no longer do so.

Religion, though, is built into the mores of American society and into virtually every social institution. Our original higher education institutions, for instance Harvard, were developed to prepare ministers for churches. The third U.S. president, John Adams (McCullough, 2001), was heavily involved in religion and several of his family members were ministers. It is doubtful that anyone could be elected president who disavowed religion, even though there are varying degrees of religious commitment among the presidents of the United States. Ronald Reagan for example, spoke often and emotionally about religion and its importance. However, he was not a particularly regular churchgoer. Jimmy Carter was probably the most religiously active of recent presidents although all in the 20th and 21st centuries have had some connections with religion. Presidents speak to religious conventions. They associate closely with religious leaders such as Billy Graham. They sponsor prayer breakfasts. And even when the Democratic Party nominated the first non-Christian for Vice President in American history, Joseph Lieberman, they chose a Jewish man who is exceptionally observant of Jewish law and exceptionally involved in Jewish worship and ritual.

My personal impression and hypothesis is that many social workers, particularly social work educators, by and large, have an ambivalent approach to religion and spirituality. On the one hand, we know how important it is to many of our clients, for a variety of reasons. For that matter, social workers are likely to have grown up in religious homes and likely to have been active in their religious bodies. Many social workers begin their careers in religious organizations. So many social work organizations are sectarian in sponsorship and operation that the connection between social work and religion is critical. On the other hand, it is also likely that large numbers of, perhaps most, social workers are nonsectarian in their lives and possibly even antireligious or at least highly skeptical of religion. That is partly because of the high degree of education of most professional social workers. Dedication to religion seems to decline as people gain years of schooling. After 12 years of elementary and secondary schools, 4 years of college, and 2 years of master's studies, with a heavy exposure to science, that explains away many of the things that religion teaches, skepticism may well follow. For social work educators, the large majority of whom now have doctorates or are approaching doctorates, there is even more opportunity to be dissuaded about the importance of and validity of religion.

This is all despite the fact that there are institutional arrangements and organizations in social work that especially pursue religious and spiritual activity. The Catholic, Lutheran, and Jewish social welfare organizations are highly organized and sponsor or are associated with many religiously-based organizations such as Catholic Charities, the Catholic Youth Organization, Lutheran Social Services, Jewish Community Centers, Jewish Family Service, as well as children's homes and institutions, services for older adults, and multiple other agencies and programs. In addition, a large number of homes for the aged, senior centers, and group child care facilities, are associated with the various Baptist faiths, the Presbyterian Church, the Episcopal Church, and many other Protestant denominations. These are additional examples of the close association between social work and religion.

It may not pay to be personal on matters such as this and it may not be relevant either. I personally came to social work as did many of the other people I know, however, for religious reasons. The Jewish youth organization that wanted to hire me when I finished college (at a Presbyterian university) said that part of my obligation would be to earn the MSW. So they sent me to MSW school, which led to an interest in many other kinds of social work and ultimately to social work education. I recall that on my first education job, after writing my very first article in the professional literature, about a Jewish community experience, which was also the only experience that I knew very well, one of my new faculty colleagues said she was struck by the importance placed on Jewishness in the community I served, as evidenced in the article. In fact, she was taken aback by its being such an important matter. It had never occurred to me that there was any question about the importance of Jewishness in that community or in the importance of other religions to others. I wasn't yet 30 years old, so there was a good bit I needed to learn. I assume she was a nonbeliever.

Of course, I later found that many of the people I worked with in Jewish life were also nonbelievers. One of the interesting sidelines to being Jewish is that one can fully identify with the ethnic group without especially believing anything about a Supreme Being or the sanctity of the Bible, or anything else. One can be fully secular and fully Jewish—although Jewish clergy would not necessarily concur. I'm not sure it's possible to be any kind of Christian and to not believe anything of a spiritual nature. It's possible to be an Arab and not follow Islam, I assume, but one really can't be a Muslim and not be a follower of Islam. There are differences between ethnicity and religion but perhaps one becomes best acquainted with them if one is Jewish.

RELIGIOUSLY ORIENTED SOCIAL WORK EDUCATION PROGRAMS

Having said all of the foregoing, it should also be clear that many social workers are very closely identified with religion. Several graduate schools of social work as well as baccalaureate programs are closely identified with one religion or another. The Wurzweiler School of Social Work at Yeshiva University is the best example of a Jewish school of social work. Brandeis University in Massachusetts originally pursued a mission of Jewish identification. Although it is still supported by members of the Jewish community, the academic programs are secular, and the Florence Heller School of Advanced Studies in Social Welfare—originally identified with social work—now does not particularly identify with social work or the Jewish community.

There are several programs that are associated with the Seventh Day Adventist Church, including Walla Walla College and Loma Linda University. Catholic University of America has a venerable school of social work and St. Louis University, a Roman Catholic institution, does as well. Fordham University is a leading Catholic institution. There are many schools and programs that have either strong or nominal relationships with churches and, therefore, much of social work education is highly influenced by religion.

For example, the University of Southern California School of Social Work has a dual degree program with the Jewish Institute of Religion in Los Angeles. The University of Maryland school has associations with a Jewish program. Several schools have dual degrees with Christian theology programs, so many people may earn the Master of Social Work and the Master of Theology. The social work program at Brigham Young University is closely affiliated with the Church of Jesus Christ of the Latter Day Saints, often called the Mormons. Abilene Christian University, affiliated with the Church of Christ, has discussed the possibility of embarking on a MSW degree program. Oral Roberts University in Tulsa, Oklahoma, is named for a prominent evangelical minister and has a longstanding baccalaureate of social work program.

SOCIAL WORK VALUES AND RELIGIOUS VALUES

One of the issues of concern for some social work educators is that some churches and some religious organizations specifically disassociate themselves from some kinds of behavior and lifestyles. Social work education has had an ongoing conflict about how to handle the issue of sexual orientation, especially gay and lesbian sexual orientation, in its curriculum standards.

It is part of the doctrine of some religions that gay and lesbian as well as bisexual sex violates biblical injunctions and, therefore, has to be prohibited among the student body and faculty. The social work education posture on this is to require teaching about gay and lesbian issues, lifestyles, and behavior as part of the curriculum. Gay and lesbian people are included in the discussions of oppressed groups.

There are social work educators and other advocates who would like to see a demand for equal opportunity and affirmative action for people of bisexual, gay, and lesbian sexual orientation in the eligibility standards for social work. Upon advice from legal counsel, however, the Council of Social Work Education has determined that it could not do so and that requiring equal opportunity for gay and lesbian people would violate some religious groups' rights to follow their religious convictions and doctrines. Therefore, religious schools that object to gay and lesbian faculty and students on the basis of their religious beliefs are not required to include gay and lesbian people in their affirmative action plans. Affirmative action plans are one of the eligibility standards for having an accredited social work program but religious institutions need not protect or take affirmative action for gay and lesbian people.

CURRICULUM AND RELIGION

Although we don't say very much in our accreditation standards about religion or spirituality, nevertheless, they are important subjects to cover in every sequence of the foundation social work curriculum. It seems to me that there are close associations between spirituality and every aspect of the social work curriculum. In fact, it is probably a necessity for baccalaureate and master's programs to include material on religion and spirituality because of their central place in American life.

Field Practicum

Although field practicum is usually the last part of the curriculum discussed in comprehensive articles such as this, it should probably be the first that comes to mind when dealing with this subject because so many social work field instruction placements are with religious organizations and institutions. The Salvation Army, Jewish Community Centers, Catholic Youth Organizations, and the many church related children's and senior programs are important examples of field instruction that occurs in religious and spiritual settings. In many cases, these field instruction agencies do not limit their field instruction students to adherents of their faith. They do pursue religious agendas, however, and generally insist upon students respecting and supporting the religious ideas of the organization. That does not mean every participant has to be a believer but it means that every participant must be respectful of believers and must avoid antireligious statements, particularly statements and actions contrary to the religion that is the sponsoring organization for the program.

It is a requirement of a sound field instruction program to orient students to all dimensions of an agency's philosophy and point of view. Therefore, instruction about the religious tenets of the organization and its significance is a part of the field instruction orientation that is necessary in placing a student in a sectarian agency. For example, Orthodox Jewish organizations are closed on Saturdays or limit their activities. Seventh Day Adventist organizations also observe Saturday for the Sabbath but have activities on Sunday.

Dietary preferences are also an issue. Orthodox Jewish and Muslim organizations do not serve or allow pork on their premises. Seventh Day Adventists maintain a largely vegetarian diet and also avoid caffeine; the Mormons also avoid tea and coffee. There are literally thousands of dress, dietary, and other regulations that affect sectarian organizations. Information about them must be part of the orientation of field instruction students to their agencies, if those agencies are religious in nature.

SOCIAL WELFARE POLICY AND SERVICES

It is probably valid to assume that social welfare and policy content should include material on religion and religious policy in the United States. The interface between social policy and religious doctrine is great. Also, social policies affect the ways in which people are free to express their religious preferences and ideals in American life.

There is also significant misunderstanding among Americans about American law, constitutional decisions, and religious issues. Among the major policy issues under discussion in recent years is what President George W. Bush called his "Faith-Based Initiative," as mentioned earlier. The intention was to direct more money for human service programs to religious organizations. The issue was controversial in ways that it probably should not have been because the delivery of social services by religious organizations is as old as social welfare. But the initiative raised policy issues that students need to understand.

For example, when government funds are provided through religious organizations, the recipients cannot discriminate in their delivery of services. That is, they cannot favor any one group in providing the help for which they have contracted, such as members of their own congregations. Although there was some attempt to make exceptions to the rules, in the ultimate implementation, it was clear that religious recipients of government grants could not follow their doctrines if those doctrines condemned or discriminated against people of, for example, non-heterosexual orientation. That is, they could not discriminate against gay men and lesbian women, even if their doctrinal positions supported the notion that homosexuality is forbidden and not to be sanctioned. So, in order to receive and correctly use federal funds, religious organizations would have to equally treat all those who sought their services, believers and nonbelievers, homosexual and heterosexual alike. Primarily, though, students need to understand that many social services have always been delivered by religious organizations and that there is nothing especially unusual about that.

Politics are also heavily influenced by religion. Politicians appeal to varying religious groups in support of their various doctrines. Political theorists and poll takers analyze election campaigns according to the religious affiliations of various groups. Fundamentalist Christian groups have been an important influence in many state elections and in presidential elections for the past several years. The Jewish vote, the Roman Catholic vote, and in some states, particular groups such as Mormons, are important political factors.

SEPARATION OF STATE AND CHURCH

Perhaps the major social policy issue that social work students need to understand with regard to religion is the doctrine of separation of state and church. As mentioned earlier, the United States is one of the few nations that provides for the strict separation of church and state. Ironically, as discussed in the introduction to this chapter, it was because the United States was settled by many groups, large numbers of them deeply religious, that this doctrine became a major issue in the writing of the Constitution of the United States.

The sources for these ideas can be found in the debates over the content of the U.S. Constitution and in some of the discussions leading to the adoption of the Constitution in 1789. *The Federalist Papers* (Fairfield, 1966) is one of the best sources of information on the subject. These papers, which were written in the pseudonyms of several prominent colonial leaders of the time (Alexander Hamilton, James Madison, John Jay) argue the major points of the Constitution that was finally adopted and that was quickly amended with the first ten amendments—the Bill of Rights—the first of which guarantees freedom of religion and separation of state and church, freedom of speech, and freedom of assembly—some of the most important fundamental freedoms of Americans. The irony is that the many deeply religious people of the time determined that the best way to guarantee their religious freedom was to leave government completely out of religion and spirituality so that government could neither support nor harass religious bodies. The exact wording of the separation of church and state doctrine in the Constitution is "Congress shall make no law respecting an establishment of religion, or prohibiting the free exercise thereof . . . "

The issues are not as clearcut and simple as they might seem from reading the Constitution. For example, the Constitution is clear that the government may not establish any church and that makes it clear that the United States, unlike Italy, some South American nations, Israel, and the United Kingdom, and many of the Middle Eastern countries, cannot organize or endorse a particular church. However, many public policies turn on religious issues.

Abortion and Stem Cells

For example, the issue of abortion is largely a religious matter having to do with what the U.S. government and U.S. citizens, at a particular time, might consider to be human life and the appropriate disposition of human life. Those decisions are more a matter of religious ideology than of science. The idea that human life begins at conception is the essential reason for opposition to abortion and that doctrine is supported by the Roman Catholic and other churches. For those who believe that life begins at birth, there is no particular moral or religious conflict with abortion—although some may oppose it on grounds other than religious or moral.

The same is true of stem cell research, a very current issue in the United States. Stem cells come from fertilized ova, many of which are produced in the process of assisting those who have difficulty conceiving children with the typical conception, pregnancy, and childbirth. Some stem cells from these organisms are used in medical research. Scientific researchers believe that stem cells, properly reformulated and used, have the potential for curing or at least containing conditions such as diabetes, ALS, some forms of cancer, Lupus, Parkinson's disease, and many other neurological and systemic health problems. The current president and U.S. Congress oppose the use of created stem cells, however, which they might refer to as cloning because they believe that the process is one that creates and then destroys human life for research and treatment of health conditions.

These medical issues, that some say should be treated strictly as matters of privacy and health between physicians and their patients, become religious and spiritual issues when religion and spiritual matters are associated with their morality. Contraception, itself, is a religious and moral issue that plays out differently in different places. For some time, before the constitutional decisions that invalidated them, some states had laws that forbade any kind of contraception. The states were usually heavily influenced by the Catholic Church, which takes a strong position against contraception by mechanical or medical means because it believes that sperm and ova are living organisms. In some nations that are heavily influenced by the Roman Catholic Church, spermicidal jellies and creams are not available to the public, although condoms and birth control pills may be. Aside from these medical issues, there are many other policy issues that are heavily influenced by religious and spiritual matters.

Sabbath Observation

For example, Sabbath observation is a major issue out of which public policies have been constructed in many places. Sunday closing laws, sometimes called Sunday Blue Laws, restrict business on Sundays, because that is the Christian Sabbath and a Christian day of rest. As the United States becomes increasingly multicultural, however, the broad acceptance of Sunday as the Sabbath in a particular state and in the nation becomes a complicated issue. For Seventh Day Adventists and Jews, Saturday is the Sabbath and, as indicated earlier, many Jewish establishments close down as early as Friday afternoon, because Jewish Sabbath observance, and all Jewish holidays, begin on the evening before the day of observance. Some Jews who do not operate their businesses on Friday afternoons, Friday evenings, and Saturdays, think they ought to be able to conduct business on Sunday, which is an ordinary day for observant Jews. However, state and local laws sometimes prohibit such activities for either all or part of Sunday. Muslims observe Friday as the Sabbath or holy day of the week. Observant Muslims may believe that since they do not engage in work on

Fridays, they ought to be allowed to operate their businesses and work on Sundays.

Depending upon the nature of the business, Sunday observance laws discriminate significantly against those who do not observe Sunday as a special day. For example, in many places, alcoholic beverages cannot be sold in retail stores on Sunday. Observant Muslims do not use alcohol, but they may derive their living by selling it to those who do use the substance. The same may be true for Jewish liquor store owners or for others who derive a living through the marketing of alcohol but who do not observe the Sunday Sabbath.

Perhaps the most dramatic example of this problem was the amendment of the Constitution to forbid the sale of alcohol in the United States. Exceptions were made for people who used alcohol for religious purposes. The same kinds of things are true for the sale of alcohol in restaurants and taverns. In South Carolina, in order to serve alcohol on Sunday, an establishment needs a special license, that is sometimes more expensive than the license for the other 6 days of the week. Many establishments such as bars, taverns, and restaurants, derive a major part of their income from the sale of alcohol. If they cannot sell alcohol, they cannot operate their businesses profitably. Therefore, many South Carolina restaurants, particularly those that are independently owned and that rely on small numbers of customers, simply close on Sundays because they cannot profitably purchase Sunday liquor sale licenses. The issue of prohibition and sale of alcohol on Sundays is essentially a religious and spiritual matter and has differential impact on different religious groups.

Of course, some nations that have Islam as a state religion do not allow the production or even the consumption of alcohol at any time. That is a reasonable public policy position for a nation with a state religion that does not omit religion from government.

Prayer in Schools

One of the more complicated and controversial issues governing religion and social policy in the United States is the question of whether or not prayer is permitted in the public schools. For much of American history, many school systems engaged in religious observation in the public schools. Bible reading, recitation of psalms, the memorization and recitation each day of the Lord's Prayer, and religiously oriented Christmas pageants, were all part of the educational purposes of the public schools until the mid-

20th century, when the Supreme Court decided, in a number of decisions, that prayer in the public schools and religious teaching were unconstitutional and therefore forbidden. There are several other court decisions on other practices that have impacted religion in the public schools over the years. For example, the courts have held that schools can provide release time for religious instruction off the school's grounds and in religious institutions without violating the Constitution. There are still issues about whether or not schools can have student-led prayers at football games and other public events without violating the Constitution. The latest decisions indicate that it is not permissible for high schools to do so.

Religious Displays

Whether or not government organizations can display religious objects or doctrines in public buildings is another example of these complexities. A current judge elected in Alabama has placed the Ten Commandments on the walls in his courtroom. Of course, the Ten Commandments are common to Christians and Jews but they are not part of the doctrine of Muslims, Buddhists, Hindus, or atheists. Therefore, it is likely improper for public facilities to display religious icons, symbols, or language on public property. The same holds true for municipalities that have chosen to place crèches, symbolizing the birth of Jesus, in public squares at the time of Christmas. Some communities have attempted to resolve that concern by placing Jewish symbols such as Chanuka Menorahs in the squares at the same time. That may satisfy some Jewish citizens while some others hold to the strict separation of state and church and want no religious symbols, including those of their own faith, on public property at any time of the year. In addition, of course, they do nothing to resolve the concerns of people who are neither Christian or Jewish. The courts have held that such symbols may not be displayed by government bodies on public property at any time. Of course, placing religious symbols on private property such as shopping malls, is not a violation of the Constitution or the separation of state and church since private property owners may do whatever they please, within health and safety limits, with their property.

It would seem that the standards for defining religious organizations and clergy are rather flexible. Religious organizations may have massive buildings and multimillion dollar budgets or, at the other extreme, a mailing list and a few pamphlets. Ministers may be people who studied for years in sophisticated postcollege programs as well as others who pay a few dollars and receive credentials as ministers in return. All are generally recognizable by government, and authorize adherents to perform marriages and funerals and preside over other governmentally-approved functions that require licenses.

The list of these scenarios goes on and on. State legislatures have chaplains and prayers at their sessions. The military has chaplains of various faiths, who minister to the religious needs of the troops. These kinds of activities have not been held to be in violation of the Constitution.

Taxation

Religious institutions cannot be taxed in the United States. The doctrine is that the power to tax is the power to destroy (*Marbury vs. Madison*, 1803). Therefore, since the United States must be neutral toward religion, it cannot subsidize, which would amount to the establishment of a state church, nor penalize, through taxation, religious organizations. Therefore, religious organizations receive major financial benefits from their nontaxable status. Even when churches own income-producing property—and many own real estate, businesses, publishing companies, and the like—those activities cannot be taxed which, some private property business people say, gives an unfair advantage to religious organizations. Religious organizations need not be nonprofit. They need only be religious. Of course, all this begs the question of what comprises a religious institution. There have been efforts to limit the definition of what exactly qualifies as a religious institution. The Church of Scientology, for several years, was denied tax exempt status because it was not considered a religion, but it has now regained that status. Germany, of course, does not grant such status to Scientology, which it does not view as a religious operation.

Out of the Mainstream Religions

Of course, there are many different and various kinds of religions in the United States and by Constitutional law, government cannot discriminate in favor of the mainstream or best-recognized religious groupings. For example, some groups called cults, such as the Hare Krishnas, the Unification Church of Reverend Sun Yun Moon, and others are all recognized as religions. Reverend Moon served a federal prison sentence for violation of tax laws but that was for reasons other than any sort of discrimination against his religious body.

Who is a clergyman or an ordained minister is also an issue in the United States but, again, very broad definitions are given to the category. It is possible to subscribe to a religious group and receive credentials as a clergyman for a very small fee. In fact, anyone can establish a church and market religious credentials in the United States. So long as there is no evidence of fraud, establishing a religion is a legitimate function. And persons with any sort of religious credentials are generally granted credentials to perform such state functions as performing marriages, presiding at funerals, and otherwise carrying on spiritual activities that are sanctioned by the state and that may require state licenses.

Informing Social Work Students

Social work students are generally not well informed about these matters of religion and spirituality as they interface with social policy and it is important that they understand them. Many social work students come from religious backgrounds and may hold strong doctrinaire positions. Of course, it is important that they understand concepts of religious liberty and the separation of church and state, which are generally supported by the profession of social work. Becoming an effective social worker means understanding the broad range of U.S. social policy and certainly these issues of religion and spirituality are critical for anyone who practices social work in the contemporary U.S.

Some Americans believe that the United States is, always has been, and should be a Christian nation. They object to such restrictions on public religious expression as requiring prayer in the public schools, displaying the Ten Commandments in public buildings, and placing Christmas displays on courthouse lawns. The national government has, however, as already noted, since its beginnings separated government and religion. It forbids the government from establishing—or favoring—any religion over any other. The balance of the amendment guarantees freedom of speech and assembly making it what many believe is the most important of the Bill of Rights. Social work students may be as negative about the constitutional prohibition against government's support of religions as are other citizens. However, many have not thought through the consequences of a possible close connection between government and religion or the establishment of an official national religion.

Extreme Consequences of State Religion

Of the many nations that have official religions, Afghanistan is one of the most committed to its status as an Islamic nation. In 2001, a German social welfare organization, Shelter Now International, found 24 of its staff detained by Afghanistan's government for trying to convert Afghans to Christianity. According to MSNBC (8/9/01) 16 of the 24 were Afghans, 4 were Germans, 2 came from Australia, and 2 from the United States.

In Afghanistan, a country with an established religion, it is a criminal violation for anyone to try to convert Afghans. The Bible and other religious material located in the organization's headquarters convinced the Afghan authorities that the group was attempting to convert the people of the nation to Christianity. Initially, it was believed that all of the 24 could be tried and sentenced to death. However, a later examination of the law showed that foreigners preaching other religions to Afghan Muslims would be held in prison for 3 to 10 days and then deported. It is possible, though, that the local 16 Afghans could be tried and executed for converting to another faith. Had they dropped their faith and converted to Christianity, that could be treated as treachery and such treachery could be punished by death.

Of course, most nations that have government religions do not threaten execution of those who do not adhere to the official faith. The Afghanistan example is extreme. It does illustrate the wisdom of keeping church and state separate, though, an approach that has served the United States well for its more than 200 years.

Specific Prohibitions and Rights

By and large, U.S. policy, which is composed of statutes passed by legislatures and the Congress, as well as the Constitution and the judicial interpretation of that document, forbids the practice of religion within government functions, especially when those practices are imposed upon all citizens or participants. Similarly, Americans have an absolute right to exercise their religious and spiritual beliefs, whatever they happen to be. Both concepts are important for social work students.

Public school officials must be neutral about religion, neither supporting nor endorsing any particular religion. In schools, for example, even though prayer and Bible reading are prohibited in the classroom, the courts have held that students have the absolute right to pray any time they want to.

Prayer organized by students, themselves, in groups, in school buses, in after-hours religious clubs, in school hallways, in cafeterias, and in class-rooms before and after class is legal (Robinson, 1998–2000). The essence of the issue is that we have a right to pray and we also have a right to avoid having prayer thrust upon us.

There have been recent conflicts over prayers at public school graduation ceremonies, and the legal decisions on these are mixed. Some courts have held that since they are one-shot experiences, prayers at graduations are acceptable. Others view them as violations of the religion-government separation. However, there are concrete differences between school-orga-nized graduation prayers and those organized by and carried out by stu-dents. The U.S. Supreme Court ruled in the case of *Lee v. Weisman* (1992) that public school district employees cannot induce, endorse, assist, or promote prayer at graduation ceremonies—whether by school officials or local clergy. The court has yet to rule on two other issues. One of those is the legality of student-initiated and student-led prayers, which the 5th Circuit Court of Appeals said was constitutional if the prayer was approved by most of the graduating class and given by a student. It also had to be nonsectarian and not one that proselytized, although neither of those terms is exactly defined. Perhaps that means a prayer cannot mention God because not all religions have a personal God. Courts and schools themselves, however, in several states have forbidden prayers at graduation ceremonies, while another permitted prayers at a graduation organized as a public forum rather than an official action and, therefore, was not in violation of the Constitution (Robinson, 1998–2000).

Of course, none of the issues of religion and government separation are simple. For example, the U.S. Army provides Christian and Jewish chaplains for troops but adherents to Wicca, a nature-based religion, want equal treatment. It is not Satanic but it ties to terms such as witch and witchcraft (Robinson, 1998–2000). Many prisons and other institutions provide Mus-lim chaplains to work with those who are followers of Islam, a group that is growing in the United States because of immigration from predominantly Islamic nations and also because many African Americans are born into or convert to Islam.

Other issues, as mentioned, are the posting of the Ten Commandments in public places, including courtrooms. When adjudicated, such actions are invariably held as in conflict with the Constitution. According to Robinson (1998–2000), the Ohio state motto, "With God all things are possible," which comes from Matthew 19:26, was found unconstitutional in 2000 by a three-judge panel of the U.S. 6th Circuit Court of Appeals, because it was a government endorsement of the Christian religion. Many of the major religion and spirituality issues fall into the Social Welfare Policy and Services (SWPS) area of the social work curriculum.

HUMAN BEHAVIOR AND THE SOCIAL ENVIRONMENT

This is probably the next most important area of the curriculum, after separation of church and state, for the coverage of religious and spiritual matters. In keeping with social work's multiple emphasis on different size systems, it is important for students to understand the impact of religion on individuals, families, groups, and communities, as well as the organizations associated with religious institutions themselves.

One popular human behavior and social environment (HBSE) text (Schriver, 2001) distinguishes between religion and spirituality, as do the authors of a frequently cited article in the social work literature (Cowley & Derezotes, 1994). Schriver (2001) accepts the distinctions and definitions offered by Canda (1989). Canda says spirituality is the "general human experience of developing a sense of meaning, purpose, and morality" (p. 39). He says religion is "the formal institutional contexts of spiritual beliefs and practices" (p. 39). Canda is also the co-author of a spiritual diversity text (Canda & Furman, 1999). Ellor, Netting, and Thibault (1999) offer slightly different definitions. For them, religion is "a social group or institution that ascribes meaning and value to individual life as well as to all of creation" (pp. 6–7). Spirituality pertains to a person's inner resources and ultimate concerns, providing the basic values around which one grounds other values; one's central philosophy of life—religious, nonreligious, antireligious—which guides conduct; and the way one relates to supernatural and nonmaterial dimensions of human nature. These concepts of spirituality were postulated by Moberg (1971). It is notable that they include nonbelievers as well as believers in spiritual beings and higher powers. In other words, one may have a spiritual orientation that is not only divorced from religion but may even be antireligious.

Schriver (2001, p. 77) offers nine dimensions of spirituality:

1. Transcendent dimensions
2. Meaning and purpose in life
3. Mission in life
4. Sacredness of life
5. Material values

6. Altruism
7. Ideals
8. Awareness of the tragic
9. Fruits of spirituality

For many American individuals and families, religion is an all consuming emphasis. Decisions about employment, leisure time, values, place of residence, and all of the fundamental issues are, in families that are observant, affected by religious identification and spiritual matters. Who people choose as friends, what kinds of education they pursue, how they deal with family problems, and how they address issues such as mental illness, physical illness, and economic and social difficulties are all colored by their religious associations and affiliations.

Of course, the influence of religion is differential. That is, not all families and not all individuals are religious and some are influenced less by religion than others. However, those who are also influenced are greatly affected by their religious associations and affiliations. A matter such as dealing with serious physical illness can be affected by a family's religious association. Religions such as Christian Science, Jehovah's Witnesses, and Roman Catholicism all have some specific positions on medical treatments.

For example, novelist Rosamunde Pilcher reports growing up in a family with a mother who was a Christian Scientist and who opposed modern medicine. She remembers that she and her sister simply thought beautiful thoughts when they should have gone to the doctor. Her childhood was plagued with ear- and toothaches, she says (Cheakalos & Biddle, 2001). Of course, she was fortunate. Some Christian Science families reject any medical treatment whatsoever and family members may die because of that religious principle.

Jehovah's Witnesses are basically opposed to blood transfusions, based upon their interpretation of scripture. There have been court decisions that dealt with the requirement for families to provide necessary medical treatment to preserve the life and health of children but, presumably, competent adults may die for lack of medical treatment because of religious doctrine.

Modern concepts of mental illness and modern treatments with psychoactive agents are frowned upon by some religious bodies. Abortion, birth control, and other family acts have different responses because of different religious affiliations. Dietary laws affect the kind of food that people can consume and limit the places they can go. For Orthodox Jews, the lack of kosher foods may make it impossible for persons to attend their professional meetings or their family weekend or a training session.

Unquestionably, religion has a great affect on large numbers of people as well as many families. It is also noteworthy that there are differential affects of religions, depending not only upon their religion itself, but also on the ethnic group. The African American Church is a major institution in the African American community. Many adherents to the churches spend great amounts of time in them, devote a good portion of their income to support of the churches, and take their values from the churches and the ministers who lead them.

It is also likely that a sound approach to understanding religion and spirituality would also discuss the religious institutions. Churches, synagogues, mosques, and congregations in general, are very specialized kinds of social institutions that require careful understanding for people who work in U.S. communities. They must come to know the churches and deal with them directly in their day-to-day activities in fields such as community organization, social planning, and advocacy.

So helping students understand church structure is critical. And, of course, there are many kinds of church structures. The Roman Catholic Church and some Protestant denominations have various kinds of centralized authority that make decisions about individual churches. In other cases, churches are independent, employ their own pastors, and make their own decisions about all issues.

As indicated in the discussion of social welfare policy and services, churches affect the way people vote, the kinds of candidates they support, and the kinds of social policies they oppose and support. Religious affiliation is also critical in understanding reactions to matters such as sexual orientation, marital patterns, and almost every other issue.

Students also need to understand that not everyone in the United States is religious. It is likely, however, that there are more religiously active people in the United States than in almost any other Western democracy. Ethnic groups other than African Americans have special connections with their religious groups. The Italian American community and the Irish American community have some traditional association with their own Catholic Churches. So do Hispanic groups, including Mexican Americans and Puerto Ricans. The Korean American community is by and large Christian and divided among Presbyterian, Baptist, and Roman Catholics, with some fundamentalist religious associations that are independent of mainstream churches.

A word of caution—it is not necessary or desirable to teach students about all religions or even most religions. There are certain broad definitions of what various religions believe and do but, in the large sense, it is very difficult and not particularly valuable to generalize. Students may end up with what appear to be prejudices that stereotype various religious groups, although that may not be the intention of the instructor.

Speaking as an observer of writings about Jewish life, I also find that popular press coverage of Jews is incomplete and often wrong. I think other religious groups have the same experience. It is important for students to learn to listen to others who can tell them about their religions and affiliations.

As part of human behavior and the social environment education, it is important for students to know something about the religious affiliations of Americans. According to the U.S. Bureau of the Census (1993), the group with the largest religious identification is Catholics, with 26.2% of adherents. The percentage of Baptists, who are divided among several different groups, most without any connections among them, comes second at 19.4%. Christians of all sorts constitute the large majority of the religious population. Krantz (1997) says that of the 200 U.S. denominations, 21 follow the Baptist faith, 14 the Methodist, 30 the Pentecostal, 14 identify as Lutherans, and 4 as Latter Day Saints (the rest are very small or independent). Of the Baptists, the largest group is the Southern Baptist Convention, which is also the largest Protestant church. Three of the Baptist groups are predominantly African American—the National Baptist Convention, USA; the National Baptist Convention of America; and the Progressive National Baptist Convention. Overall, the American population is 86.2% Christian. Slightly less than 2% of Americans are Jewish. One half percent are Muslim. About 10% either refuse to say what their religion is or identify themselves as nonbelievers.

There are also socioeconomic differences among spiritual groups. Jews, Episcopalians, Unitarians, and Agnostics, are the most affluent. The more fundamentalist Christian groups, Holiness and Pentecostal, are the least affluent (Woodward, 1993). This kind of information is important for helping students understand the dimensions of religion and spirituality.

SOCIAL WORK RESEARCH

There are many issues in social work research that interface with religion and spirituality. Certainly religious research projects can be conducted—or projects that deal with religious issues. The human subjects protections associated with religion are also of significance and bear discussion. Not revealing the religious affiliations of subjects may be critical in certain kinds of research projects.

It is likely that research about religion and its significance in the lives of clients can be effectively communicated in research courses. In some ways, reactions to the scientific method are a matter of religious responses, too. The debate over creationism and evolution is another of those issues that is religious or spiritual in nature.

Some social work literature is also research based or can refer readers to research oriented work. One book, by Ellor, Netting, and Thibault (1999), is an example of a heavily researched text that refers to many social work and social science studies. Essentially, religion lends itself to research. Although the content of religion may be a matter of faith and even mystery, religion, religious affiliation, religious policy, and other such matters can lend themselves to research—and students need to know that.

SOCIAL WORK PRACTICE

Of course, the social work practice field of study is the most important for preparing social workers and ideally it would also include some education for sensitivity about religion and religious differences. Work with individuals and families often must be appropriate to the religious affiliation of those families. A family may need to receive its services from a sectarian agency or a service that is religiously affiliated. Matters of child custody, foster care, and adoption are all critically associated with religion.

Perhaps most importantly, social workers need to learn to assess the importance of religion and spirituality among all their clients, based upon individual conferences and evaluations rather than stereotypes. That is, not all Italian Americans, Hispanics, and Irish Americans are Roman Catholic. Many may be Protestant. Not all African Americans are members of predominantly African American churches. Many are affiliated with religious organizations that are primarily White. There are some African Americans who are Jewish and large numbers of African Americans who are Muslim. Not all Jews are observant of dietary laws or Jewish worship, although some of them may strongly identify as Jewish. There is often a tendency, sometimes unwitting, to pigeonhole members of specific groups to specific kinds of religious affiliations and behaviors when, in fact, they may not fit at all.

Similarly, although some members of religious groups prefer living in the same neighborhoods, many prefer to live away from such neighborhoods. I once turned down a well-paying, prestigious social work education position when I was told what neighborhoods in the large city were Jewish. In West Virginia, there were no Jewish neighborhoods—a phenomenon I liked.

CONCLUSION

Because religion and spirituality are such important forces in the United States—some suggest that the United States is one of the most religiously observant nations in the world, perhaps the most religious in the Western world—not paying attention to spirituality and religion leaves wide gaps in the understandings of social workers who practice with clients and client systems.

In effect, a social worker needs to know the social welfare policy and services, human behavior and the social environment, research, and social work practice dimensions of religion and spirituality. There are also opportunities to apply such learnings in field instruction placements, both those that are primarily sectarian and those that serve a more general population, which would invariably include large numbers of people who are quite religious and whose spirituality is a major force in their lives.

On the other hand, social workers need to be cautious about generalizing about religion and spirituality and stereotyping clients and client systems because of their ethnic affiliations. Not understanding religious and spiritual matters is a source of deficit in the effectiveness of social workers. Over-understanding or drawing conclusions that are not necessarily valid about such matters is equally a deficit.

It is also important for social workers to understand the precise legal status of religion and spirituality in the United States. These are complicated matters that are not fully resolved for at all times. Additional public policy issues regarding church and state relations continue to emerge. It is important for social workers to understand with some sophistication just what those policies, court decisions, and current practices are. That is probably especially true for social workers who are employed by religiously affiliated organizations, but it is also important for social workers who serve a more general population to understand the legal dimensions of religion and spirituality in the United States.

REFERENCES

Beckett, J. O., & Johnson, H. C. (1995). Human development. In R. L. Edwards et al. (Eds.), *Encyclopedia of social work* (19th ed., pp. 1385–1405). Washington, DC: NASW Press.

Canda, E. R. (1989). Religious content in social work education: A comparative approach. *Journal of Social Work Education, 25*(1), 36–45.

Canda, E. R., & Furman, L. D. (1999). *Spiritual diversity in social work practice.* New York: Free Press.

Cheakalos, C., & Biddle, N. (August 13, 2001). Country comforter people. *People,* 101–104.

Cowley, A. S., & Derezotes, D. (1994). Transpersonal psychology and social work education. *Journal of Social Work Education, 30*(1), 32–41.

Ellor, J. W., Netting, F. E., & Thibault, J. M. (1999). *Religious and spiritual aspects of human service practice.* Columbia, SC: USC Press.

Fairfield, R. P. (Ed.). (1966). *The federalist papers.* Garden City, NY: Anchor.

Krantz, L. (1997). *The definitive guide to the best and worst of everything.* Paramus, NJ: Prentice-Hall.

Lee v. Weisman, 112 S. Ct. 2649 (1992).

Marbury v. Madison, 5 U.S. 137 (1803).

McCullough, D. (2001). *John Adams.* New York: Simon and Schuster.

Moberg, D. O. (1971). Spiritual well-being: Background and issues. Subjective measures of spiritual well-being. *Review of Religious Research, 25*(4), 4.

MSNBC. (2001, August 9). [On-line]. Available: http://www.msnbc.com/news/609839.asp

Robinson, B. A. (1998). *Religious tolerance* [On-line]. Available: http://www.religioustolerance.org/

Schriver, J. M. (2001). *Human behavior and the social environment: Shifting paradigms in essential knowledge for social work practice* (3rd ed.). Needham Heights, MA: Allyn and Bacon.

U.S. Bureau of the Census. (1993). *Statistical abstract of the United States, 1993* (113th ed.). Austin, TX: Reference Press.

Woodward, K. I. (November 29, 1993). The rites of Americans. *Newsweek,* 80–82.

Chapter 8

SECTARIAN ORGANIZATIONS SERVING CIVIC PURPOSES

Nieli Langer

RELIGIOUSLY MOTIVATED HELPING

The desire to help others and, therefore, the beginning of social welfare, appears to have developed as a part of religion. In past centuries, the only moral code was one that was based on a spiritual, religious standard. Almost all religions have obligated their followers to engage in acts of charity, sometimes only to members of their creed and sometimes to anyone in need. All major religions have to some extent stressed mutual responsibility, kindness or justice to the needy, and self-fulfillment through service (Macarov, 1978, p. 76).

Since colonial times, religious congregations and religious organizations in the United States have been providing not only for the spiritual needs of their congregants, but for their social welfare as well. The history of the United States is, to a great extent, a history of religion's role as a prod to social justice and inclusion. Religiously motivated service, currently referred to as the sectarian agency, responded to the needs of communities before state or federal governments assumed this responsibility or before the evolution of the social work profession (Ortiz, 1995, p. 2109). Indeed, until the close of the 19th century, religious groups were virtually the nation's sole provider of social services and " . . . religious ideas were the most important intellectual influence on American welfare institutions . . . " (Leiby, 1978, p. 12).

The Gallup organization has tracked America's religious beliefs for over 60 years, with consistent results over time. Greater participation in worship and interest in religion is found in America than in any other Western nation, including the United Kingdom, Australia, Canada, and Europe (Gallup Poll, 1998). The United States is noteworthy not only for its high level of religiosity, but also for the variety of its religions. The United States enjoys religious freedom, and, therefore, many religions have prospered here. The story of religion in the United States is the story of immigration. Ongoing waves of new settlers to its shores have assured that there have been not only dramatic changes in the religious makeup of the nation throughout its history, but also a generous variety of faiths to choose from. Now as before, with President Johnson's signing of the 1965 Immigration and Nationality Act, immigrants are gradually changing the face of U.S. religion. Since the signing of the Immigration Act has greatly facilitated the arrival of Asians, religions such as Buddhism, Hinduism, and Islam are now firmly rooted in America.

Jews and Christians are the two religious groups that are most involved in sectarian practice in the United States. Both groups have had a significant presence in American social welfare from the early days of immigration to the present. The American approach to welfare and the evolution of the social work profession have their foundations in both religious traditions (Ortiz, 1995, p. 2110).

Probably the most significant advance of Jewish charitable thought was the assertion that individuals have a positive obligation to perform acts of helping and doing good for others, which contrasts with the ancient Egyptian concept of charity as mainly the avoidance of doing harm to others. Judaism bases its requirements for altruism on essentially two concepts: *Tsedakah*, a mixture of charity and justice, and *Chesed*, loving kindness. Not only did people have an obligation to help those in need but also the needy had a right to receive aid. Charitable acts were to be done simply because they were the right thing to do and the giver should expect no repayment from the recipient (Johnson & Schwartz, 1988). The Jewish philosopher Maimonides outlined eight degrees of charity, from lowest to highest:

> Give, but with reluctance and regret. This is the gift of the hand but not of the heart.

> The second is to give cheerfully, but not proportionately to the distress of the sufferer.

The third is to give cheerfully and proportionately, but not until we are solicited.

The fourth is to give cheerfully and proportionately, and even unsolicited; but to put it in the poor man's hand, thereby exciting in him the painful emotion of shame.

The fifth is to give charity in such a way that the distressed may receive the bounty and know their benefactor, without being known to him.

The sixth, which rises still higher, is to know the objects of our bounty, but remain unknown to them.

The seventh is still more meritorious, namely, to bestow charity in such a way that the benefactor may not know the relieved persons, nor they the name of their benefactor.

Lastly, the eighth and most meritorious of all, is to anticipate charity by preventing poverty; i.e., to assist a reduced person so that he may earn an honest livelihood and not be forced to the dreadful alternative of holding up his hand for charity. (Macarov, 1978, p. 76)

From these tenets, along with the Ten Commandments, the Proverbs, teachings from the Old Testament books of Leviticus and Deuteronomy and the Talmud, the roots of Jewish social welfare practices were established. The social welfare foundation of the Jewish community is reflected in an enumeration from a morning prayer. The list is not far removed from some basic "social work" functions: clothing the naked, educating the poor, providing poor girls with a dowry, providing food for Passover, caring for orphans, visiting the sick, caring for the elderly, consolation of the bereaved, and providing burials (Dolgoff, Feldstein, & Skolnik, 1993, p. 32).

From a social welfare perspective, several important themes have their roots in Jewish religion. Social welfare became institutionalized in two important respects: in regard to expected behavior and in provision for the poor in essentially non-stigmatizing ways. Therefore, Jewish welfare tradition precludes means testing and advocates that the provision of resources is a right or entitlement. In addition, individuals and the society in which they live will be judged on the degree to which they provide for the poor without demeaning them (Dolgoff, Feldstein, & Skolnik, 1993, p. 32).

To the moral teachings and concept of justice from the Old Testament, the early Christians added an emphasis on love and compassion. With the development of Christianity, two themes were introduced that influenced social welfare for over 1,500 years, and remain with us today. Charity was to be administered without regard to a person's social status or ethnicity.

A second theme derived from Christian thought was the denigration of conspicuous consumption. These two Christian themes brought with them several significant social welfare themes such as relief for the poor, aid to widows and orphans, and hospitality to the homeless. Both love of Jesus and love of people were necessary for the Christian life. Judgment was to be on the basis of how one treated those who were hungry, strangers, sick, or in prison since Jesus was considered present in all such people. While Christians placed emphasis on giving alms to the poor, early Christians also held strong beliefs about the necessity of work so that Christians need not be a burden to others. In addition, it was important for Christians of means to divest themselves of property to support those in need in order to show signs of one's Christian commitment (Dolgoff, 1993, pp. 32–33).

The early Christian church, and the generations that followed, took seriously the command of Jesus to express love and carry out charitable acts. Since its earliest days, the church has engaged in at least 12 areas of social ministry: care of widows, orphans, sick, poor, disabled, prisoners, captives, slaves, victims of calamity; burial of the poor; and provision of employment services and meals for the needy (Brackney & Watkins, 1983, p. 7). Because the roots of the Christian church are in Judaism, the charitable activities of the two groups are very similar.

Services to congregants and communities have been conceptualized and implemented during different historical periods in response to prevailing needs. Furthermore, religious denominations have selectively implemented these services with some groups providing one service more than others. For example, Baptists have been active in providing homes for children; Catholics, in health care and the needs of children, especially orphans; the Salvation Army has provided emergency services to the poorest and most neglected people in our society. The denomination's underlying ideological orientation is often the key to understanding the sectarian agencies, for they influence the agencies' missions, programming, and staffing and motivation of their workers. The doctrinal orientations are often at the core of professional dilemmas or conflicts experienced in particular sectarian agencies (Ortiz, 1995, pp. 2110–2111).

Sectarian agencies in the United States grew with migration and proliferated in the late 19th century, operating independently to meet community needs. With the advent of the Charity Organization Societies after the Civil War, sectarian agencies became permanent sources of social service agencies on the U.S. welfare landscape, soon competing with one another and with nonsectarian agencies for both private and eventually public funding (Ortiz, 1995, pp. 2110–2111).

The provision of social services under Catholic auspices is usually centrally structured and administered, often operating under the jurisdiction of the local dioceses with local bishops assuming control. The National Conference of Catholic Charities is the umbrella organization that coordinates and supports these local agencies (Reid & Stimpson, 1987, pp. 545–556).

Protestant services that are locally organized are more independently operated. They fall under one of three categories: *church related* (the Salvation Army which is really a church and a social welfare organization combined, or Latter Day Saints agencies which are extensions of the Mormon Church); *autonomous* organizations, which are administered by board members from a church or denomination that represent a community with a set of beliefs incorporated into their bylaws (e.g., Episcopal Charity organizations); and *interdenominational* agencies that are administered by a coalition of religious groups, representing various faiths, agreeing on a common ecumenical purpose and organized to address a particular community need (Rahn & Whiting, 1965, pp. 567–600).

Jewish services operate independently from organized religious groups and tend to be nationally organized by areas of service, that is, families, health care, the elderly, and community services. These national organizations do not provide funding to local affiliates but regulate services through accreditation and provide information and consultation. Federations of locally organized service agencies representing both the agencies and the communities assume the responsibility for program planning, fund-raising, and fiscal policy. The Council of Jewish Federations as a national umbrella organization has assumed this responsibility for local service agencies (Reid & Stimpson, 1987, pp. 545–556).

Sectarian agencies respond to community needs and today are rarely bound to their historic target population or field of service. They are no longer solely dependent on their sponsoring denominations or constituent groups. Due to limited funding, however, they must often make difficult decisions about what and how much to fund a particular cause. Today, their funding sources are increasingly derived from fund-raising groups such as United Way and from government contracts, a trend that has accelerated exponentially since the turn of the century (Netting, 1986, pp. 50–63). Second only to government contracts, it is the religious groups that support welfare agencies (Popple & Leighninger, 1993, pp. 95–96).

SEPARATION OF SACRED AND SECULAR

Since the early 1930s, when the U.S. government began to support social welfare measures, there has been a public debate over public funding of sectarian agencies. Debate for some has targeted government funding of religious activities, and for others, especially administrators and religious sponsors of agencies, the threat of a potential loss of an agency's historical mission by acceptance of public funds. The massive funds generated and distributed to sectarian agencies during the War on Poverty during the 1960s is a striking example that despite the church-state issues, the purchase of services from sectarian services was a well accepted practice. Scholars, journalists, and other professionals have called attention to the vital and unique role that sectarian agencies play in social restoration. In light of the continuous struggle to allay a confounding array of poverty-related social ills—inadequate education, family disintegration, substance abuse, violent crime, and inadequate health and child care, public officials are unusually open to cooperation with the private religious sector to address these problems. The source of this openness for collaboration and cooperation is the recognition that many of the nation's social problems have both moral and spiritual roots. The evidence, though not conclusive, strongly suggests that religion can make a difference in the lives of people.

Despite this potential, public-private cooperative efforts involving sectarian agencies have been constrained by the current climate of First Amendment interpretation of separation of church and state as set forth in *Everson v. Board of Education* (1947). The Court's interpretation in this case was "no aid to religion." However, the courts have not provided decisive definitions of what constitutes a religious-based program and as a result of this legal confusion, some agencies that receive government funding pray openly with their clients, while other agencies have been banned from displaying religious symbols.

Consistent application of the no aid to religious organizations principle to sectarian agencies that currently receive funding would create havoc in government administration of social welfare services. The Supreme Court's restrictive and ambiguous rulings on public funds to support sectarian agencies are a barrier to the government's overtures to develop and enhance greater public/sectarian solutions to societal problems. In addition, the no aid to religion principle is inevitably discriminatory when the Court interpretation of the First Amendment favors programs rooted in a secularly-based faith commitment over ones rooted in a religiously-based faith commitment. If a sectarian agency must downplay its religious principles in order to receive the public funding that a comparable secular organization receives, public policy is interfering with its free exercise of religious freedom (Pavlischek, 1997, pp. 47–50). As a result, the sectarian agencies are reluctant to expose themselves to risk of lawsuits while public authorities, although confused about what is permissible, often look the other way when faith-based social service agencies include substantial religious programming.

An alternative First Amendment interpretation identified as the "equal treatment" strain by Stephen Monsma (1996), emerged with the Court's rulings in *Widmar v. Vincent* (1981) and *Rosenberger v. Rector* (1995). In these rulings, the Court upheld the principle that public access to facilities or benefits cannot exclude religious groups. It may one day be the argument for defending cooperation between public and sectarian agencies where the offer of public funds is made available to any qualifying agency.

The federal government's latest welfare overhaul, the Personal Responsibility and Work Opportunity Reconciliation Act (1996), includes what has been labeled the "Charitable Choice" provision. This historic welfare reform turned over the welfare administration into the hands of state governments. The revolutionary feature of the new legislation was its support for cooperation between states and faith-based charities, based on their exemplary efficiency and success rate despite government restrictions. Churches have long contracted with the government, but the difference was that churches ran their social service projects through separately incorporated entities. The law provides public/sectarian cooperation by prohibiting the government from discriminating against nonprofit applicants for certain types of social service funding on the basis of their religious foundation. Charitable Choice also protects sectarian agencies that receive government funds from pressure to alter their religious focus while prohibiting these religious nonprofit organizations from using these funds for overt religious activities, that is, sectarian worship, instruction, or proselytization. It encourages states to use faith-based organizations in serving the poor and needy, and provides protection for the religious integrity and character of these organizations that are willing to accept government funds. Advocates of enlisting faith-based organizations in the provision of public services argue that the dangers posed by the social problems, such as drug addiction, outweigh any threat to the separation of church and state posed by the use of faith-based organizations.

Charitable Choice attempts to make religiosity secondary to the public-private cooperative efforts and projects that may alter the current blight of social ills. It also strives to protect clients' First Amendment rights by ensuring that services are not conditional on religious practice, and that nonsectarian service providers are available alternatives. Charitable Choice alters the focus of church-state interactions away from the religious constructs of sectarian social service agencies, and onto the common goals of helping the indigent and fostering constructive cooperation between church and state in addressing the nation's most serious social problems and, in turn, enhancing the fabric of our society. In light of the above issues, however, making Charitable Choice work remains an enormous challenge because we will still have to grapple with First Amendment rights. Religious groups may worry that acceptance of government funds may require them to weaken their faith commitments. While organizations such as Catholic Charities and the Jewish Federation have long received large subsidies from the federal government, such traditional charities have pursued their efforts in a nonsectarian manner. Critics argue that newer faith-based approaches rely explicitly on proselytization as the means of effecting behavioral change. The use of Bible studies and prayers are central to the success of projects such as Teen Challenge and Prison Fellowships. To take away the religion of the organization's policies is to take away the very effectiveness that is lauded by governments and churches alike. At the same time, there is a legitimate fear that supporting the religious groups with the highest success rates will translate into government aid to those organizations that require the strongest religious commitment from clients (Dionne & Dilulio, 1999, pp. 4–9).

In the changing fortunes of the initiatives to finance social programs of religious charities, supporters and critics have failed to assuage persistent fears that the initiatives would undermine Constitutional guarantees separating church and state. Massive legal and practical confusion continues to reign. In the current political climate when there is growing appreciation of the enormous and indispensable role played by sectarian agencies in addressing dire social problems, serious legal and Constitutional obstacles still exist for these organizations. Apart from a few extreme separationists, however, no one wants public funding of religiously-based social organizations to end, largely because these agencies are so effective (Pavlischek, 1997, pp. 47–50).

FAITH-BASED SOCIAL PROGRAMS

Despite the secular evolution of the welfare state, religious congregations have continuously provided social services throughout our history. As the nation's social needs have become more urgent over the past few decades, religious congregations have responded. President Bush, in a speech delivered on January 30, 2001 took this position:

> Government cannot be replaced by charities, but it can and should welcome them as partners. We must heed the growing consensus across America that

successful government social programs work in fruitful partnership with community-serving and faith-based organizations—whether run by Methodists, Muslims, Mormons, or good people of no faith at all. (President George Bush,
2001, Foreword)

The consensus cited by President Bush runs wide and deep. Survey data
compiled by Gallup and associates has consistently indicated that most
U.S. citizens believe that religion can help "answer all or most of today's
problems" (Gallup & Lindsay, 1999). *Independent Sector,* an umbrella organization representing nonprofits both religious and secular, estimates that
the United States is home to over 300,000 community-serving religious
congregations, 4 out of 5 of which provide services *without* regard to the
religious identities (if any) of those whom they serve (Independent Sector,
2000). The Pew Charitable Trusts recently released a national poll showing
that most Americans believe "local churches, synagogues or mosques,"
together with "organizations such as the Salvation Army, Goodwill Industries and Habitat for Humanity," are top problem-solving organizations in
their communities (Morin, 2001).

Partners for Sacred Places, an organization dedicated to saving historic
church buildings, commissioned Ram A. Cnaan of the University of Pennsylvania to study what kind of services and to whom were inner-city
congregations providing in order to address the social needs of their neighborhoods. Professor Cnaan conducted a survey of 113 congregations in
Chicago, Indianapolis, Mobile, New York, Philadelphia, and San Francisco.
He compiled a multi-city database that documents how congregations serve
America's poorest urban communities (Cnaan, 2000). He and his associates
report that

1. over 90% of urban congregations provide social services that include
   soup kitchens, preschool programs, prison ministries, health clinics,
   literacy programs, day care centers, and much more.
2. congregation members performed these services primarily on behalf
   of poor neighborhood children, youth, and families who are *not*
   members of the congregations that serve them.
3. *almost none* of these sectarian agencies make receipt of services
   contingent upon any profession of faith or performance of religious
   rituals of any kind.
4. the people most influential in initiating social services in the sample
   were the clergy and individual members of groups in the
   congregations.

As a result, Professor Cnaan calls community-serving congregations America's "hidden safety net" (Cnaan, 2000).

Using a nationwide survey of 766 nonprofit organizations, Stephen Monsma documented the nature of government support of nonprofit organizations and their relationship. He found that most sectarian nonprofits that receive public funds are more than nominally religious and that even highly religious organizations receive large amounts of public monies yet report little overt pressure on their religious practices from government (Pavlischek, 1997, pp. 47–50). Monsma's study focuses primarily on organizations that are fairly well established and have the experience of negotiating with government bureaucracies and defending themselves against government encroachment. Although information about smaller organizations with fewer political resources might provide a more balanced picture of government pressure on religious practices, Monsma is more concerned with offering a menu of prescriptions that will allow nonprofit congregational organizations to function for the public good without compromising their religious beliefs (Pavlischek, 1997, pp. 47–50). Monsma contends that regardless of church-state issues, *for decades* the sacred and the secular have mixed in the administration of hundreds of taxpayer-supported programs (Monsma, 1996, pp. 37–41).

The increased interest in providing public social services under the rubric of faith-based organizations is a result of several factors. First, there are some organizations that have been very successful in reducing or alleviating social problems in troubled communities. The Azusa Christian Community in Boston, under the leadership of Reverend Eugene Rivers, has been credited with lowering the juvenile murder rates in that community to almost zero.

Second, social science data has increasingly documented a strong inverse correlation between religious commitment and social pathologies. In the initial work on religion reducing deviance, the Harvard economist, Richard Freeman, found that Black urban youth who were religious were less likely to be criminal than those who were irreligious (Freeman, 1985). Using a more multidimensional measure of religious commitment than churchgoing, Larson and Johnson (1998) found that religion is indeed a powerful predictor of escaping poverty, crime, and other social ills, more powerful even than such variables as peer influences. Like Freeman, Larson and Johnson conjecture that the potential of church-going and other religious activities to improve the life prospects of poor black urban youth is in part a function of how church-going and other faith factors influence how young people spend their time, the extent of their engagement in positive structured activities, and the degree to which they are supported by responsible adults (Larson & Johnson 1998). Their research speaks powerfully to the need for researchers and others to start remembering the faith factor and to take religion as an ally in repairing lives, saving children, and resurrecting the civil society of inner-city neighborhoods.

Third, dissatisfaction with the outcome of government programs has led both to reduction in federal welfare spending and increased pressure to enlist the help of faith- and community-based organizations in caring for the poor. One example is Teen Challenge, the largest residential drug rehabilitation program, with a reported success of 70%, a higher success rate than most other programs at substantially lower cost. There is no systematic evidence as to whether these programs are working for many participants, but ample testimony that they do work in a small sense. Religion may be a key variable in escaping the inner city, recovering from alcohol and drug addiction, keeping marriages together, and staying out of prison (Institute for Communitarian Policy Studies, 2001). There are many people involved in comparable projects in cities all across America who have faith motivation at least to provide these services.

Black Americans are in many ways the most religious people in America (Gallup Poll, 1998). In many of our most difficult communities, the Black church is the asset; it is the predominant, most significant asset in the community. The Black church is not only a vehicle to disseminate the faith, but it is also an organizational framework. In the Black church, when it is successful, you learn not only about Jesus but about mentoring, growing up, and facing up to responsibilities, and where the price of admission is not that you necessarily accept the faith. Voluntary associations as exemplified by the Black churches can be valuable allies in the battle against social pathologies. People who for many reasons fear church-state partnerships should focus more on the consistent finding that faith-based outreach efforts benefit poor unchurched neighborhood children most of all.

REDEFINING THE RELATIONSHIP BETWEEN RELIGION AND SOCIAL LIFE

Many sectarian agencies have remained dynamic and have adapted to the changing needs of society. Many religious groups are altering their traditional services, however, opting instead to sponsor innovative grass-roots, empowerment, justice oriented services (McDonald, 1984, pp. 20–

24). Religious congregations are enhancing local quality of life and contributing to the formation of civil society. These institutions are the least studied and least understood actors in contemporary public life, but they are rapidly gaining attention because of the numerous examples of positive results produced in the communities where they are most active. This endeavor is different from the sectarian model that has been a fixture in U.S. welfare. These faith-based organizations are a natural site for delivering services, identifying community needs, and using untapped resources such as volunteers and laypersons to meet pressing needs (Ortiz, 1995, pp. 2115–2116).

> For my own part, I pray that broadly based, deeply rooted, powerfully led, spiritually anointed movements in our most disadvantaged communities will not just be tolerated by our public institutions, but that as a nation we will find ways of supporting these communities of faith as they seek in mysterious ways to transform, and to transcend, the social reality. (Loury, 1999, pp. 2–3)

Private charities, not the government, should be the resource of first resort. In the real world, private charities have made the most significant changes in people's lives, not government programs. If religion is an important source of possible personal transformation yet direct financial transactions between the government and religion will be denied by the Court, then we should remove subsidies for faith-based groups and take private charities off the federal payroll. Instead, encourage the passage of legislation for tax and regulatory reform that will make charitable giving more attractive. These initiatives do not require tax dollars and would circumvent the debate over subsidies to church-based organizations, and subsequently pacify the argument over separation of church and state in the dissemination of social services.

A great deal of money goes from individual Americans to religious groups. It is the power of millions of Americans who give voluntarily to right a wrong and correct society's problems. The spirit of private giving is an invaluable resource that no amount of government financial support can replace. Corporations contribute large amounts to nonreligious organizations, however, such as schools, hospitals, and cultural enterprises. U.S. corporations advise their employees that they will match money up to a certain amount that is donated to a charitable organization. They will match funds allocated for nonsectarian institutions but not to religious organizations. If there is no legal deterrent, corporations should change their giving patterns and modify the way they match contributions so that faith-based organizations may be included (Wilson, 1999, pp. 36–41).

Wilson refers to a "United Way for Religious Outreach" that would identify *useful* faith-based outreach programs aimed at alcoholism, crime, delinquency, drug abuse, and single-mom pregnancies—issues about which Americans are deeply concerned. Useful, as defined by Wilson, would include "a program that is aimed at reaching people at risk for harmful behavior, and is financially honest and intellectually serious" (Wilson, 1999, pp. 36–41). This organization would provide guidance for corporations willing to match funds of corporate employees eager to contribute to a particular kind of church outreach.

Sectarian and community initiatives must be supported in the interests of improving government performance and enhancing public trust. Congregations are extensively involved in social service in their communities and their voluntary efforts provide a vital backbone for civic society in the United States. That congregations throughout the nation come together to help those in need is a uniquely American social institution. But it will be pluralistic dialogues, not polarizing labels, that will unite the efforts of faith-based and community initiatives on behalf of the least advantaged in our society (Dilulio, 2001). Religion's role in renewing society will most often begin at the level of the individual, not the government. Religion's chief contribution is in empowerment, that is, an individual's recognition that he/she can transform their lives. Churches are the base operators of great community organizing where people are brought together to do for themselves. Yet, no matter how much congregations exert themselves, they cannot fill the gaps created by the devolution of federal responsibility for social welfare to states and localities. The recent interest in faith-based congregational efforts to alleviate social ills should be seen as a promising aspect of a larger transformation in the evolution of religion and politics in the United States. It should be viewed as a gadfly for us to rethink the relationship of religion and social life in America today.

In a surprising turnaround, the religion-based initiative has caught the attention of many states, where local officials are making unprecedented efforts to encourage religious charities to apply for government money. An article entitled, "States Steer Religious Charities Toward Aid" in the *New York Times*, July 21, 2001 described government liaisons brokering new collaborations between clergy members and state social service departments—two groups that heretofore shared little contact or trust. Other states are sponsoring conferences where religious leaders are being taught the arcane rules of government contracting.

States had been required to make it easier for religious groups to win contracts to run social service programs since the passage of the legislation overhauling welfare in 1996. Until recently, however, they had remained lukewarm to the idea. Now, after 6 years of hesitation, states are taking the initiative to form relationships with religious ministries, many with good intentions, but little experience either as government contractors or as social workers. In the past, religious leaders were hesitant about using government funds but today, as described in the aforementioned newspaper article, "many are prepared to jump through the hoops because the financing amounts to more than they could raise passing the plate." Many people believe that religiously inspired social services can reach some troubled people who do not respond to other programs. The question is whether federal subsidies for such faith-based groups can exist comfortably with the constitutional ban on government involvement in religion. Our political debate is often organized as a debate about whether you want the government or the market to do something. We do not live in one or the other, however, the government or in the market; we live in civil society. We need to acknowledge that "although the government need not continue to be the dominant supplier, religion and government are of the society; let both contribute to it" (Dionne & DiIulio, 1999, pp. 4–9).

REFERENCES

Brackney, B., & Watkins, D. (1983). An analysis of Christian values and social work practice. *Social Work and Christianity, 10*(7).

Cnaan, R. (2000). *Keeping the faith in the city: How 401 religious congregations serve their neediest neighbors.* Center for Research on Religion and Urban Civil Society, CRRUCS Report 2000–2001, University of Pennsylvania, Philadelphia, Pennsylvania.

Delivery of Social Services Through Faith-Based Organizations, Institute for Communitarian Policy Studies. (2001). The George Washington University. Washington, D.C. http://gwis.circ.gwu.edu/~icps/faithb.html

DiIulio, J. J. (March 7, 2001). *Compassion in truth and action.* Speech delivered at the National Association of Evangelicals, Dallas, Texas.

Dionne, E. J., & DiIulio, J. J. (1999). What's God got to do with the American experiment? *Brookings Review, 17*(2), 4–9.

Dolgoff, R., Felstein, D., & Skolnik, L. (1993). *Understanding social welfare.* New York: Longman.

Everson v. Board of Education of Ewing Township, 330 U.S. 1 (1947).

Freeman, R. (1985). *Who escapes? The relation of church-going and other background factors to the socio-economic performance of black male youths from inner-city poverty tracts.* Working Paper, Number 1656, National Bureau of Economic Research, Cambridge, MA.

Gallup, G., Jr., & Lindsay, M. D. (1999). *Surveying the religious landscape: Trends in U.S. beliefs*. Harrisburg, PA: Morehouse Publishing.

Gallup Poll. (1998). *Public opinion 1997*. Wilmington, Delaware: Scholarly Resources, Inc.

Independent Sector is a coalition of nonprofits, foundations, etc. representing over 700 organizations and it publishes a newsletter as referenced. See *www.IndependentSector.org*

Johnson, L., & Schwartz, C. (1988). *Social welfare: A response to human need*. Needham Heights, MA: Allyn & Bacon.

Larson, D. B., & Johnson, B. R. (1998). *Religion: The forgotten factor in cutting youth crime and saving at-risk urban youth*. Report 98-2. New York: The Jeremiah Project, Manhattan Institute for Policy Research.

Leiby, J. (1978). *A history of social welfare and social work in the United States*. New York: Columbia University Press.

Loury, G. (1999). "God talk" and public policy. *Brookings Review, 17*(2), 2–3.

Macarov, D. (1978). *The design of social welfare*. New York: Holt, Rinehart, and Winston.

McDonald, J. (1984). Survey finds religious groups strongly favor more collaboration. *Foundation News, 35,* 20–24.

Monsma, S. V. (1996). *When sacred and secular mix: Religious nonprofit organizations and public money*. New York: Rowman and Littlefield.

Morin, R. (February 1, 2001). Nonprofit, faith-based groups near top of poll on solving social woes. *The Washington Post*, p. 5.

Netting, F. E. (1986). The religiously affiliated agency: Implications for social work administration. *Social Work and Christianity: An International Journal, 13*(2), 50–63.

Ortiz, L. (1995). Sectarian agencies. In R. L. Edwards (Ed.), *Encyclopedia of social work* (19th ed., pp. 2109–2116). NASW Press.

Pavlischek, K. (1997). [Review of the book *When sacred and secular mix: Religious nonprofit organizations and public money* by Stephen V. Monsma]. *First Things: A Journal of Religion and Public Life, 72*(April), 47–50.

Popple, P., & Leighninger, L. (1993). *Social work, social welfare, and American society*. Boston: Allyn and Bacon.

President George W. Bush, *Rallying the Armies of Compassion*, Washington, D.C. January 30, 2001, Foreword.

Rahn, S., & Whiting, N. (1965). Protestant social services. In H. L. Lurie (Ed.), *Encyclopedia of social work* (15th ed., pp. 567–600). New York: National Association of Social Workers.

Reid, W., & Stimpson, W. (1987). Sectarian agencies. In A. Minahan (Ed.), *Encyclopedia of social work* (18th ed., Vol. 2, pp. 545–556). Silver Springs, MD: National Association of Social Workers.

Rosenberger v. University of Virginia 515 U.S. 819 (1995).

States Steer Religious Charities Toward Aid. (July 21, 2001). *New York Times*, p. 1.

Widmar v. Vincent, 454 U.S. 263 (1981).

Wilson, J. Q. (1999). Religion and public life. *Brookings Review, 17*(2), 36–41.

PART III

NEW MODELS FOR THE 21ST CENTURY

Chapter 9

THE KOREAN AMERICAN CHURCH AS A SOCIAL SERVICE PROVIDER

Gil Choi

The Korean American church has been the primary mediating institution between Korean immigrants and their adjustment process to a new life in the United States, and continues its role as the primary social service provider for their unmet needs (those to which the formal service agencies are unable to respond). It functions as a social center and a means of cultural identification, serves an educational function, and takes a role as a broker between its congregants and the bureaucratic institutions of the larger society.

THE GROWTH OF CHURCH IN KOREA

The roots of Christianity in Korea go back to the late 18th century. It was in 1784 that Korean scholars who were studying in Beijing, China became acquainted with Jesuit missionaries and brought the Catholic doctrine to Korea. After an initial period of favor, Catholics were subject to persecution from the late 18th to the late 19th centuries. The first Korean Catholic martyr was executed in 1791, and official persecutions were mandated in 1801, 1839, and 1866. As a result of these persecutions, Catholics remained a small and embattled religious group until the 20th century, when the

155

religion began to attract followers once again (Kim, Warner, & Kwon, 2001).

The Korean government entered into a formal treaty with the United States in 1882, opening its doors to Americans. In 1883 two Protestant missionaries, Horace G. Underwood, a Presbyterian, and Henry G. Appenzeller, a Methodist, arrived. They were soon joined by other American, Canadian, and Australian missionaries and began a program of building churches, schools, and hospitals. They translated the Bible into the *hangul* script (Korean written language), that had been disdained in favor of classical Chinese writing by the Confucian literati, and thus they laid the foundation for mass literacy and the modern Korean educational system. Many Koreans were favorably impressed with the missionaries' activities and began to think of Protestant Christianity as a positive, modernizing force (Kim et al., 2001).

For the last few decades, the Korean church has grown enormously. Han (1983) argued that the involvement of the Korean church in social justice, nationalism, and human rights contributed significantly up to the time of national independence from Japan in 1945. The church in Korea has kept up with a tradition of social justice and human rights by standing up for the underprivileged, who were disenchanted with the authoritarian and bureaucratic system of government and by siding with the women's movement (Kim, 1985). It has also been deeply involved in the development of educational systems and social welfare policies. Some other factors contributing to the growth of the Korean church have included the rapid industrialization and urbanization since the early 1960s, and a threat of communism. Ro (1983) pointed out that political insecurity and social instability caused by a constant threat of Communist attack during the Cold War era had led Koreans to look for spiritual security. Ro also claimed that political, social, cultural, and religious circumstances have also been favorable for the rapid growth of the church. One fourth of South Koreans are now reportedly Christians. It is also noteworthy that the largest church in the world is in Korea, with a membership of over 850,000.

THE GROWTH OF THE KOREAN CHURCH IN THE UNITED STATES

Korean immigration to the United States began in the early 1900s. After the Chinese Exclusion Act of 1882, which became permanent in 1902, Hawaiian sugar plantation owners turned to Koreans as a possible source of labor. Between 1900 and 1905 approximately 7,000 Korean immigrants found work laboring under harsh conditions for long hours on sugar plantations or as cooks, janitors, and launderers at meager wages within the confines of the plantations (Yun, 1979). After 1905, the number of Korean immigrants to Hawaii dwindled sharply as the Korean government became reluctant to permit further immigration after learning of the extremely poor working conditions and low wages (Jo, 1999).

All Korean immigration to Hawaii and the mainland of United States ended after the Immigration Act of 1924 became effective. This Act created an apportionment formula for the allowable number of foreigners into the United States based on national origin. Northern and western Europeans were allotted fairly large quotas while all Asian nations were given token annual quotas of 100 (Jo, 1999). The Immigration Act of 1965, which abolished the quota system based on national origins, opened a door for a great number of Korean immigrants. For example, in 1965, 3,130 Korean immigrants came to America (Hurh & Kim, 1990). A decade later the number reached 28,362 (Immigration and Naturalization Service, 1979). The number of Koreans increased fivefold from 1970 to 1980 and 227% from 1980 to 1990. The latest U.S. Census (U.S. Department of Commerce, 2001) reported 1,076,872 Koreans living in the United States.

The Korean church has grown enormously in numbers, not only in Korea but also in many parts of the world, particularly in the United States. For example, the number of Korean churches in the United States increased from less than 75 in 1970 to 1,624 as of January 1986 (Shin & Park, 1988). With an estimated total size of 750,000 Korean Americans in 1986, the population/church density was approximately one church per 462 Korean Americans. Korean immigrants are known as churchgoers.

THE CHURCH AS A SURROGATE FAMILY FOR KOREAN IMMIGRANTS

The vast majority of Korean immigrants living in the United States are affiliated with the Christian church. Kim's (1978) study on Asian Americans in the Chicago area found that the church participation of Korean immigrants was greater than that of any other Asian group except the Filipinos. The study reported that about 32% of Chinese samples, 28% of Japanese samples, and 71% of the Korean samples were affiliated with Christian churches. In two separate studies that Hurh and Kim (1984, 1988) conducted, they found that 69.9% of Koreans living in Los Angeles and 76.8%

of Koreans in Chicago were affiliated with Korean churches. These empirical data indicate that church involvement is indeed a way of life for the majority of Koreans in the United States. By contrast, only 13% of the total population in South Korea in 1982, 18%–21% in 1986, and 25% in 2000 were reportedly churchgoers (Choi, 1999).

The propensity of Korean immigrants to establish a church is well expressed in a Korean anecdote (Kim, 1985): "When two Japanese get together, they set up a business firm; when two Chinese get together, they open a Chinese restaurant, and when two Koreans get together, they establish a church." This may be an overgeneralized and ethnocentric remark, but it appears to be associated with psychosocial, sociocultural, emotional, and spiritual needs stemming from Korean immigrants' experiences in the process of acculturation. Korean immigrants have become involved more actively in church activities, compared to their pre-immigrant years in Korea, perhaps because of their heightened needs for a communal bond, such as social belonging and psychological comfort, in socially and culturally different foreign environments. The theoretical implications of Korean immigrants' needs for church affiliation may be based on the notion of "the marginal man" (Gordon, 1964; Hughes, 1949; Park, 1928; Shin & Park, 1988). Gordon (1964) wrote that "the marginal man is the person who stands on the borders or margins of two cultural worlds but is fully a member of neither" (p. 64). From the marginality theory an argument can be derived that Korean immigrants feel not only "in between" or "on the boundary" but also "outside," or at the periphery of the mainstream culture (Lee, 1980). The comfort theory of religion (Glock, Ringer, & Babbie, 1967; Glock & Stark, 1965) may provide another perspective that explains the needs and motivations for Korean immigrants' overwhelming enthusiasm for involvement in church. The theory views religion as essentially providing comfort, serenity, and reassurance to those who are deprived, troubled, alienated, or disturbed (Greely, 1972). As the Black church has traditionally played a crucial role in not only providing its members with a refuge in an unfriendly and hostile White society but also in being the main arena of social life in which Blacks could aspire to become the leaders of their community (Frazier, 1974; Taylor, Thornton, & Chatters, 1987; Walls & Zarit, 1991), the Korean church is the primary source of comfort, belonging, emotional support, spiritual recharge, and information exchange for Korean immigrants (Hurh & Kim, 1984). Most of the Korean churches are small and play a role of surrogate family in meeting the congregation's needs for social interaction.

In a study that investigated religious participation of Korean Americans, Hurh and Kim (1990) tested four propositions. First, "religion becomes a way of life for Korean immigrants" (p. 22). Generally speaking, immigrants participate more actively and in greater numbers in religious activities in the host country than in their homeland. Second, "religion provides meaning, belonging, and comfort" (p. 22). Third, "mental health and life satisfaction of Korean immigrants are positively related to their participation in church" (p. 23). Fourth, "religion either promotes or slows mobility/assimilation" (p. 23). The first three propositions were supported by their empirical data. As other authors point out, church is one of the most important integral aspects of Korean immigrants' life (Kim, 1996; Kwon, Ebaugh, & Hagan, 1997; Min, 1990; Shin & Park, 1988).

Why does the Korean church occupy such an important place in the lives of Koreans residing in the United States? In addition to what has already been mentioned, the answer seems to be that the church, staffed by Korean speaking and educated ministers, serves the common interests of its congregants in ways that no other formal service agencies can do. As Kim (1982) argued, various Korean associations, such as Korean community associations, business associations, political associations, alumni associations, sports clubs, and so on, "are incomparable to the Korean churches in terms of function, influence, size and organizational structure" (p. 11). The Korean church has been the major center of ethnic identification and social interaction for Koreans throughout the history of their immigration to the United States. Responding to the needs of each wave of Korean immigrants, the church has performed different service roles at different times.

INFORMAL SERVICES PROVIDED BY KOREAN AMERICAN CHURCHES

Kim (1985) pointed out a few factors that make the Korean church unique for its members. First, Korean immigrants have organized churches to meet the need for a religious and ethnic fellowship, given their marginal socioeconomic status in the alien environment of urban America. Second, the inclusive nature of the church as a social community has attracted the participation of immigrants who seek a community with a "family atmosphere" for their psychosocial needs. Kim (1985) indicated that by serving as a surrogate for the extended family, "Korean churches have become a focus for strengthening the immigrants' psychological defenses against the dominant institutions and culture of the larger society" (p. 234) and have been a center of social morale for the immigrants' daily survival.

Helping New Immigrants

As soon as Korean immigrants arrive at a respective city for settlement, most of them make a visit to a Korean church. This is mainly because they are already well informed that the church is a place where they can meet other Koreans and where they can obtain the information they need in order to establish themselves.

The resources provided through a church network are particularly important to newcomer Korean immigrants. The church provides services, such as aid in opening a bank account, buying a car and auto insurance, getting a driver's license, finding housing, obtaining job referrals, child care referrals, social security information, translating services, making airport pickups, registering children for school, applying for citizenship, getting legal aid, offering English conversation classes, making an appointment with a doctor, offering family counseling services, and so on. This implies that the newcomers have significant service needs in these areas and that the Korean church pastors are currently the major gatekeepers for the newcomers. The services, provided mostly by the pastor and sometimes by volunteer church members are critical in helping newcomers facilitate the settlement process. The church is the most well-established social, cultural, and educational center for Koreans in the United States. It functions as a reception center for newly arrived immigrants and a shelter for the settlers. Regardless of age, gender, education, or socioeconomic status, the church is the most inclusive and accessible social service center for Korean immigrants.

Keeping Ethnic Identity Intact

The Korean church takes a significant role in helping the immigrants maintain their ethnic identity, cultural traditions, and language. For example, the Korean language and customs are more strictly observed inside the church than outside of it. Sermons, hymns, and liturgy are delivered in Korean for almost all adult worship services. Most churches run a Korean ethnic school to help children maintain "Koreanness." The school teaches Korean language, history, culture, heritage, folk dance, games, etiquette, music, and art so that ethnic identity can continue. Some churches offer these classes before or after the Sunday service, but others provide various programs on Saturday. Contributions that church language schools make to maintaining the language and culture are significant, particularly because there are only a few communitywide language schools not affiliated with the church and because most parents have little time to teach their children the language at home. Exposure to Korean culture at church is not limited to the Korean language. The Korean church is a primary institution helping Korean youths maintain their ethnic identity, language, and culture. All Korean immigrant churches celebrate religious and traditional holidays by serving a variety of Korean foods. On Korean holidays many people come to church in traditional Korean costumes to preserve the tradition. Churches teach children traditional values such as filial piety to help them grow with respect for their parents and grandparents.

Pastors often emphasize Korean values in their sermons. They tie their sermons to Korean national holidays, such as the March First Independence Movement Day and Independence Day. Churches help the congregants remember their homeland and Korean identity by inviting ministers and professors from Korea to give sermons or lectures. Min's (1990) survey found that 78% of Korean churches in New York have had at least one visiting preacher or lecturer from Korea over the last year. Through these activities, churches contribute to helping Korean immigrants maintain their cultural and ethnic identity.

Providing Emotional Support

In addition to practical, tangible services, the church also functions as a provider of emotional support. Korean immigrants find emotional comfort from the stress and pressures of their difficult lives in a culturally and socially new environment. They have no difficulty finding sympathetic listeners for their problems and struggles, who understand what they are going through because they have already been there before. The immigrants gather together in the church not only to meet their spiritual needs but to meet friends and to see new faces other than their family members and relatives. Missing their old formal and informal social networks in Korea, they come to church to get their unique social and emotional needs met. This may explain why a high proportion of Korean immigrants attend their ethnic churches regardless of their level of acculturation. This phenomenon calls the Korean church to be sensitive and responsive to the psychosocial needs of their ethnic group. Through the church, immigrants find friendships, a sense of security, and emotional support, in addition to addressing the existential meaning of life. The human need for spirituality and for belonging, comfort, and security appear to be met for Korean immigrants by attending their ethnic churches. Undoubtedly, the Korean church functions to buffer recent immigrants from culture shock and to help their settlement process with tangible and intangible support.

In addition to pastoral counseling, some big churches provide counseling services for domestic violence, juvenile delinquency, marital conflicts, alcohol/drug/gambling addiction, racial discrimination, and so on. One of the biggest concerns for the pastors is to provide family counseling and mental health services. Immigrants are often so preoccupied with problems of economic survival, in particular, during the first few years in their immigrant lives that they have little time to concern themselves with interpersonal problems. Thus, latent family problems emerge. The generation gap creates serious conflicts in the family when children embrace values that are incongruent with those held by their parents. The relationship between wife and husband becomes aggravated when the wife increases her economic independence as a contributor to family income. With limited church resources and limited counseling skills, pastors do their best to provide services for the family but often feel unprepared and inadequate.

Caring for the Elderly

Korean family values demand that children respect and honor their parents as well as all elderly. This value is strictly observed and any deviation is discouraged. Someone who refuses to accede to the wishes of the family and the community may be shunned, or even ostracized. A person who is disrespectful of his/her parents or the elderly is referred to as *Sangnom* (a beast). Filial piety is a theme that is at the heart of Korean family values. A young child is taught at home to show reverence to parents and grandparents. By the time the child reaches school age, it has already been inculcated in him/her to treat teachers with the same respect. In Korean culture, there are many ways to show filial piety to the elder. For example, the younger is expected to rise when an elder enters a room. The younger will not take a seat until the elder does so first. The younger must not drink alcoholic beverages, smoke a cigarette, speak in a loud tone of voice, or in any other way behave aggressively or inconsiderately in the presence of elders. The younger must always defer to their parents' ultimate ethical and moral guide. The notion of filial piety is not only limited to practice only within the family, but rather governs the relationship with elders in any social situation.

In the Korean church, the older adults are always the most courteously treated. The pastor and the lay leaders are sensitive to the needs of the older adults and do everything possible to accommodate them as much as possible. In responding to the traditional family values and the unique needs of the elderly living in the United States, Korean churches are actively involved in providing services for their elderly congregants. In a study that investigated the availability of church-based programs and activities for older adults, Choi and Tirrito (1999) found that a great deal of resources of Korean churches are directed toward serving the elderly. For example, of 34 Korean churches in the southeastern United States, pastoral home visits were the most frequently reported service program. Over 97% of churches reported providing regular pastoral visitation to older adults who are homebound. Other types of programs reported in the study include visitation for the hospitalized (94.1%), pastoral counseling (88.2%), helping older adults become actively involved in church affairs (88.2%), group tours (82.4%), making doctors' appointments (79.4%), providing transportation (76.5%), continuing education for affirming values and dignity of older adults (73.5%), seminars on physical health and mental health (26.5%), English class (26.5%), lectures on aging issues (17.6%), caregivers' training on stress management and care-burden (14.7%), and crafts (2.9%). The same study reported that only 13% of the older adults had visited social service agencies or had used social services, in spite of many unmet mental and social service needs.

The study by Choi and Tirrito (1999) indicates that older Korean adults derive much of their happiness with life from participation in church activities. The more frequently they attend Sunday services and church activities, the happier and more satisfied they are with life. Factors such as reading the Bible, praying, and listening to religious programs via radio, television, and tape also contribute to their happiness and satisfaction with life. The practice of prayer and its provision of sense of connection with God and with fellow church members may serve as a source of comfort, peace, strength, harmony, and support.

Choi and Tirrito (1999) observed a crucial role Korean church pastors play in providing services for older adults. Pastors set the tone in terms of the number and kinds of programs offered to the older congregants. The role of the pastor as program developer and service provider has important implications for practice. The use of Korean pastors as primary care providers and brokers to provide links with formal service agencies would be ideal. Formal service providers must develop a partnership with Korean churches to deliver cost-effective and culturally relevant services to Korean older adults. These approaches may warrant intervention research to substantiate the potential of Korean churches to augment formal service programs, as well as to identify barriers to formal service delivery.

Brokering for Korean Entrepreneurs

Many Koreans who immigrate to the United States are educated professionals, and their primary motive for immigration is to pursue a profession.
However, they soon find it impossible to translate their Korean credentials
into American careers and to communicate well in English with their
coworkers and bosses at work. Due to the reality that many obstacles are
stacked up against their ideas of becoming white-collar professionals, they
find another alternative, which is to open small businesses. Thus, a large
number of Korean immigrants, regardless of their background in Korea,
find themselves gravitating toward a small business for various reasons
(Min, 1983).

According to Min's (1991) survey in 1986, 75% of Korean immigrant
adults in Los Angeles and Orange County in California were either self-
employed or employed in Korean firms, and in New York City almost 86%
were also self-employed. Based on the reports of the U.S. Bureau of Census,
Yoon (1997) found that Korean immigrants showed the highest rate of
self-employment among 17 immigrant groups that came to the United
States between 1970 and 1980. The church is involved deeply in helping
Korean owned businesses. For example, churches make official announce-
ments during Sunday services about the opening of new businesses by
their members. Members who own a business often invite the pastor to
their shops to conduct a short service of blessing. The pastor in particular
helps the business owners hire newly arrived immigrants and advertise
their services and goods. The pastor pays a regular visit to each business
owned by his church members and often brings members in need of services
provided by a particular business enterprise. If a church member expresses
the need to buy a car, he/she is referred to a church member in the car
business. The business transaction usually takes place in a trusting and
courteous way. The buyer is often referred to another member in the
church in the car insurance business. If the church does not have a business
network within the church to help members meet their needs, the members
are often referred to Korean businesses owned by others outside the church.
This process of networking and referrals helps meet the needs of newcomers
who are unfamiliar with services in new surroundings. Newcomers receive
the support and services they require without going through the exhausting
and often discouraging process of searching for information and services
from people who do not understand Korean language and customs. Business owners, on the other hand, benefit from the business brought in
by the church's involvement. For the entrepreneurs serving the Korean

community, the church network system can generate an important pool of customers. The church also benefits from the business connections it facilitates as more people are attracted to the church.

It is apparent that the relationships between the Korean business community and the church are mutually beneficial. Newcomers benefit from receiving services from Korean businesses arranged through the church networking systems. The church also benefits by attracting members who use church networks for business and employment opportunities.

Facilitating Community Relations with Other Ethnic Groups

The friction between Koreans and the African Americans in Los Angeles in particular has become so contentious that it has led to physical assaults, destruction of property, even murder and civil disturbances. This heightened strife has directed national attention to the conflict. Sources of conflict between these two groups are complex and deeply rooted. Basically, Black residents accuse the Korean business owners of overcharging them for goods and services, blatant price gouging, discourteous and rude behavior, taking over Black businesses, taking dollars away from the Black community, and giving little back to the Black community. To such charges, Koreans have responded that the major cause of conflict is simply a misunderstanding caused primarily by the language barrier or cultural differences. They also insist that they are not taking over Black businesses in the community.

Both Korean and African American communities are church oriented, and thus pastors play important roles in both. Some Korean churches and pastors concerned about conflicts between Koreans and African Americans have acted to bridge the gap between the two groups. Korean churches have provided their congregants with seminars on Black culture and racial harmony and have set up scholarship programs for Black youths. Two Korean churches in Brooklyn, New York hired African American ministers for youth ministry. Korean churches in Los Angeles have made greater efforts to reduce intergroup tensions and facilitate communication with the African American community. Their efforts include cultural exchanges, joint religious services, and scholarship programs. For example, beginning in 1984, the Oriental Mission Church, the largest Korean congregation in the U.S., with over 7,000 members, has held several joint services and exchange of choirs with African American churches. Also since that time, the church continues to provide scholarships of $5,000 a year for African

American students (Min, 1996). Other churches have made contributions to African American residents and churches by donating Korean food, turkeys, and other charitable items. For example, Hebron Presbyterian Church, located in an African American neighborhood in Los Angeles, has given residents a Thanksgiving party with Korean food, traditional Korean songs, and traditional dances every year since 1988. More than 1,000 African American residents attended the party in 1990 alone (Min, 1996).

In February 1985, Korean and African American church leaders initiated a sister-church program in which about 20 Korean churches in Los Angeles would maintain close relationships with a similar number of African American churches through choir exchanges, joint services, and cultural exchanges (Dart, 1985). In 1985, about 130 Korean and African American churches participated in a joint Easter Sunday service held near Koreatown in Los Angeles (Chang, 1990). In 1991, Korean and African American church leaders established the African/Korean American Christian Alliance (AKACA) to improve the relationship between the two communities (Min, 1996). Thanks to the sponsor of AKACA, more than 3,000 Korean and African American Christians gathered together for reconciliation, dancing and singing together, hand in hand.

Even after the 1992 Los Angeles riots, Korean churches have continued to play a pivotal role not only in helping reduce Korean-African American tension, but also in building community-based programs for better relations with African American communities in Chicago, Los Angeles, New York, and other major cities. The Community Mediation Project (CMP) was initiated by the church to encourage Korean American merchants to play a more visible and active role in community affairs where their stores are located and to educate them on African American culture, customs, and history. Under the CPM, multiple programs were put together to build a strong and healthy relationship between the two communities. For example, geographic area committees have provided a common ground for Korean American merchants and African American residents to engage in face-to-face discussions and solve problems. As a way of supporting the community, a scholarship program was established for African American high school students. Cross-cultural exchange concerts, athletic programs, youth exchanges, journalistic exchanges, workshops and seminars, and joint worship services were initiated. Community policing began to strengthen a relationship with police by helping area police departments become more sensitive to the needs of the Korean merchants and African American residents. The Korean church continues to strive with its full strength to build a good relationship with other ethnic communities, in particular with the African American community, and to foster justice and equality inside and outside the Korean community.

IMPLICATIONS

The Korean church has been the primary mediating institution between Korean immigrants and their adjustment process to a new life in the United States and is the primary social service provider for their unmet needs to which formal service agencies are unable to respond. The difficulties that Korean immigrants face in their daily struggles lead them to turn to their pastors and churches for assistance. It appears that the critical shortage of professionally ethnic social service providers in the Korean community will insure the need for the Korean church to continue its present role in service delivery to Korean immigrants. It is imperative that the church continues to serve as a locus of preventive interventions that provide a variety of educational and supportive activities for the newcomers. Among such services should be an English language class to assist participants in their functioning in the community and orientation to American life, and in finding ways to acquire information on finding a job or establishing a business. Seminars geared toward teaching effective parent-child communication skills and to strengthening marital relationships can be provided to both the settled and newcomers after Sunday services. Educational programs must focus on helping immigrants to enhance their coping and adaptive skills.

Due to the lack of resources and trained human service professionals, Korean church-based service programs are run by paraprofessionals. In order to better serve its congregants and the Korean community as a whole, the church and the Korean business community are urged to provide scholarships to support Korean students who are seeking to enter the helping professions. Schools of social work should be encouraged to review their admission policies to insure that they are responsive to the needs of ethnic minority applicants.

In the resource development effort, special attention must be directed to the role of the Korean pastor's wife. Due to the unique role she plays in the Korean church, she becomes well aware of particulars in church members' families and enjoys their trust. She is the first person female church members usually contact when they have a personal or family problem. She is more readily available than the pastor and is less burdened with church mission. She can be trained to become not only a service provider but also an agent who can make referrals to professional service agencies on behalf of the families and individuals needing services that the church is not equipped to provide. The church's further involvement in service delivery requires linkage with community resources. For example, the church needs to consult with experienced and knowledgeable professionals for their suggestions before a program is developed. Thus, the church-based social services must advance from charitable work activities to professional services that are theory-guided and evidence-based. It is apparent that the Korean church is overburdened and is unable to cope with the expanding demand from a rapidly growing number of Korean immigrants. A linkage between the Korean church and formal service providers must be built and strengthened. Formal service providers can make much better use of the Korean church to provide preventive services and to identify those in need, by becoming their allies in service provision.

REFERENCES

Chang, E. (1990). *New urban crisis: Korean-Black conflicts in Los Angeles.* Unpublished doctoral dissertation, University of California, Berkeley.

Choi, G., & Tirrito, T. (1999). The Korean church as a social service provider for older adults. *Arete, 23*(2), 69–83.

Choi, M. (1999). *Korean churches and social welfare.* Seoul, S. Korea: Nanumeau Jeeb (in Korean).

Dart, J. (1985, November 9). Korean immigrants and blacks use churches as bridge to ease tensions. *Los Angeles Times,* p. 8.

Frazier, E. (1974). The Negro church: A nation within a nation. In R. Richey (Ed.), *Denominationalism* (pp. 209–226). Nashville: Abingdon.

Glock, C., Ringer, B., & Babbie, E. (1967). *To comfort and to challenge.* Berkeley: University of California Press.

Glock, C., & Stark, R. (1965). *Religion and society in tension.* Chicago: Rand McNally and Co.

Gordon, M. (1964). *Assimilation in American life: The role of race and national origins.* New York: Oxford University Press.

Greely, A. (1972). *Denominational society: A sociological approach to religion in America.* Glenview, IL: Scott, Foresman and Co.

Han, W. (1983). Quantitative growth of Korean church and the values of Korean Christians. In W. Han (Ed.), *The modernization of Korea and Christianity* (pp. 121–156). Seoul, S. Korea: Sungjon University (in Korean).

Hughes, E. (1949). Social change and status protest: An essay on the marginal man. *Phylon, 10,* 58–65.

Hurh, W., & Kim, K. (1984). *Korean immigrants in America: A structural analysis of ethnic confinement and adhesive adaptation.* Cranbury, NJ: Associated University Press.

Hurh, W., & Kim, K. (1988). *Uprooting and adjustment: A sociological study of Korean immigrants' mental health.* Final report submitted to the National Institute of Mental Health, US Department of Health and Human Services.

Hurh, W., & Kim, K. (1990). Religious participation of Korean immigrants in the United States. *Journal for the Scientific Study of Religion, 29*(1), 19–34.

Immigration and Naturalization Service. (1979). *Annual reports.* Washington, DC: Government Printing Office.

Jo, M. (1999). *Korean immigrants and the challenge of adjustment.* Westport, CT: Greenwood Press.

Kim, B. (1985). The explosive growth of the Korean church today: A sociological analysis. *International Review of Mission, 64*(293), 61–74.

Kim, B. L. (1978). *The Asian Americans: Changing patterns and changing needs.* Montclair, NJ: Association for Korean Christian Scholars in North America.

Kim, C. (1982). The way the Korean church should take. *The Koreans in America, 4*(9), 11–15.

Kim, I. (1985). Organizational patterns of Korean American Methodist churches: Denominationalism and personal community. In R. Richey & K. Rowe (Eds.), *Rethinking Methodist history* (pp. 54–76). Nashville, TN: Kingwood Books.

Kim, J. (1996). The labor of compassion: Voices of "churched" Korean American women. *Amerasia Journal, 22*(1), 93–105.

Kim, K., Warner, R., & Kwon, H. (2001). Korean American religion in international perspective. In II. Kwon, K. Kim, & R. Warner (Eds.), *Korean Americans and their religion* (pp. 3–24). University Park, PA: Pennsylvania State University.

Kwon, V., Ebaugh, H., & Hagan, J. (1997). The structure and functions of cell group ministry in a Korean Christian church. *Journal for the Scientific Study of Religion, 36*(2), 247–256.

Lee, S. (1980). *Called to be pilgrims: Toward a theology within the Korean immigrant context.* An unpublished mimeograph. Princeton Theological Seminary, Princeton, NJ.

Min, P. (1983). The Korean American family. In C. Mindell, et al. (Eds.), *Ethnic families in America: Patterns and variations* (pp. 88–103). New York: Elasevier Press.

Min, P. (1990). The structure and social functions of Korean immigrant churches in the United States. *International Migration Review, 26*(4), 1370–1394.

Min, P. (1991). Cultural and economic boundaries of Korean ethnicity: A comparative analysis. *Ethnic and Racial Studies, 14*(2), 225–241.

Min, P. (1996). *Caught in the middle: Korean merchants in America's multiethnic cities.* Berkeley, CA: University of California Press.

Park, R. (1928). Human migration and the marginal man. *American Journal of Sociology, 33,* 881–893.

Ro, B. (1983). Non-spiritual factors in church growth. In B. Ro & M. Nelson (Eds.), *Korean church explosion.* Seoul, S. Korea: Word of Life Press (in Korean).

Shin, E., & Park, H. (1988). An analysis of causes of schisms in ethnic churches: The case of Korean-American churches. *Sociological Analysis, 49*(3), 234–248.

Taylor, R., Thornton, M., & Chatters, L. (1987). Black American's perceptions of the sociohistorical role of the church. *Journal of Black Studies, 18*(2), 123–138.

U.S. Department of Commerce. (2001). *Census 2000: Profile of general demographic characteristics for the United States.* Washington, DC: U.S. Government Printing Office.

Walls, C., & Zarit, S. (1991). Informal support from black churches and the well-being of elderly blacks. *The Gerontologist, 31*(4), 490–495.

Yoon, I. (1997). *On my own.* Chicago, IL: The University of Chicago Press.

Yun, Y. (1979). Early history of Korean immigration to America. In H. Kim (Ed.), *The Korean diaspora.* Santa Barbara, CA: Clio Press.

Chapter 10

THE FAITH-BASED COMMUNITY ACTION MODEL

Terry Tirrito

The basic philosophy of this book is that faith-based organizations should be and can be involved in community action programs. From the literature, practice wisdom, and current political trends, it is clear that faith-based organizations can fill an essential role in providing programs and services to local communities.

The Faith-Based Community Action (FBCA) model is a method that faith-based organizations can use to develop community action programs. Adapted from community organization principles, this 12-step model provides faith-based organizations with a step-by-step plan for community action programs. In an effort to identify the variations in perceptions of different position-holders regarding the need for faith-based programs, the author met with church leaders, congregation members, and agency leaders. During discussions with these various groups, the conversation often moved to this issue: *How* does a church implement community action programs? Community planning models in the social work literature present several approaches for assessment and identification of community needs and for empowering community groups into social action (Rothman, 1979; Weil & Gamble, 1995). Some scholars believe that church members, church leaders, social activists, or academics should take responsibility for developing and initiating community action programs in faith-based organizations (Wineburg, 2001). Church leaders, academics, and social activists are important in the process, but a significant barrier for these community activists has been the absence of a method to develop community action programs. The FBCA model was developed for this purpose. Although the FBCA model in this chapter illustrates the development of community action programs for older adults, it is a model that can be used to develop faith-based community action programs for any constituency.

RELIGION AND COMMUNITY ACTION PROGRAMS

The social importance of religion has been debated for centuries. Philosopher Emile Durkheim describes religion as "something eminently social" (Durkheim, 1915/1961, p. 22). Durkheim believed that religious organizations have a function "to help us live" and that "nearly all the great social institutions have been born in religion" (p. 466). Historically, religion has been intertwined with social institutions and the church was a provider of services for the poor, the elderly, the orphaned, and the needy. Simmons (1991) states that it would be immoral not to help those in need. Moberg (1962) describes the function of the church as a social institution that supports and reinforces the functions of other basic institutions in society. If local citizens, clergy, agency planners, or scholars choose to look closely at the evolution of human services in communities across the United States, they would find that the path has been laid for bringing religious, government, and private nonprofit agencies to the planning table (Wineburg, 2001, p. 32).

While politicians argue the pros and cons regarding the provision of social services by religious organizations, President Bush is leading an initiative to bring faith-based social services to local communities. The end of welfare as we knew it in the 1990s resulted in cuts in food stamp programs, Supplemental Social Insurance, Medicaid, and child welfare programs. The government is struggling to provide for the social needs of its citizens, as the author will demonstrate is the situation for older adults in the United States. The devolution revolution indicates a trend in governments, both national and state, to move the provision of social services to the local level though local communities can not afford to provide services (Sherman & Viggiani, 1996). Religious organizations can provide these services.

FAITH-BASED ORGANIZATIONS, SOCIAL SERVICES, AND OLDER ADULTS

In the United States there are 34,933,000 persons over 65 years of age and 4,368,000 over 85 years of age, with 68,000 persons over 100 years of age

(U.S. Census, 2000). Improved medical care contributed to longer life spans while increases in Medicare and Medicaid spending demonstrate that it is not clear where funding will be found for future geriatric health care.

Eighty percent of persons 65 and older are members of a church or synagogue, and 52% attend church at least once a week (Koenig & Weaver, 1998). Some studies report a strong link between religiosity and life satisfaction (Koenig, Smiley, & Gonzales, 1988). Religious older persons are happier, have better coping mechanisms and better physical and mental health than those who are not religious (Johnson, 1995). Koenig and colleagues documented the positive association between religion and health, particularly mental health, in studies from Duke University (Koenig, 1995). The literature is clear that clergy are very often the first persons contacted when families are in crisis (Gulledge, 1992).

A review of the literature clearly documents the importance of the church in the lives of older adults and the reluctance of older adults to use current community social services (especially community mental health services) (Koenig & Weaver, 1998) and their willingness to use social services in their religious organizations. In one study over 70% of the older adult respondents reported a willingness to attend programs at their places of worship (Tirrito & Spencer-Amado, 2000).

Thibuault, Ellor, and Netting (1991) found evidence that older adults, particularly ethnic older persons, underutilized community social services. Koenig, George, and Schneider (1994) found that older adults infrequently use community mental health services and consequently, older adults are more likely to go untreated for depression, dementia, and alcohol and drug abuse. While 10% to 30% of older adults have emotional problems that are reversible when treated, less than 20% of older adults with a mental health diagnosis receive treatment. This treatment can be provided by mental health clinics in places where older adults are comfortable. In 1957 and 1976, seminal studies reported that high church attendees were more open to the use of professional help for psychological problems. Older persons (aged 55 and over) who attended church regularly were more likely to accept formal help for problems. The researchers reasoned that devout elderly persons may have a trusting relationship with members of the clergy (Veroff, Kulka, & Douvan, 1981).

Simmons proposes that the church family "may be called on to serve as surrogate family for the treatment of a variety of ills which the family of birth is unable to handle" (Simmons, 1991, p. 24). The church has a long history of support and aid to social problems (Taylor, 1993; Tobin, Ellor, & Anderson-Ray, 1986).

It seems logical that since religious institutions serve an important role in the lives of older persons, the church is the ideal place to provide these social services. The programs traditionally provided by community social agencies, such as family counseling, mental health counseling, crisis counseling, support groups, respite services, educational programs, caregiver training, and a variety of health and nutritional programs can be made available by faith-based organizations. With an increase in the aging population and the gap created by cuts in public funding, the religious organization can play a critical role in filling this gap as a service provider for older adults. As stated by Simmons (1991), "If we don't, who will? The church has a moral responsibility to provide for its community."

FAITH-BASED HUMAN SERVICES AND PROGRAMS

Religious organizations are sometimes defined as ontological communities that symbolize communities of meaning. Ontological communities often become the heart of a community (Bruggemann, 2002). Ontological religious communities are cultural, social, and ethnic centers for members of particular groups such as Muslims, Jews, Asians, or African Americans.

Religious institutions form the largest network of voluntary associations in U.S. society. Statistical data report about 500,000 local churches, synagogues, temples, and mosques in the United States (Bruggemann, 2002). Ontological communities can supplement missing components of modern life. When primary social systems fail, ontological communities fill the gap. In some cities of the Northeast, the bulk of social services are provided by religious organizations (Bruggemann, 2002).

There is evidence that religion is significant in the lives of people of all cultures but the church is a very integral part of the support networks of African Americans and Hispanic Americans (Atchley, 1998). A study of over 1,800 Hispanic Americans reports that Hispanic Americans over age 55 were twice as likely to seek help from the church than from any other community agency (Koenig & Weaver, 1998).

Billingsley (1999) surveyed nearly a thousand Black churches across the country to examine social service activities provided by African American churches. He found a variety of programs, including family support, parenting, substance abuse, youth-at-risk, role-modeling, job training, and financial assistance. The Brookland Baptist Church of South Carolina developed a credit union to provide funds for its members to start small minority businesses (Billingsley, 1999, p. 190). In the Black community religion is a major social, political, and economic force.

In ethnic neighborhoods the religious organization actively helps immigrants from various ethnic groups to adapt to a new culture (Choi &

Tirrito, 1999). The religious organization serves as a community center providing social services for new families and a place where friendships and links are formed to ease adjustment into the new culture. Immigrants prefer help from religious organizations rather than government agencies (Choi & Tirrito, 1999). Religious organizations support and build housing for the elderly, the handicapped, and the poor. In cities and in rural areas religious organizations provide new homes, housing loans, and refurbished housing. Faith-based organizations support and staff day care programs, respite care programs, and shelters. St. Joseph's Respite Program in Columbia, South Carolina, will be discussed later in this chapter.

Around the world, faith-based organizations provide social services to communities. Cnaan, Wineburg, and Boddie (1999) and Wineburg (2001) conducted studies to determine the extent to which religious organizations are involved in the provision of social services in two cities in the United States: Greensboro, North Carolina and Philadelphia, Pennsylvania. The studies found that the religious community is extensively involved in the delivery of social services. The Greensboro study examined community social service delivery in a small southern city and reported the following:

- 84% of responding congregations offered at least one in-house service, such as counseling.
- 39% offered services to members of the community.
- 89% had counseling services.
- 34% housed programs such as Alcoholics Anonymous, Narcotics Anonymous, Al-Anon, Alateen, and/or Overeaters Anonymous.
- 87% provided volunteers for shelters and feeding programs.
- 44% worked with neighborhood groups.
- 40% gave food to the food bank.

In a 1996–1998 study of religious-based service provision in Philadelphia, congregations were asked to identify from a list of 200 social and community programs their participation in these programs. Twenty-five percent to 58% of congregations were involved in social and community programs in Philadelphia (Cnaan et al., 1999).

Several examples of faith-based social services in the literature include New York City's Partnership for the Homeless, started in 1982, by a handful of religious leaders. It addresses the needs of the overwhelming number of homeless persons in that city. The Oakhurst Baptist Church in Atlanta inspired over 70 other congregations to provide services for the homeless in Atlanta. Catholic orders of nuns and brothers provide church-based services for people with mental health problems including Alzheimer's disease, child welfare programs, and health services. The First Baptist Church in Philadelphia provides Alcoholics Anonymous and Narcotics Anonymous programs for an average of 500 persons a day (Cnaan et al., 1999). An innovative program is the Willow Creek program in Illinois which offers an active car repair service. Weekend repairmen repair the cars of fellow parishioners who cannot afford professional services. In 1993 this congregation gave away 85 automobiles to poor single mothers (Cnaan et al., 1999). Confiscated drug money funds community programs, according to the Daytona Beach News Journal, June 14, 2002. Drug money seized by law enforcement has been donated to support Florida's Sheriff's Youth Ranch ($20,000) and the House Next Door counseling center ($10,000). Other community organizations are targeted for these drug forfeiture funds (http://www.n-jcenter.com/2002/Jun/14/V3.htm). These programs are community programs.

RESOURCES OF RELIGIOUS ORGANIZATIONS

In the United States, religious communities are involved in social service programs "to a degree unimagined and unacknowledged" (Cnaan et al., 1999, p. 157).

The Protestant church, the Catholic church, Buddhist temples, and Muslim mosques can play vital roles in providing social services to congregations and communities. Rozen developed a typology of churches and describes some congregations as Civic-Oriented (Wineburg, 2001).The FBCA model helps civic-oriented churches and community leaders to develop collaborative partnerships in their communities. Seven assets that a faith community can offer to its community partners are

1. Mission to Serve—Faith communities bring a mission to help those in need.
2. Pool of Volunteers—Communication through sermons and newsletters and committee structure with missions to help those in need.
3. Sacred Space—Usable space for community meetings and community activities.
4. Funding Potential—Raising funds for designated causes.
5. Political Strength—Large numbers of people.
6. Moral Authority—Moral influence and a value system.
7. Creativity and Experimentation—Partnerships can encourage experimentation and creative programs (Wineburg, 2001, p. 3).

Faith-based organizations can develop programs that prevent, intervene in, and ameliorate social problems, for example, bereavement groups, divorce, caregiving, and drug and alcohol abuse support groups. Some religious places provide space for Alcoholics Anonymous meetings (Cnaan et al., 1999). Religious places can be used as counseling centers, respite programs, support groups, and/or referral centers. They can offer educational programs for health promotion and nutritional or exercise programs.

Most religious congregations include professionals from various disciplines such as medicine, nursing, law, business, pharmacy, social work, and allied health disciplines. These people can be invaluable to a community action program based in a religious organization. In the United States, religious communities are involved in social service programs "to a degree unimagined and unacknowledged" (Cnaan et al., 1999, p. 157) but many more can become involved. The question is this: How do we begin?

COMMUNITY PLANNING

Comprehensive local planning is essential in building partnerships with religious organizations. Wineburg (2001) urges the academic community to participate in faith-based community programs and recommends areas of research to develop partnerships. He suggests studies to provide information on

1. Understanding emerging and historical partnerships at the local level between the religious community and social service providers.
2. Learning more about the capacities of congregations and faith-based charities to handle more service responsibilities, and building those capacities.
3. Deciphering the process by which faith-based organizations choose to become involved in volunteering and providing other resources for community projects.
4. Evaluating the effectiveness of involvement in community projects for the client, faith-based organizations, other members of the partnership, and the local community.
5. Determining outcomes—whether the effort solved, managed, or prevented the problems it was designed to tackle.
6. Understanding and delineating the roles and functions of faith-based organizations.
7. Determining training requirements.

8. Measuring costs of service and contributions of volunteers and other in-kind resources.
9. Understanding how the interaction of the efforts noted above contribute to local policy development.
10. Comparing different communities in order to develop new and testable policy theory (Wineburg, 2001, pp. 48–49).

Community action planning models vary and include the social planning models, the community liaison models, and the community development models. Congregational decisions in community social issues are not random ones and "a social ministry requires a need to be identified and that someone, usually a leader in the congregation advocates for a service to be delivered and developed" (Cnaan et al., 1999, p. 239). Random selection of programs is haphazard. Planning is essential for community action programs.

In a Philadelphia study researchers found that those persons who were most influential in initiating social service programs were the clergy (49.44%), followed by individual members (33.71%), congregational committees (16.85%), and staff members (14.61%) (Cnaan et al., 1999). The following community practice models are most popular in the literature and are described in Table 10.1.

The Faith-Based Community Action model includes

• concepts from the above planning models;
• methods that are useful in faith-based organizations involved in community action planning;
• concepts relating specifically to the implementation of community action plans for faith-based organizations; and
• approaches to determining community views.

DETERMINING COMMUNITY VIEWS

Determining community views is critical to community action planning for faith-based organizations. A planning model cannot be successful without input from community members and an assessment of the community's needs. Three community group approaches are commonly referred to in the literature to determine community views. One of these approaches can be used to achieve consensus regarding community needs.

TABLE 10.1 Current Models of Community Practice for Social Work

Comparative Characteristics	Neighborhood and Community Organizing	Organizing Functional Communities	Community Social and Economic Development	Social Planning	Program Development and Community Liaison	Political and Social Action
Desired Outcome	Develop capacity of members to organize; change the impact of citywide planning and external development.	Action for social justice focused on advocacy and on changing behaviors and attitudes; may also provide service.	Initiate development plans from a grass-roots perspective; prepare citizens to make use of social and economic investments.	Citywide or regional proposals for action by elected body or human services planning councils.	Expansion or redirection of agency program to improve community service effectiveness; organize a new service.	Action for social justice focused on policy or policy makers.
System Targeted for Change	Municipal government: external developers; community members.	General public; government institutions.	Banks; foundations; external developers; community citizens.	Perspectives of community leaders; perspectives of human service leaders.	Funders of agency programs; beneficiaries of agency services.	Voting public; elected officials; inactive/potential participants.

(continued)

TABLE 10.1 (*continued*)

Comparative Characteristics	Neighborhood and Community Organizing	Organizing Functional Communities	Community Social and Economic Development	Social Planning	Program Development and Community Liaison	Political and Social Action
Primary Constituency	Residents of neighborhood, parish, or rural county.	Like-minded people in a community, region, nation or across the globe.	Low-income, marginalized, or oppressed population groups in a city or region.	Elected officials; social agencies and interagency organizations.	Agency board or administrators; community representatives.	Citizens in a particular political jurisdiction.
Scope of Concern	Quality of life in geographic area.	Advocacy for a particular issue.	Income, resource and social support development, improved basic education and leadership skills.	Integration of social needs into geographic planning in public arena; human services network coordination.	Service development for a specific population.	Building political power; institutional change.

Adapted from Weil, M., & Gamble, N. (1995). Community practice models. In R. Edwards (Ed.), *Encyclopedia of Social Work* (19th ed., Vol. 1, pp. 577–593). Washington, DC: National Association of Social Workers.

1. *Community Forum.* This approach consists of an open meeting to which all members of the community are invited and at which all participants are urged to present their views regarding the human service needs in a particular social service area.

2. *Nominal Group Approach.* The nominal group approach is principally a noninteractive workshop designed to maximize creativity and productivity and to minimize the argumentative style of problem-solving and competitive discussion.

In this format a select group of community residents is invited to share group subject views regarding community needs or to identify barriers to relevant, effective human service delivery in a social service area. The nominal group approach is most appropriate to obtain citizen and consumer input into the need assessment and program planning process.

3. *Delphi Approach.* This approach to need identification includes the development of a questionnaire, that is then distributed to a panel of resource persons and/or a select group of community residents whose opinions on a particular issue or issues are highly valued. From their responses, a perspective can be derived regarding the human service needs of the community. This technique is quite useful and most appropriate when respondents have a minimal amount of time available for an identification effort.

Another popular method for determining community ideas is the Community Impressions Method. Three steps to this assessment procedure approach are a) a small but representative group of individuals is interviewed regarding their views of human service needs; b) this information is then integrated with existing data taken from public records and other assessment efforts to yield a richer understanding of the community needs; and c) the resulting community portrait is then validated and/or revised according to information gained from various groups in the community through the community forum process (Tropman, Erlich, & Rothman, 1995). Any of these approaches can determine the views of community residents.

The FBCA model adapted material from Cohn's Community Impressions Approach (Tropman et al., 1995). This approach gathers data on the group in a community with the greatest human service needs and the community's impressions about those needs. First, key informants offer impressions of those persons living and working in the community. Next, the information is integrated into existing data from a variety of sources. Last, the group identified as having the greatest human service needs, verifies the findings in a community forum.

The Community Impressions Approach is particularly useful with religious organizations because it includes key players in the congregation and the community. The planning group can move ahead with the confidence that needs are correctly identified, meet the expectations of community members, and have the support of local community agencies.

Case Example: A Respite Program at St. Joseph's Church

St. Joseph's Respite Program in Columbia, South Carolina, began in 1994. Sister Andrea Callahan began and continues to direct the Respite Program. Sister Andrea was interviewed for this book to determine the steps that she used in developing this successful program, which is a citywide model program local faith-based organizations are replicating (personal communication, June 2001). Sr. Andrea states that she was intuitively using some of the steps of this model but she would have avoided mistakes and used her time more effectively if she had been aware of this type of model. Sr. Andrea did not have any previous training in program development.

Sr. Andrea describes her church leader as a visionary leader who understands the needs of older persons in the community. When she was assigned as the Director of Senior Ministry, she called together a planning group from members of the congregation to determine the needs of the community. From this planning group, it was evident that the community needed a respite program. Sr. Andrea and the members of the group consulted with a gerontology expert in the community, met with community leaders from the state Department of Aging, Council of Aging representatives, professionals, and community older persons.

An advisory board of 15 members was created. The board meets 1 to 2 hours each month to assess the program, develop marketing strategies, and to develop gerontological education workshops for the community. The board members are ethnically and religiously diverse. They prepare a monthly schedule of volunteers and invite experts to work with the participants from the fields of music and art, exercise, nutrition, and health. The respite program meets once a week and 6 to 8 people attend each week. Over the years about 30 persons have participated in the respite program. Volunteers from the church's congregation receive training regarding the needs of frail older adults and methods for interaction with the participants. The program is well established and strongly supported by the pastor, as well as the entire church community.

The program has its own house with furnishings donated by the members of the congregation. The program is free of charge to any member of the community. Participants who are accepted require constant supervision, are sufficiently mobile to participate in activities, and can meet basic hygiene needs with minimal help. Volunteers provide supervision and companionship, working in pairs to lead activities at St. Joseph's Respite House.

Crucial to success of all programs is the leadership role of the church leader, pastor, minister, and rabbi, or members of the congregation. The members of the advisory board are leaders from social agencies and other interfaith programs. Sr. Andrea frankly admits to floundering in numerous directions in her efforts to develop this program. Sr. Andrea intuitively used some of the concepts included in the FBCA model to develop St. Joseph's Respite Program.

THE FAITH-BASED COMMUNITY ACTION (FBCA) MODEL

The Faith-Based Community Action (FBCA) model includes concepts from several community planning models that are applicable to faith-based organizations planning community action programs. (Figure 10.1 lists the 12 steps involved in the FBCA model.) In Step One, the forming of a planning group is based on the models that intend to develop the capacity of members to organize for change.

In Step Two, the faith-based organization must determine its priorities and capabilities to undertake community action programs. The commitment of church leaders and parishioners is essential for success. Developing a network of relationships (Step Three) is based on coalition-building principles for community action programs. Building a multi-organizational power base to influence program direction or draw on resources is essential in community planning.

Planning a flexible agenda (Step Four) allows for community and congregational input, permits ownership of the project, allows for critical evaluation of the planning process and incorporates diversity in the planning process. Taking steps in defining the community problem to be addressed (Step Five) is basic community planning practice. Deciding on a community action program with consensus and recognition of the limitations of resources (Step Six) is realistic and incremental social planning. Asking for commitment and support from key persons in the community and congregation (Step Seven) ensures a collaborative effort to support the project and ensures resources will be available for the project.

Involving community agencies (Step Eight) develops additional resources from local government and state officials as well as community

FIGURE 10.1   The Faith-Based Community Action model.

Step One	Form a planning group.
Step Two	Define the church's mission in meeting community needs.
Step Three	Develop a network of relationships.
Step Four	Plan a flexible agenda.
Step Five	Define the community problem.
Step Six	Decide on a community action program.
Step Seven	Ask for commitments and support from key persons.
Step Eight	Involve community agencies.
Step Nine	Investigate other churches with similar programs.
Step Ten	Involve as many church members as possible.
Step Eleven	Prepare alternative solutions. (Preparing alternative solutions allows members to select other programs that may be more useful to the congregation.)
Step Twelve	Monitor, evaluate, and provide feedback.

Step One: Form a Planning Group

Determine the needs of the community and interest in community action programs.

1. Invite community leaders, church leaders, members of the congregation.
2. Use the Community Impressions Model and invite key informants to discuss their views of community needs.

Step Two: Define the Church's Mission in Meeting the Community's Needs

Essential questions for congregations to ask themselves and their church leaders determine the church leaders' and members' willingness to become involved in community action programs.

FIGURE 10.1   (continued)

1. Determine whether the church's mission is a social mission or a spiritual mission.
2. Is this a civic-oriented church?
3. Is this a church whose mission is evangelical and proselytizing?

Step Three: Develop a Network of Relationships

A network of relationships is essential for successful community action programs.

1. Develop an advisory board of members.
2. Ten to fifteen members are recommended for a cohesive group.
3. Select members from the congregation, from other churches, from community agencies, and from business and political arenas.
4. Select those who are interested in community action and who are willing to commit time and resources to the project.

Step Four: Plan a Flexible Agenda

Being prepared with an agenda that includes examples from other community action programs is efficient and convincing that faith-based community action programs can be successful.

1. Develop an agenda of service needs for persons in the community but be prepared to change some of the program planning.
2. Be flexible and listen to community members.

Step Five: Define the Community Problems but Select One Problem for Action

After a comprehensive assessment of the community's needs, select one group and one problem for action. A lack of focus and resources that are not used wisely will contribute to failure.

FIGURE 10.1   *(continued)*

1. Define the community's needs but agree on one problem.
2. Do not try to solve all of the community's problems.
3. Select one problem to be addressed and gather information from experts about causes and solutions.

Step Six: Decide on a Community Action Program

The experts in the community can provide information on successful and unsuccessful programs. Decide on a program that is feasible at the present time.

1. Select professional volunteers in the community to take active roles in the implementation of the solution. For example, nurses, doctors, lawyers, social workers, and business leaders in the congregation.
2. Choose a community action program to implement, with agreement and commitment from the members.

Step Seven: Ask for Commitments and Support From Key Persons

When the program is selected, include as many members of the community as possible for supportive roles.

1. Seek support from church administration for space, advertising, outreach efforts, volunteers, et cetera.
2. Use designated church space for meetings, et cetera.
3. Use newsletters to reach congregation for donations and volunteers and to provide ongoing information about the program.
4. Use volunteers to help with securing community support.

Step Eight: Involve Community Agencies in the Planning Process

Community agencies are essential to provide additional services beyond the scope of faith-based organizations. Their collaboration is essential for success.

FIGURE 10.1 *(continued)*

1. Involve a community agency and arrange for consultations by professionals for follow-up for referrals or treatment interventions.
2. Some examples are health screenings, medication checks, a mental health clinic, Alzheimer's referral center, or a geriatric assessment clinic.

Step Nine: Investigate Other Churches, Synagogues, Temples, Mosques With Similar Programs

Learning from other programs avoids costly mistakes. Duplication of services is not cost effective.

1. Assess the possibility for collaboration and interfaith coalitions. Investigate to find whether there are similar programs in other neighborhoods or nearby cities.
2. Consider collaboration with other groups.
3. Collect materials from other programs.
4. Visit other programs if possible.

Step Ten: Involve as Many Church Members as Possible in a Collaborative Coalition

Collaboration is key in community action programs. Involvement of members and community leaders is an essential ingredient to success.

1. Present the plan to the community, to church members, and to decision makers, like local business leaders, local politicians.
2. Gather support from as many as possible.

Step Eleven: Prepare Alternative Solutions for Reaching the Goal

Alternative solutions may be necessary. Have other options prepared and commitments from community providers for alternative solutions.

FIGURE 10.1 *(continued)*

Step Twelve: Monitor, Evaluate, and Provide Feedback

Monitoring is necessary to evaluate results of the program. Positive and negative results must be provided to key players to determine whether goals were met.

1. Provide feedback to the church leaders, community planners, and community agencies.
2. Questions to ask are: How is the program working? What are the positives and negatives? How can services be improved?

These twelve steps offer a method for faith-based organizations to implement community action programs. This model incorporates basic principles of community planning and adapts these principles for faith-based organizations.

---

policy makers. Investigating other programs (Step Nine) and involving other churches in the project (Step Ten) ensures political support from key community members rather than competition and conflict. Evaluation (Step Twelve) is a key component of accountability and promotes support for continuing action-based programs.

SUMMARY

How a religious organization implements community action programs is the basis for the development of the Faith-Based Community Action Model. In examining the rationale for the religious organization as a service provider for older persons, the literature points to the failure of community agencies and the inability of government programs to provide needed social services. There is evidence that older persons appear to be receptive to programs and services based in religious organizations.

The FBCA model is a 12-step method that religious organizations can use to develop community action programs. The religious community has the potential to develop partnerships with the neighborhood community, but social planning is essential for effective partnering. While good intentions are critical, knowledge is essential.

REFERENCES

Atchley, R. (1998). The importance of being religious. *American Society on Aging Newsletter*, March/April, 9–12.

Billingsley, A. (1999). *Mighty like a river: The black church and social reform* (pp. 190–191). New York: Oxford University Press.

Bruggemann, W. G. (2002). *The practice of macro social work* (2nd ed.). New York: Brooks/Cole Publishing.

Choi, G., & Tirrito, T. (1999). The Korean church as a social service provider for older adults. *Arete*, 23(3), 69–83.

Cnaan, R., Wineburg, B., & Boddie, S. (1999). *The newer deal: Social work and religion in partnership*. New York: Columbia University Press.

Durkheim, E. (1915/1961). *The elementary forms of the religious life*. Translated by J. W. Swain. New York: Collier Books.

Gulledge, K. J. (1992). Gerontological knowledge among clergy: Implications for seminary training. *Educational Gerontologist*, 18, 636–644.

Koenig, H. G. (1995). *Research on religion and aging*. Westport, CT: Greenwood Press.

Koenig, H. G., George, L. K., & Schneider, R. (1994). Mental health care for older adults in the year 2020: A dangerous and avoided topic. *The Gerontologist*, 34(5), 674–679.

Koenig, H. G., Smiley, M., & Gonzales, J. (1988). *Religion, health and aging: A review of theoretical integration*. Westport, CT: Greenwood Press.

Koenig, H. G., & Weaver, L. (1998). Religion provides counseling tool. *American Society on Aging Newsletter*, March/April, 9–12.

Moberg, D. O. (1962). *The church as a social institution* (p. 445). Englewood Cliffs, NJ: Prentice Hall.

Rothman, J. (1979). Three models of community organization practice: Their mixing and phasing in. In F. Cox, J. L. Erlich, J. Rothman, & J. E. Tropman (Eds.), *Strategies of community organization* (4th ed., pp. 125–145). Itasca, IL: I. F. E. Peacock.

Sherman, L., & Viggiani, P. (1996). The impact of federal policy changes on children: Research needs for the future. *Social Work*, 41(6), 594–600.

Simmons, H. C. (1991). Ethical perspectives on church and synagogue as intergenerational support systems. *Journal of Religious Gerontology*, 7(4), 17–28.

Taylor, R. J. (1993). Religion and religious observances. In J. S. Jackson, L. M. Chatters, & R. Taylor (Eds.), *Aging in Black America*. Newbury Park, CA: Sage Publications.

Thibuault, J., Ellor, J., & Netting, F. (1991). A conceptual framework for assessing the spiritual functioning and fulfillment of older adults in long term care settings. *Journal of Religious Gerontology, 7*(4), 29–46.

Tirrito, T., & Spencer-Amado, J. (2000). A study of older adults' willingness to use social services in places of worship. *Journal of Religious Gerontology, 11*(2), 29–42.

Tobin, S., Ellor, J. W., & Anderson-Ray, S. (1986). *Enabling the elderly: Religious institutions within the community service system.* Albany, NY: State University of New York Press.

Tropman, J. E., Erlich, J. L., & Rothman, J. (Eds.). (1995). *Tactics and techniques of community intervention* (3rd ed.). Itasca, IL: Peacock Publishers, Inc.

Veroff, J., Kulka, R. A., & Douvan, E. (1981). *Mental health in America: Patterns of help-seeking from 1957–1976* (p. 108). New York: Basic Books.

Weil, M., & Gamble, D. (1995). Community practice models. In R. Edwards (Ed.), *Encyclopedia of social work* (19th ed., pp. 577–593). Washington, DC: NASW Press.

Wineburg, B. (2001). *A limited partnership: The politics of religion, welfare and social service.* New York: Columbia University Press.

U.S. Census. (2000). *Washington, D.C. Population Estimates Program, Population Division* [On-line]. Available: http://www.census.gov/population/estimates/nation/intfile2-1.txt

CONCLUSION

This book embarked on an ambitious mission. We have attempted to explore the scope and breadth of religious organizations in social work practice. We trace the origins of the social work profession back to the earliest of civilizations and their religious traditions. In this way, we demonstrate the inextricability of the profession from religious doctrine. We also examine how religion affects people as individuals. This book, as well as many other works in the professional literature, demonstrates the profound impact that religion has on the physical and emotional health of its adherents. This book also examines the similarities and differences between spirituality and religion as concepts and the current debates regarding these terms in the literature. Further, we explore the changes in religious and spiritual observance throughout the life cycle, demonstrating that this facet of life, like many others, is dynamic and interactive.

This book then takes a broader perspective and looks at the role of congregations in the wider community. It explores the many social welfare functions that religious organizations perform for their congregants as well as the community at large. Looking at this information, we see that religious provision of community services is not something that happened before the advent of the welfare state. Indeed, it is a current reality, and religious organizations are vital members of the welfare community, providing space for meetings, therapeutic services, soup kitchens, and financial assistance, among many others.

We explore this phenomenon in depth through the example of the Korean church. The author here demonstrates the invaluable assistance that the church provides to Korean immigrants, helping them to navigate the social welfare maze and acculturate to their new surroundings, not to mention providing valuable social support to a people very far from their native land. Based on this example and others like it, we also provide a model to facilitate social welfare systems and religious organizations to work together to provide important services in the best manner possible to people in need.

Finally, we explore the place of religion in social work education, demonstrating that the effect of religious organizations on social welfare extends beyond the general community to social work training as well.

In all of these ways, it has been our attempt to portray religious organizations in the social welfare arena as dynamic and vital. They are and always have been an integral part of the social welfare system. Despite people's objections to the commingling of religion and social welfare, this is a fruitful partnership, and services are extended to people who might otherwise not receive help. Furthermore, this aid, provided under religious auspices, is accepted by those who otherwise might choose to go without rather than approach the public social welfare system. Religious social welfare fulfills a vital need in the community. It is our obligation as social workers to provide services to people in a way that meets their needs, and in working with religious organizations, we come one step closer to reaching that goal.

INDEX

Abortion, 60, 121–122
Acupuncture, 85
Adams, John, 114
Addictions, sources of, 93–94, 96
Adolescents:
  delinquency, 119
  faith development in, 66–68
Adult day care, 43
Adulthood, faith development in, 68
Adult literacy education, 43
Adversity, impact of, 64–65, 70
Advocacy, paradenominational, 27
Aerobic classes, 43
Affirmative action, 118
Afghanistan, Christian conversion, 127
African American(s):
  churches, religious traditions, 35
  community relations, 165–166
  denomination research, 36
  faith-based social programs, 146–147
  social justice experience, 54–55
African American Church, 131
African/Korean American Christian Alliance (AKACA), 166
Agape, 12
Age cohort, in faith development, 70–71
Aging population, implications of, 54, 82, 172–173
Agrarian society, 5–6
Alcohol, regulation of, 123
Alcoholics Anonymous, 37, 176–177
Almsgiving, in Islam, 16

Altar healing, 98–99
Altruism, 3
American Association of Christian Counselors, 91–92
Anatomy of the Spirit (Myss), 85
Anxiety, sources of, 82, 96
Apostles, 13–14
Appenzeller, Henry G., 156
Arca, 10
Autonomous organizations, 141
Azusa Christian Community, 146

Baby boom generation, 64, 70–71, 73–74
Baptism, 102
Baptists:
  population statistics, 132
  religious traditions, 35
  social services, generally, 53, 116
Belief system, 67–68
Bible study, 56, 94, 144
Bill of Rights, 126
Bio-psycho-social approach, 86–88
Biotechnology, impact of, 64
Blood drives, 37
Blood transfusions, 103, 130
Brookland Baptist Church of South Carolina, 174
Bruner, Jerome, 92
Buddhists/Buddhism, 75, 114, 138
Burial, charitable, 10
Bush, George W., 119, 144–145, 172

Carter, Jimmy, 115
Catholic Charities, 115, 144
Catholic Youth Organization, 115, 118
Celibacy, 59
Center for Mind-Body Medicine, 85
Chaplains, 125, 128
Character development, 68
Charismatics, 92, 94, 98–99, 102–103
Charitable Choice, 143–144
Charitable giving, 148
Charity:
    Christian foundations, 9–14
    Islamic foundations, 14–18
    Jewish foundations, 3–8, 16
Charity Organization Societies, 140
Chesed, 138
Chicano movement, 56
Child care services, 59, 116
Children, faith development in, 66–67
Children's homes, 53, 115, 140
Child welfare programs, 172
Chinese Exclusion Act of 1882, 156
Chinese medicine, 81, 85
Christianity:
    baptism, 102
    in Korea, 155–156
    sacraments in, 85
    in South Korea, 156
Christian Science, 130
Chronological aging, implications of, 74
Church attendance:
    aging population, 173
    demographic research, 31, 34
    faith development and, 69–70
    importance of, 94–95
    mental health and, 101
    volunteerism and, 42
Church of England, 114
Church of Scientology, 125
Church of the Latter Day Saints, 53,
    132, 141
Church-state separation:
    abortion, 121–122
    importance of, 120–121
    out of the mainstream religions,
        125–126

prayer in school, 123–124
religious displays, 124–126
Sabbath observation, 122–123
secular agencies and, 141–144
specific prohibitions and rights,
    127–129
stem cells, 121–122
taxation, 125
Civic-oriented congregations, 176
Civic society, 149
Clothing closets programs, 37–38
Cnaan, Ram A., 145–146
Cognitive development, 63, 66, 69
Cold War, 156
Committee meetings, 43
Community action, faith-based:
    case example, 182–183
    community planning, 177–178
    community views, determination of,
        178, 181–182
    current models, 179–180
    development of, 171–172
    human services and programs,
        174–176
    older adults and, 172–174
    religious organizations resources,
        176–177
Community action programs, religion
    and, 172
Community centers, 175
Community chests, 18
Community Forum, community action
    planning, 181
Community Impressions Method, com-
    munity action planning, 181–182
Community Mediation Project (CMP),
    166
Community planning, 177–178
Community relations, Korean American
    Church, 165–166
Community-serving congregations, 146
Compassion, 19
Complacency, 73
Complementary and alternative medi-
    cine, 83
Congregations, American:

contributions, economic value of, 43–44

core activities of, 28–29

defined, 25–26

demographics of, 30–31

ethnicity, 35–36

facilities, 25, 42–43, 45

importance of, 23–24, 44–46

number of, 32–33

outreach programs, 28, 36–39

religious organizations, relationships with, 26–28

religious traditions, 35

scholarly study, 29–30

size of, 33–34

social work, 24, 39–44

volunteerism, 26, 40–42, 45

Conjunctive Faith phase, faith development, 67

Conscience development, 71

Consciousness, altered states of, 85

Consumption, 140

Contraception, 54, 122

Coping:
  in the elderly, 82
  religious, 69, 95

Council of Jewish Federations, 141

Council of Social Work Education, 118

Counseling services, 175, 177

Crisis, religious interpretation, 100

Cults, 125

Daily devotionals, 94

Day care programs, 37, 43, 145, 175

Death and dying, spirituality in, 83–84

Delphi Approach, community action planning, 181

Demographic research, American congregations, 30–31

Denominations, demographic studies, 31

Depression, sources of, 93–94, 96

Direct service congregations, 37–38

Divine healing, 103

Drug and alcohol prevention programs, 37, 53

Durkheim, Emile, 172

Early Childhood, faith development in, 67

Eastern Orthodox, religious traditions, 35

Eastern religions, 83

Ecumenical coalitions, 27

Ego, 68

Elderly:
  community action programs, 172–174
  faith development, 70–71
  Korean immigrants, 162–163

Ellis, Albert, 91

Emergency relief services, 36–38, 59

Emotional support, 161–162

Emotion-experience-centered theology, 99–100

Empowerment:
  importance of, 86, 147, 149
  Latino population, 57
  women, 59

End-of-life care, 83

Energy healing, 85–86

Enlightened teamwork, 87

Enlightenment, 71

Entrepreneurs, brokering for, 164–165

Episcopal Church, 116

Erikson, Erik, 75

Ethnic diversity, 35

Ethnic identity, 160–161

Ethnicity, 35–36, 131. See also specific ethnic groups

Evangelicals, 92

Evangelistic work, 40

Existential well-being, 71–72, 74–76

Exposure, spiritual, 71

Extrinsically religious, 96

Facilities, for congregations, 25, 42–43, 45

Faith:
  development stages, 66–76
  significance of, 65–66

Faith-based community action (FBCA) model:
  community planning, 178

Faith-based community action (FBCA)
   model (*continued*)
   components of, 176, 183–188
   development of, 171–172, 181, 183
Faith-Based Initiative, 119, 172
Faith Communities Today (FCT), 36
Faith healers, 103
Federal responsibility, 149
Federalist Papers, The, 120–121
Fellowship, 29
Filial piety, 162
Financial assistance programs, 38
First Amendment interpretations,
   142–143
First Baptist Church, Philadelphia, 176
Five Pillars of Islam, 15
Food pantries, 37–38
Food service programs, 38
Food stamp programs, 172
Forgiveness, 72
Freedom of religion, 113–114, 121, 127,
   138, 142
Freeman, Richard, 146
Freud, Sigmund, 72, 75, 91, 103
Fundamentalist Christians, 120
Future of Illusion (Freud), 103

Gay population, social justice experi-
   ence, 59–60
Gender differences, faith development,
   69, 71
General Social Survey (GSS), 34
Glynn, Patrick, 70
God:
   existence of, 4, 71–72, 76
   faith development, 66–68
   patriarchal, 4
   relationship with, 68–69, 102–103
God the Evidence (Glynn), 70
Golden Rule, 11, 13
Good Samaritan parable, 11–13
Goodwill Industries, 145
Government funding, 120, 149–150
Graham, Billy, 115
Grassroot organizations, 147
Greek Orthodox, 114

Grief:
   grieving process, 83
   suppression of, 101

Habitat for Humanity, 145
Hajj, 15
Handbook of Religion and Health (Koe-
   nig/McCollough/Larson), 81
Hare Krishnas, 125
Healers:
   consciousness of, 85
   historical perspectives, 80–81
   religious behaviors, 103
Healing:
   altar, 98–99
   defined, 79
   divine, 103
   energy, 85–86
   historical perspectives, 80–81
   importance of, 72
   Jewish rituals, 84
   in the New Millenium, 83–86
Health, generally:
   defined, 79
   in the New Millenium, 83–86
   screening services, 37
   spiritual/religious beliefs and prac-
     tices, impact on, 81–83
Health behaviors, 82
Health care services, 59
Health care setting, 88
Health clinics, 145
Health promotion programs, 84–85, 88
Hebron Presbyterian Church, 166
Hegelian dialectic, 72
Hermeneutical psychology, 97
Hinduism, 75, 85, 138
Hispanic Americans, *see* Latino
   population
HIV/AIDS programs, 38
Holy Spirit, 98–99
Homes for the aged, 116
Homosexuality, social justice experi-
   ence, 59–60
Hope, 94
House Next Door counseling center, 176

Human behavior and social environment
    (HBSE), 129–132
Human development, 63–64
Humanistic theorists, 66

Ideology, 52
Illness:
    impact of spirituality, 82, 88, 130
    risk factors, 93
Immigrants:
    denomination research, 36, 138
    Korean, 156–160
Immigration Act of 1965, 157
Immigration and Nationality Act, 138
Immunizations, 103
Independent Sector, 145
Individuative-Reflect phase, faith devel-
    opment, 67
In-home assistance, 37
Integrity, 68
Interdenominational agencies, 141
Interfaith agencies, 27
Interfaith marriages, 71
International organizations, religiously
    affiliated, 27
Interpretation, religious, 99–101
Intrinsically religious, 96
Intuitive-Projective phase, faith develop-
    ment, 66
Isaiah, 7–8
Islam:
    belief system, 114, 138
    social welfare, 14–18

Jehovahs Witnesses, 103, 130
Jesus Christ:
    on charity, 140
    miracles of, 97
    on the poor, 11–14, 57
    relationship with, 51
Jesus Seminar, 97
Jewish Community Centers, 115, 118
Jewish Family Service, 115
Jewish Federation, 14
Job counseling, 37
Job placement services, 37

Journal of Psychology and Christianity, 92
Jubilee year, 5–6
Judaism:
    charity and, 3–8, 16
    death rituals, 84
    population statistics, 132
    religious traditions, 85
    social services, generally, 53
    social welfare organizations, 115,
        139–141
    Torah, 4–9
    Tree of Life, 85
Judeo-Christian religion, 67
Judeo-Christian tradition:
    charitable distribution, 16–18
    moral law, 75
    religious displays, 124
Jung, Carl, 72–73, 75, 83–84
Justice, principles of, 11
Justice-oriented services, 147. See also
        Social justice

Kaba-Zinn, Jon, 84
Kaddish, 84
Kinship, 5
Koenig, Harold, 65
Korea, growth of church in, 155–156
Korean American church:
    growth of, 156–157
    implications of, 167–168
    informal services provided by,
        159–167
    as surrogate family for immigrants,
        157–159
Korean American community, 131
Kosher food, 130

Labyrinthine journey of faith, 71
Late Childhood, faith development in,
        68
Late life, faith development, 67
Latino population:
    congregation research, 36
    human services and programs, utiliza-
        tion of, 174

Latino population (*continued*)
  social environment, 131
  social justice experience, 55–58
Leadership, community, 55
Lesbians, social justice experience,
    59–60
Liberation Theology, 57–58
Lieberman, Joseph, 115
Life span, 71
Literacy programs, 43, 145
Lord's Prayer, 123
Love:
  Christan, 12
  religious foundations of, 3, 10–11
Lutherans, population statistics, 132
Lutheran Social Services, 53, 115

Maimonides, Rabbi Moses, 9, 138
Marital status, religious involvement
    and, 93
Martos, Joseph, 71
Medicaid, 172–173
Medical advances, 64
Medical treatment, 103, 130
Medicare, 173
Meditation, 84
Megachurches, 29
Mennonites, 56
Mental health:
  psychopathology, 95–99
  religious behavior, 101–103
  religious beliefs and, 81–82, 91–92
  religious interpretation, 99–101
  well-being, 93–95
Methodists, population statistics, 132
Micah, 57
Middle Childhood, faith development
    in, 68
Midlife, faith development, 67, 73
Mind-body approaches, 84–85
Mind-body split, 86–87
Ministers:
  credentials for, 126
  functions of, 124–125
Ministry, 58
Mishnah, 8–9

Missionaries, 58
Mission/mission statement, 28
Mission work, 40
Monotheism, 4
Monsma, Stephen, 146
Moon, Reverend Sun Yun, 125–126
Moral development, 63, 66, 69
Mormons, 53, 119
Muhammad, 14–15
Multi-ethnic congregations, 36
Muslims, (*see* Islam):
  on alcohol, 123
  belief system, 119
  moral law, 75
  Sabbath observance, 122–123
Myss, Carolyn, 85
Mystical experiences, 82
Mythic-Literal phase, faith development,
    66

Narcissistic beliefs, 96
Narcotics Anonymous, 176
National Association of Social Workers
    (NASW), code of ethics, 53
National Baptist Convention of America,
    132
National Center for Complementary and
    Alternative Medicine, 83
National Conference of Catholic Charit-
    ies, 53, 141
National Congregational Study (NCS),
    34
National Institutes of Health, 83
National projects, 27
Native Americans, 114
New Testament:
  healing in, 97–98
  morality, 75
Nominal Group Approach, community
    action planning, 181
Nondenominational churches, 99
Nondenominational congregations, 35
Nongovernmental organizations
    (NGOs), 27
Nonprofit organizations, government
    support of, 146
Nursery schools, 43

Oakhurst Baptist Church, 175
Oblations, 10
Old Testament, 139
Ontological religious communities, 174
Oppression, 7–8, 113
Optimism, importance of, 94
Oriental Mission Church, 165
Orphans, support of, 5, 16–17, 54, 139–140
Orthodox Jewish community, 11, 102, 119, 130
Out of the mainstream religions, 125–126
Outreach programs:
    faith-based, 149
    types of, 28, 36–39

Paranormal experiences, 82
Parental influences, on faith development, 66–67, 71
Partners for Sacred Places, 145
Partnership for the Homeless, New York City, 175
Passover, 139
Pastoral counselors, 92
Pastors, Korean American church, 163
Patriarchal God, 4
Peah, 8–9
Pentecostals, 92, 94, 98, 102, 132
Personal growth programs, 40
Personality style, impact of, 94, 96
Personal responsibility, 19
Personal Responsibility and Work Opportunity Reconciliation Act, 143
Pew Charitable Trusts, 145
Philosophy of life, 129
Pilcher, Rosamunde, 130
Pilgrims, 113
Postmodern philosophy, 74–75, 97
Post-transition faith, 68
Poverty, 7–8
Prana, 85
Prayer:
    daily devotionals, 94
    importance of, 85
    in Islam, 15

mental health status and, 101
    reasons for, 98
    in school, 123–124, 127–128
    therapeutic, 99
Prayer groups, 128
Prayer meetings, 94
Presbyterian Church, 56, 116
Preschool programs, 145
Prison Fellowships, 144
Prison ministries, 145
Private charities, 148
Privativistic congregations, 39
Protestant Church:
    authority in, 131
    population statistics, 132
    religious traditions, 35
    social services, generally, 53, 116
Proverbs, 139
Psychoanalysis, 72
Psychological well-being, 93–95
Psychopathology, religion and, 95–99
Psychosocial development, 66, 69

Q Project, 97
Qigong, 81, 83
Quakers, 113
Quality of life, 44
Quiescence, 73
Qur'un, 15, 17–18

Racial diversity, 35
Rationalistic worldview, 74
Reagan, Ronald, 115
Reconciliation, 76
Recreational programs, 37
Rejection, in faith development, 68
Religion, in social work, 24
Religiosity, 51
Religious affiliation, 94
Religious behavior, 101–103
Religious beliefs, 29
Religious coping, 69, 95
Religious displays, 124–126
Religious education programs, 41
Religious identification, 132
Religious involvement, 93

Religious organizations:
congregational relationship, 26–28
federal funding, 120
Religious service attendance, see Church
attendance
Religious tradition, in congregations, 25,
35
Rental space, 42–43
Replacement value, 44
Resacralization, 65
Respite care, 175
Ritualistic practices, 102
Rivers, Reverend Eugene, 146
Robert Wood Johnson Foundation, 83
Roman Catholic Church:
authority in, 131
in Colombia, 114
on contraception, 122
in France, 114
Latino population, 56
Liberation Theology, 57
medical treatments, 130
religious identification, 132
religious traditions, 35
social services, generally, 53
social welfare programs, 1153
Romanian Orthodox Church, 114
Rorh, Richard, 71
Rosh Hashanah, 5
Rural areas:
congregations in, 32–33
human services and programs, 175
Russian Orthodox Church, 114

Sabbath observation, 122–123
Sabbatical year, 5–6
Sacraments, 85
Sacred psychotherapy, 85
Sacrifice, ritual, 4
Sadaqa, 16
St. Ambrose, 14
St. Augustine of Hippo, 14
St. Joseph's Respite Program, 175,
182–183
St. Jude society, 58
St. Maximus the Confessor, 12

Salat, 15
Salvation, religious foundations of, 3, 14
Salvation Army, 53, 58, 118, 140, 145
Sangnom, 162
Sectarian agencies, 27, 52–54, 140–141.
See also Sectarian organizations
Sectarian organizations:
church-state separation, 141–144
faith-based social programs, 144–147
religion and social life, relationship be-
tween, 147–150
religiously motivated helping,
137–141
Secularization theory, 31
Self-awareness, 85–86
Self-expression, 75
Self-help groups, 37, 40, 43
Self-improvement, 95
Senior centers, 116
Sermon on the Mount, 11, 14
Seventh Day Adventists, 119
Sex education programs, 38
Shahadatain, 15
Shakti, 85
Shamanism, 81
Shelter Now International, 127
Shiva, 84
Social capital, development of, 29
Social justice programs, 19, 38
Social movements, 54
Social programs, faith-based, 144–147
Social science, 146
Social service programs, government con-
tracting, 149–150
Social structures, faith development and,
72
Social welfare:
Christian principles of, 9–11
Islam, 14–15
Jewish, 7
policy, generally, 131
religious foundations of charity, 4

Social work, generally:
congregational, 24, 39–44

education program, *see* Social work
    education
practice, 133
research, 132–133
Social Work Code of Ethics, 86
Social work education:
    curriculum, field practicum, 118–119
    degree programs, 115–116
    human behavior and social environ-
        ment (HBSE), 129–132
    religiously oriented, 116–117
    religious values and, 117–118
    separation of church and state,
        120–129
    social welfare policy/services, 119–120
Socioeconomic differences:
    faith development, 69–70
    impact of, 132
Soup kitchens, 8, 17, 37, 145
Southern Baptists, religious traditions,
    35
Spiritual awakening, 64
Spiritual awareness, 71
Spiritual development, 64
Spiritual growth, 72, 100
Spirituality:
    defined, 79
    dimensions of, 129–130
    life cycle and, 63–76
    in the New Millenium, 83–86
    in social work, 24
Spiritual self-examination, 87
Spontaneous remission, 85
Star Wars analogy, 73
State religions, extreme consequences of,
    127
Steinberg, Milton, 76
Stem cells, 121–122
Stereotypes, faith development and, 69,
    71, 75
Stewardship, 28, 40
Strangers, in *Torah*, 5
Stress:
    impact of, 94, 96
    reduction programs, 84–85
Substance abuse:

incidence of, 82
psychological well-being and, 93, 96
self-help groups, 176–177
treatment programs, 38, 59, 149
Suburban areas, congregations in, 34
Successful aging, 70
Suicide rates, 82
Summer day camp, 37
Sunna, 15
Supplemental Social Insurance, 172
Supreme Being, 65
Symbolism, 97–98
Synthetic-Conventional phase, faith de-
    velopment, 67
Systems theory, 26

Talmud, 69
Tamhui, 8
Taxation, 125, 148
Teen Challenge, 144, 147
Templeton Foundation, 83
Temporality, 75–76
Ten Commandments, 124, 128, 139
Terrorist attacks, impact of, 88
Testimonies, religious, 102–103
Tongues, speaking in, 99
Torah, charity in, 4–94
Transcendent meaning, 73
Transcendent relationship, 72
Transportation services, 37
Tree of Life, 85
Tzedakah, 4–5, 7–9, 138

Unaffiliated congregations, 35
Underwood, Horace G., 156
Unification Church, 125
United Fellowship of the Metropolitan
    Community Church, 60
United Methodist church, 102
U.S. Constitution, 114, 120–121, 123–
    124, 127
United Way, 141
United Way for Religious Outreach, 149
Universalizing Faith, faith development,
    67

Urban congregations, social service pro-
    grams, 40, 145

Value-free morality, 75
Vision, in faith development, 67
Volunteerism, 26, 40–42, 45, 56, 94

Waaf, 17
War on Poverty, 142
Warner, Stephen, 25
Welfare policies/programs, 40, 149–150.
    See also Social welfare
Well-being:
    existential, 71–72, 74–76
    health and, 82–83
    mental health and, 93–95
    obstacles to, 52
    personal, 71
    psychological, 93–95
    spiritual, 28, 82
    subjective, 82
Western religious traditions, 82
White House Commission on Comple-
    mentary and Alternative Medicine,
    83

Whole person model, 87
Wicca, 128
Widows, support of, 5, 16, 19
Willow Creek program, 176
Women:
    abortion, 60, 121–122
    contraception, 54, 122
    faith development in, 69, 71
    lesbians, 59–60
    single-mom pregnancy, 149
    social justice experience, 58–59
    widows, support of, 5, 16, 19
Work ethic, 6
Worship, 28–29

Yahrzeit, 84
*Yearbook of American and Canadian
    Churches*, 31
Yoga, 84–85
Yom Kippur, 5
Young adulthood, faith development in,
    67–68

Zakat, 15–16, 18

Springer Publishing Company

Religion, Belief, and Spirituality in Late Life

L. Eugene Thomas, PhD and
Susan A. Eisenhandler, PhD, Editors

This volume examines the importance of beliefs in understanding psychologically-relevant issues from self-identity to recovery from grief. Thomas and Eisenhandler provide a broad framework for viewing religion in the lives of the elderly by drawing on insights derived from the humanities, and those mined from qualitative social science research, as well as from empirical and quantitative research. This book is a valuable resource for academics, gerontologists, psychologists, graduate-level students, and other professionals who are interested in the emerging study of religion, spirituality, and aging.

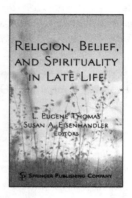

Partial Contents:

Part I: Creating and Understanding the Text of Late Life Spirituality

• A Handful of Quietness: Measuring the Meaning of our Years
  Stephen Bertman

Part II: Spirituality Writ Large and Small in Late Life

• Spiritual and Ethical Striving in Late Life: Three Paths to Integrity
  Melvin E. Miller

• Aspects of **Transcendence** in Everyday Worlds: Reading and Spirituality in Late Life, *Susan A. Eisenhandler*

Part III: The Nature of Beliefs: Cross-Cultural Perspectives

• Quarreling with God: Belief and Disbelief Among Elderly Jewish Immigrants From the Former USSR, *L. Eugene Thomas*

Part IV: Glimpses of Gendered Spirituality

• Spirituality: A Continually Evolving Component in Women's Identity Development, *Patricia Burke*

Part V: Is There a Distinctive Spirituality of Late Life?

• Late-Life Transcendence: A New Developmental Perspective on Aging
  Lars Tornstam

1999   248pp   0-8261-1235-8   hard

536 Broadway, New York, NY 10012 • Telephone: 212-431-4370
Fax: 212-941-7842 • Order Toll-Free: 877-687-7476 • Order On-line: www.springerpub.com

Springer Publishing Company

Keeping the Faith in Late Life

Susan A. Eisenhandler, PhD

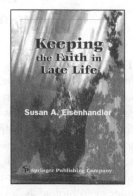

"Eisenhandler's well-grounded report of bedrock social-ization and the folkways of faith provides a long-needed counterbalance for our understanding of American elders. This book belongs on its own shelf—even better, it belongs in the hands of all who have wondered about the fate of life."

—**Robert J. Kastenbaum,** PhD
Professor Emeritus of Gerontology and Communication
Arizona State University

"Intelligently argued and compellingly written, this book is a welcome addition to a gerontological literature that now increasingly considers the place of spirituality in older people's everyday lives...Powerful and grounded in the ordinary, the book provides marvelous insights into the nexus of religious sensibility and the practice of daily living."

—**Jaber F. Gubrium,** PhD
University of Missouri

Through extensive interviews, Eisenhandler explores older adults' personal engagement with religion, the role of socialization in retaining faith in late life, and the extent to which older adults participate in religious behavior and find reli-gious beliefs relevant to their present life.

Partial Contents:
*   Introduction: Faith as a Feature of Identity and of Late Life: The Theoretical and Methodological Context of the Study
*   The Bedrock of Faith and Religion—Socialization
*   The Folkways of Prayer in Late Life
*   Other Folkways of Faith in Late Life
*   A Grown-Up Faith with Musings, Doubts, and Questions
*   Folkways of Faith in Long-Term Care Settings: Self, Soul, and Space
*   Conclusion: Beyond A Reflexive Faith
*   Appendix A: A Closer Look at Several Steps in the Research Process

2003   208pp   0-8261-1775-9   hard

536 Broadway, New York, NY 10012 • Telephone: 212-431-4370
Fax: 212-941-7842 • Order Toll-Free: 877-687-7476 • Order On-line: www.springerpub.com